IN WORD AND DEED

Evangelism and Social Responsibility

EDITOR
BRUCE NICHOLLS

GRAND RAPIDS, MICHIGAN
WILLIAM B. EERDMANS PUBLISHING COMPANY

First published 1985 by The Paternoster Press, England
This edition published 1986 through special arrangement with Paternoster
by Wm. B. Eerdmans Publishing Company, 255 Jefferson S.E.,
Grand Rapids, Mich. 49503

Library of Congress Cataloging-in-Publication Data

Main entry under title:

In word and deed.

Papers presented at the Consultation on the Relationship between Evangelism and social Responsibility, held at the Reformed Bible College, Grand Rapids, Mich., June 16-23, 1982; sponsored by the Lausanne Committee for World Evangelization and the World Evangelical Fellowship.
    1. Evangelistic work— Congresses. 2. Church and social problems— Congresses. I. Nicholls, Bruce. II. Consultation on the Relationship between Evangelism and Social Responsibility (1982 : Reformed Bible College, Grand Rapids, Mich.) III. Lausanne Committee for World Evangelization. IV. World Evangelical Fellowship.
        BV3755.I5   1986   266'.001   85-27561

ISBN 0-8028-1965-6

Contents

657

3 March 1986

72252

Preface

From June 16 to 23, 1982, some fifty evangelical leaders from six continents attended the Reformed Bible College, Grand Rapids, Michigan, for a Consultation on the Relationship between Evangelism and Social Responsibility, co-sponsored by the Lausanne Committee for World Evangelism and the World Evangelical Fellowship. The delegates comprised theologians, pastors, evangelists, missiologists, and social service and development workers, more than one-half of whom came from Third World countries.

CRESR turned out to be a model of how Christians should approach a potentially divisive issue. The planning and execution of the Consultation was marked by a spirit of humility and openness, patient listening and real effort to understand each other, willingness to submit to Scripture and eagerness to find one another under the Cross. Individuals who had published strong, divergent views on the issue served on the CRESR planning and executive committees. It was during the process of planning together that the spirit of fellowship, understanding and appreciation of one another in Christ developed which eventually prevailed over the debate at the Consultation.

Eight major papers and their responses were presented and discussed in small groups and in plenary sessions during the consultation. These papers and responses, now published in an edited form, deal with the biblical, historical, and missiological understanding of the relationship between evangelism and social responsibility. Studying them will assist readers greatly in interpreting a complex issue.

The question of Christian social responsibility has been extensively discussed within the ecumenical circle for the past two decades, and the same concern has overflowed to evangelical Christianity in recent years. Evangelical Christians who had pre-

7

viously reacted against the 'social gospel' are now awakening to
their social responsibility and are questioning their social duty in
relationship to evangelism and missions. Nevertheless differences of opinion persist among Christians as to the interpretation
of such biblical doctrines as salvation, the kingdom of God, and
eschatology, resulting in different approaches in the relationship
between the two areas under consideration.

The debate was well and truly joined as we grappled with the
issue of the exact relationship between evangelism and social
responsibility, and the related question of the primacy of evangelism, as defined in the Lausanne Covenant (paragraphs 4, 5
and 6). The plenary papers and case histories sharpened for us
the issues for debate which were approached both from Scripture
and theology, and also from the practice of the church in its
different contexts down the centuries. Ultimately the model of
the life and ministry of the Lord Jesus Christ was the most
decisive factor in arriving at the right integration of the Christian's twin duty of evangelism and social responsibility. Our
conclusion was that there are at least three relationships
between evangelism and social responsibility which are equally
valid; namely, that Christian social concern is a *consequence* of
evangelism, can be a *bridge* to evangelism, and should be a
partner of evangelism. It was especially pointed out concerning
the latter that in our Lord's ministry, proclamation and service
went hand in hand. His words explained His works and His
works dramatized his words. Both His words and works were
expressions of His compassion for people.

Having reached agreement on the different ways in which
evangelism and social responsibility are related, it was relatively
easy to reach a consensus on the primacy of evangelism. Since
Christian social concern is a consequence of evangelism, evangelism has a logical priority. Besides, one of the goals of evangelism
is good works (see Eph. 2:10; Titus 2:14). It takes socially responsible Christians to carry out Christian social responsibility.
Again, the supreme and ultimate need of all mankind is the
saving grace of Jesus Christ. Therefore a person's eternal
spiritual salvation is of greater importance than his or her
temporal and material well-being. Primacy does not necessarily
imply priority in the sequence of time. This too is obvious from
the assertion that social concern can be a bridge to evangelism.
The members of the Consultation unequivocally affirmed the
priority of evangelism in the report.

Although the Consultation did not come up with a neat
definition of social responsibility, it sought to distinguish
between two forms of it, namely social service and social action.
Social service covers activities related to relieving human need,

philanthropy, seeking to minister to individuals and families, and works of mercy. Social action has to do with removing the causes of human need, political and economic activity, seeking to transform the structures of society, and the quest for justice. There remain a number of problematic areas that require attention. What is the definition of Christian social responsibility or of evangelism? How can we determine a proper balance in our distribution of church resources (i.e., funds and personnel) between the ministry of evangelism and teaching on one hand and the ministry of social service on the other? Does this social concern eventually lead to a place of confrontation with government which is often unsympathetic toward Christianity?

The aim of the Consultation was that God's people may commit themselves to a yet more effective proclamation and service in reaching the unreached peoples with the Good News of Jesus Christ. To this end guidelines were drawn up to assist local churches to become more involved in evangelism and social responsibility according to their particular situation and opportunities.

We recommend this book to theological schools, local churches and individual Christians who are interested in further studies in this area.

The final statement of the Consultation appeared in 1982 as the Grand Rapids Report, *Evangelism and Social Responsibility: an Evangelical Commitment*. This 64-page report provides a succinct summary of the relationship between evangelism and social responsibility from an evangelical perspective. It is available as Lausanne Occasional Paper No. 21.

It is our sincere hope that this book will serve as a tool to further our understanding of the Lord's Great Commission, thereby accelerating our attempts in the evangelization of the world.

We acknowledge with gratitude the help of many people who have given time and effort to make publication of this book possible.

Bong Rin Ro
Gottfried Osei-Mensah

1

The Perspectives of Church History from New Testament Times to 1960

BONG RIN RO*

Synopsis   Dr. Bong Ro asks, 'Has the Church throughout the centuries given evangelism priority over social responsibility or has the Church stressed evangelism and social responsibility equally as her mandate?' and 'Is the Church's expression of concern for the poor and for social justice the same today as it was in the past?'

Dr. Ro examines eight periods of Church history surveying the motives and responses of ecclesiastical leaders to the Church's role in evangelism and social concern and justice and the relationship between them. Political, economic and social factors as well as religious and theological movements are discussed and evaluated as to their influence on the issues under discussion.

Different models of relationship develop during this span of history from the simplicity of faith and service of the New Testament and early apostolic times to the identification of Church and State model of the mediaeval period and its modification during the era of the European Reformation. The recovery of biblical preaching and evangelism alongside social action characterized the Protestant Reformation.

The evangelical revival movements of European pietism, the Wesleyan Revival in England and the Great Awakening in North America are shown to have stimulated evangelism, missions and

*Dr Bong Ro is Executive Secretary of the Asia Theological Association, Taichung, Taiwan.

social responsibility in the period of rapid social change from the 17th to mid-19th centuries. Jonathan Edwards and Charles E. Finney worked for justice in society as well as continuing their evangelistic campaigns. However, division over absolutist views on social issues, differing attitudes to slavery and conflicting millennial views contributed to the decline of evangelical social concern. Then followed the rise of higher criticism, humanism, rational and evolutionary philosophies and theologies leading to the dominance of the Social Gospel. In the early twentieth century evangelicals reacted sharply against social and political involvement and devoted their energies to evangelism and missions. Social activity was viewed as the means to or the fruit of evangelism.

The relationship of the Kingdom of God to social concern and the priority of evangelism over social responsibility have become major issues in contemporary evangelical theology.

Finally, Dr. Ro outlines factors that have contributed to the diversity of positions held by Third World evangelicals.

———————————

An article entitled 'What is the Church's Mandate?' in the *Asia Theological News* (April-June 1982, pp.4–5, 16–18), (a quarterly magazine of the Asia Theological Association) presented the opinions of two outspoken exponents of two distinctive evangelical views on this issue. One of the questions asked in the article was: 'What is the key issue in recent years in the evangelical dialogue on the relationship between evangelism and social responsibility?'

Arthur P. Johnston, Professor of World Mission and Evangelism at Trinity Evangelical Divinity School, Illinois, replied: 'The church has one mission, evangelism, but many responsibilities—such as baptism, teaching, worship, and doing good to all men (Gal. 6:10).' Ronald J. Sider, associate professor of theology at the Eastern Baptist Theological Seminary, Philadelphia, answered: 'Evangelism and social concern are equally important but distinct aspects of the total mission of the church.'[1]

Which reply corresponds to the church's historical response? Has the church throughout the centuries given evangelism priority over social responsibility or has the church stressed evangelism and social responsibility equally as her mandate? Is the church's expression of concern for the poor and for social justice the same today as it was in the past? Is this concern expressed differently in this century than it was in previous centuries? How has the Christian church over the centuries worked to change religious values and social structures in order to improve the living conditions of the poor?

The following discussion surveys church history from New Testament times to 1960. Because there are so many current definitions of 'evangelism' it is necessary for this author to define his understanding of the term. He takes evangelism to mean the proclamation of the good news that God sent his only begotten Son to redeem man from his sin in order to restore him to fellowship with God and to serve God in his Church.[2]

The main thesis of this paper is that evangelism and social concern are both intimately related in the history of the church, though they are expressed in different ways in different periods of history. Christians in the early church simply believed in Jesus Christ for their salvation and shared their faith both in words and deeds. The contemporary theology which relates the kingdom of God to social concern and the current debate as to the priority of evangelism or social responsibility are recent developments. Only in the past one and a half centuries have these become major theological issues in the church worldwide.

1. The New Testament Church and the Apostolic Fathers (–150 A.D.)

A. *The New Testament Church (–95 A.D.)*

The relationship between evangelism and social responsibility in the early church should be looked at from two perspectives: the Jewish-Roman-Hellenistic context into which the church was born and grew, and the teachings and impact of the New Testament upon the Christian community.

The Christians in the early church represented a very small minority. They were often misunderstood by the Jewish-Roman-Hellenistic world. Knowing that they were a small minority, the Christians were challenged to grow numerically and spiritually by faithful witnesses in words and deeds. The Christians suffered persecution under the Roman emperors. Foxe's *Christian Martyrs of the World* describes ten major persecutions against Christians beginning with Emperor Nero (64) and ending with Emperor Diocletian (303)[3] Widespread persecutions were launched, especially by the Emperor Decius Trajan (250–251 A.D.) with his edict of 250 and Emperor Diocletian (284–305 A.D.) with four edicts (303–304 A.D.) Thousands of Christians were tortured and executed mercilessly for their faith. To be a Christian was a matter of life and death.

During the first century, many Christians were very conscious of their Jewish background. By the second century most Christians were Gentiles who had come out of a pagan, syncretistic Graeco-Roman background. The gospel of Christ was radically new to these Gentile converts. The newness was something to share with their pagan associates. Like many Asian Christians today, they developed their ethical teachings out of a Gentile world view rather than out of the world view shaped by the Torah of the Old Testament.

The early church was strongly oriented towards the second coming of Christ. Those Scripture passages which speak of the imminent return of Christ (Mk. 1:15; 1 Thess. 5:2; Jas. 5:4; and Phil. 3:13–14) made a significant impact on their life style. Believers eagerly anticipated going to be with Christ in the heavenly city.[4]

The early church's tremendous concern for the 'lost' caused it greatly to emphasize evangelism. The early church's concept of 'conversion' was unique. It demanded a complete break from the past pagan life to a new life in Christ. *Evangelism in the Early Church*, by Michael Green, devotes a whole chapter to the obstacles to evangelism in the Jewish and Graeco-Roman world.[5]

> At whatever level in society it was attempted, evangelism in the early church was a very daunting undertaking. It was a task involving social odium, political danger, the charge of treachery to the gods and the state, the insinuation of horrible crimes and calculated opposition from a combination of sources more powerful, perhaps, than at any time since.[6]

With simplicity of faith and zeal for evangelism, the early Christians shared their possessions with the needy. As described in Acts 4, Christians in the Jerusalem Church shared their possessions with each other. Such generosity, motivated by deep love for the Lord, made a profound impact on the early church and on society. This willingness to sacrifice self interest for the sake of others and for the furtherance of the gospel made it possible for Christians to evangelize the Graeco-Roman world by the end of the 5th century. The sacrificial love of these humble believers was the professed allegiance of the overwhelming majority of the population of the Roman empire.

B. *The Apostolic Fathers (95–150 A.D.)*

Anyone who reads the Apostolic Fathers will realize that they had a meaningful experience of Jesus Christ, cherished their salvation, and had a deep desire to obey the Great Commission in their pagan world. Their faith was simple. They believed in the imminent return of Christ, were afraid of his judgment, and called people to repentance and faith in Christ. The *Shepherd of Hermas* reveals their values: 'Have simplicity and be innocent and you shall be as the children who do not know the wickedness that destroys the life of men.'[7]

Furthermore, this faith in Christ was not expressed in words only. Their faith was translated into actions through love and concern for needy people around them. Practical social concern was the inevitable result of their spiritual conversion.

Clement of Rome explained this intimate relationship between justification and good works:

> . . . through faith, by which Almighty God has justified all men from the beginning of the world . . . What shall we do, then, brethren? Shall we be slothful in well-being and cease from love?
>
> Let the strong care for the weak and let the weak reverence the strong. Let the rich man bestow help on the poor and let the poor give thanks to God, that He gave him one to supply his needs.[8]

The Epistle of Barnabas spoke of the Two Ways: 'The Way of Light' (chapter 19) and the 'Way of Darkness' (chapter 20). One way that the light can be shown is:

> Thou shalt share all things with thy neighbour and shalt not say that they are thy own property; for if you are sharers in that which is incorruptible, how much more in that which is corruptible?[9]

The Shepherd of Hermas said:

> The rich man, therefore, helps the poor in all things without doubting. But the poor man, being helped by the rich, makes intercession to God, giving him thanks . . . Therefore, the two together complete the work . . .[10]

The simplicity of faith and consistent Christian life and testimony of these second century Christians caused the rapid growth of the church.

2. The Old Catholic Church (150–325 A.D.)

During the second and third centuries Christianity spread south into North Africa, north to Lyon, and east into the Tigris-Euphrates valley (Edessa), Armenia, Arabia and India. By 180 A.D. Christianity was established in all of the Roman Empire. The church's self identity became strong enough to defend Christianity from attacks from outside the church and to repudiate false doctrines within the church.

Skilful apologists such as Justin Martyr (150–163) and

Tertullian of Carthage (150–225) rebutted false charges of atheism, cannibalism, incest, indolence, and antisocial actions which pagan writers such as Celsus brought against Christianity. These apologists also showed how Judaeo-Christianity was different from pagan religions.[11]

The polemicists in the late second and the early third centuries attacked the false teachings of heretics. Origen of Alexandria wrote *Against Celsus* to protect the church from pagan intellectuals while Irenaeus of Lyon wrote *Against Heresies* to refute heretics within the church. The apologists were first generation Christians while the polemicists enjoyed a Christian cultural background.[12]

The motivation for Christian charity changed during this time. During the period of the Apostolic Fathers, Christian charity was the result of spiritual conversion. Good works were one of the fruits of a believer's new life in Christ. But during the period of the Old Catholic Church, one of the motives for Christian charity became the hope of future reward. During this period, an organized structure was developed to take care of Christian social activities on a large scale. Although Christians confined their charity largely to their own community, they also supported the unemployed, orphans, widows, the injured, the sick, and travellers. Churches sent relief goods to other churches during famines and other calamities. Christians were encouraged to fast to help the poor. The church in Rome supported 1,500 widows and persons in need.[13] Some time after the death of Constantine, the church in Antioch supported 3,000 widows, virgins, sick people in inns, prisoners, and many other poor people.[14]

In his *First Apology* Justin Martyr defended the church by saying that the early Christians had started a common fund and shared their goods, meals, and everything with those in need. The only persons excluded from this fund were the wives of the Christians—in contrast with the pagans who were more willing to share with their wives than with anyone else.[15] Justin also severely criticized the public exercise of prostitution practised in his time, as a great injustice.[16]

Tertullian encouraged each Christian to deposit a small amount on a certain day of the month according to his or her ability to help the needy:

> The money therefrom is spent not for banquets or drinking parties or good-for-nothing eating houses, but for the support and burial of the poor, for children who are without their parents and means of subsistence, for aged men who are confined to the house; likewise, for shipwrecked sailors, and for any in the mines, on islands or in prisons.[17]

3. Post-Constantine Era: the Supremacy of the Old Catholic Church (313–590 A.D.)

The despised became the despiser. With close co-operation between church and state, the church became a very powerful institution. Both evangelism and social concern became a joint endeavour of the church and state. This was the beginning of the time later described as the 'identification model'.

The continual hope of early Christians for freedom from official persecution and social contempt became real through the Edict of Milan (313 A.D.) of the Emperor Constantine. Constantine and his successors continued and broadened the policy of favouring the church so that by the time of Theodosius I (379–392 A.D.) Christianity became the official state religion through the edicts of 380 and 381. Theodosius I through the Edict of Constantinople (392 A.D.) banned pagan sacrifices and attendance at pagan temples. In the Eastern Empire Justinian (527–565 A.D.) ordered the closing of the pagan school of philosophy in Athens in 529 A.D.[18]

What a contrast to the evangelism of the pre-Constantine era! State support meant that the church now had the immense task of evangelizing not only those who were already living in the Roman Empire but also the great mass of Barbarians (Teutonic, Viking, Slav, and Mongol people) who had migrated into Europe from the north and east between 375 and 1066.[19]

The close co-operation between the church and state during this period brought radical changes into the church. Dr. Robert E. Webber in *The Secular Saint* summarizes the Constantine era as the 'identification model' in church-state relations.[20]

1. The church became a wealthy institution. In the past, it had tried to support itself through small business enterprises as well as through the donations of its members. But during the identification period, the rapid expansion of Christianity required extensive income for its church buildings, art galleries, and elaborate administrative system.

2. Nominal Christians began to fill the church. The previous emphasis on a conversion experience declined. Evangelism was no longer a personal matter but a matter of joining an institution and following its rituals.

3. The church lost the sharp distinction between the ideal of the kingdom and the ideal of humanitarianism. Many Christians became more interested in the kingdom of this world and in their own personal security than in the future kingdom of God.

4. The church became a powerful institution. In co-operation with the state, it supplied Christian politicians and adminis-

trators for government posts. These Christians tried to make the
empire Christian by means of government regulations.[21]

From among the numerous early church fathers, I have selected
two spokesmen for the post-Constantine period: St.
Augustine of Hippo (354–430), who represents the Latin Church, and St.
Basil of Caesarea (c.329–379), who represents the Eastern
Church.

St. Augustine's strong interest in winning pagans to Christ
sprang from his own experience of living in deep sin before his
conversion. He described in *The Confessions of St. Augustine* how
only the grace of God can bring new life to a man.

In *The City of God* he sought to explain the distinctive
difference in the life styles of the city of God and of the city of
man. Here he presented his concept of the Christian's relationship to the world. He said that the city of God consists of those
who follow the true God and the city of man consists of those
who worship false gods. A constant battle rages between the two
cities. Christians are citizens of the city of God but they live in
the city of man in order to demonstrate God's love to mankind.

> The two cities then were created by two kinds of love: the earthly
> city by a love of self carried even to the point of contempt for God,
> the heavenly city by love of God carried even to the point of
> contempt for self.[22]

St. Augustine's concern for the poor was expressed well when
his congregation sang the psalm, 'Blessed is the man who
regarded the needs of the poor.' St. Augustine praised the rich
who helped the poor, the church, and the monasteries:

> They are the cedars of Lebanon. See how many sparrows—how
> many, that is to say, of the little ones of this world, who have given
> up their little bit of goods and gear and family life to make a new
> home upon these heights of the spirit—see how many of these have
> built their nests in these cedars.[23]

In regard to the slavery issue, St. Augustine, like Paul and all
other early church fathers, was concerned more with the proper
relationship between master and slave than he was with
abolishing slavery and with reconstructing the social order.
Every home had a large number of slaves and wealthy homes
kept hundreds of slaves. Many slaves did not want to be freed
because then they had difficulty finding new jobs. Although it
was considered a 'good work' for Christians to liberate slaves, St.
Augustine never in his writings advocated the wholesale liberation of slaves.[24]

St. Basil, Bishop of Cappadocia and noted theologian, was
renowned for his application of the gospel to society. He saw in

his time a tremendous gap between the rich and the poor. The poor were so destitute that many sold their children into slavery in order to support the family. St. Basil condemned irresponsible wealthy people as 'thieves and robbers'.[25] Basil himself possessed nothing 'but a cloak and a few books'. In his *Ta Ethika* he instructed Christians to use any possessions beyond their basic necessities to help needy people. Everyone who can help others should do so. St. Basil concluded his lecture in ethics by asking: 'What is the mark of a Christian?' His answer: 'To love one another, even as Christ also loved you. To see the Lord always before him.' And, 'To watch each night and day and in the perfection of pleasing God by being ready, knowing that the Lord cometh at the hour he thinketh not.'[26]

St. Basil developed a collective Christian social service by establishing hospitals and shelters for travellers and the poor. These were so widespread and numerous that they were known as the 'new city'. Dr. Forell comments: 'A key to this development may have been Basil's unique combination of theology and ethics, of pastoral and social concern, of faith and love.'[27]

4. The Early Mediaeval Church (590–1300 A.D.)

Politically, by the year 1000 A.D. the church was co-operating more and more with the secular rulers in Europe, thus creating tensions and conflicts. The new empires in the West, such as the Merovingian (Frankish) Empire which arose after the fall of the Roman Empire in 476, the Carolingian Empire of Charlemagne (751–), and the Holy Roman Empire (962–1806), all began with the blessings of the mediaeval church. In the East the Byzantine Empire (395–1453) continued until Constantinople fell to the Turks in 1453.

Religiously, the rise of the papacy during this time gave birth to a legacy of conflict in the Roman Catholic Church. Papal power increased rapidly with Gregory the Great (590–604). Pope Gregory VII (1075–85) degraded the Emperor Henry IV of the Holy Roman Empire by forcing him to stand barefoot in the snow in 1077 at Canossa in order to gain papal clemency. Papal power reached its peak during the time of Pope Innocent III (1195–1216), and the church exterminated opposers through excommunication and inquisition. A new monastic movement developed in reaction to the institutionalization and secularization of the church. Monastic orders such as the Benedictine Order (529–), Cluny Reform (910–1790), Cistercian Order (1098–), Franciscan Order (1209–), Dominican Order (1216–)

Augustinian Order (1256–), and others provided not only discipline for the monks in their prayer and studies but also a social service for the people.

The early mediaeval social structure with its decentralized administrative system was basically feudalistic. The development of commerce and industry beginning with the twelfth century gradually changed this social structure. New factors such as urbanization, the cavalry and new political and social classes of merchants, artisans, and feudal lords contributed to these changes.[28]

The mediaeval concept of the relationship between evangelism and social responsibility can be understood only within the context of the institutional church. The mediaeval church taught that God has provided salvation for mankind through Jesus Christ and that this salvation can be obtained only through God's grace. But the only way to secure this grace was through the medium of the church which was headed by the Pope, the Vicar of Christ and successor of St. Peter.

Earning merit for salvation through asceticism and good works became so important that the doctrine of indulgence developed in the eleventh century. Evangelism was interpreted as not only bringing people to Christ but also bringing them to the church. Since salvation rests only within the church, the role of parish priests became very important.[29]

Christian social concern in the mediaeval church was strongly influenced by the concept of the *corpus Christianum*. Advocates of this concept believed in a universal Christian state in which both church and state are God's instruments to achieve God's purpose for man. It was, therefore, the responsibility of both church and state to promote evangelism and social responsibility. It was the duty of popes, councils, monks, and clerks in the mediaeval church to regulate feudalism, protect labourers, and establish educational and charitable institutions. And it was the duty of the state to support these programmes. This close co-operation of church and state provides us with a perfect example of the 'identification model' in church-state relations.

Among the mediaeval church fathers, one of the best fleshed-out examples of evangelism and Christian charity was St. Francis of Assisi (1182–1226), founder of the Franciscan Order. His guileless simplicity and love for others were emulated by many followers.

St. Francis is called the 'Apostle of Love' because of his God-given generosity. He became known throughout the mediaeval and modern world for his love for the poor as expressed in his desire to marry 'the noblest, richest, and most beautiful girl,' whom he called 'Lady Poverty'—a symbol for his commitment to the needy. Thomas of Celano, who was St. Francis's first and most reliable biographer, describes Francis:

> If any of the poor people asked for his help as he walked along the streets he gave them money or, if short of it, his hat or his belt rather than leave them with nothing. He would go so far as to take off his shirt in some dark corner and ask the poor man to take it for the love of God. When his father and his brother were away, he saw to it there was as much food as if the whole family were at home. When his mother asked why he insisted upon this, he explained that the extra was for his brothers, the poor.[30]

He also required the same concern for others and poverty of his monks. According to the Rule of the Franciscan Order, they should possess nothing but rather seek alms as our Lord made himself poor for us in this world.

5. The Renaissance and the Reformation (1300–1600 A.D.)

A. *Late Mediaeval Church (1300–1500)*

The political, socio-economic, and religious climate changed during the Late Mediaeval Age (1300–1500). Feudalism began to decline and strong central monarchical governments were established in Europe.

The Renaissance promoted humanism with the revival of Greek and Latin learning, the development of science, and new tendencies in the arts. The nominalism of William of Ockham (c.1280–c.1349) and of Gabriel Biel (1420–95) challenged the early mediaeval philosophy and theology of universalism.

Religiously, the supremacy of the papacy began to be seriously challenged from the time of Pope Boniface VIII (1294–1303). Ecclesiastical chaos prevailed throughout the Babylonian Captivity (1307–78) and the Great Schism (1378–1417). The conciliar movement and other reform movements failed to bring reconciliation and spiritual and moral revival to the corrupt Roman Catholic Church. In the East the Ottoman Turkish Empire attacked the Byzantine Empire until Constantinople finally fell to the Muslims in 1453.

Economically, the continual development of trade and industry encouraged a capitalistic economy and changed the social structure. Large influxes of migrant peoples into towns for new jobs brought economic impoverishment to large sections of society, especially peasants and country gentry.

From the fourteenth century onwards the peasants were often restless because they suffered from growing economic pressures from landlords whose land was declining in value and who

demanded more remuneration because of increases in the costs of
the life style of the nobility. Suffering from these injustices and
the burdens of famine, pestilence (such as the Black Death from
1348–49), and war (such as the One Hundred Years war from
1337–1453), the peasants revolted against both secular and
religious rulers. The peasant revolts in Flanders in 1323, in
France in 1358, in England in 1381, and in Germany in 1524–25
forced the ruling classes to make economic reforms. Christ's
example of poverty, the monastic emphasis on poverty, and
asceticism in some segments of the mediaeval church were not
enough to suppress the aspirations of the town populations for
freedom from the oppression of the church and state. The town
populations demanded even more radical changes in the social
structure.

B. *Protestant Reformation (1517–1600)*

The reformers' doctrines of *sola gratia*, *sola fide*, *sola scriptura*,
and *soli Deo gloria* challenged every major tenet of the Roman
Catholic Church. For the reformers, evangelism meant the
restoration of the erring church to the Scripture's teachings.
Their doctrine of justification by faith downgraded the mediaeval concept of meritorial works to obtain salvation through the
sacramental system of the church. *Sola gratia* simplified the
complicated Roman Catholic soteriological system, and *sola
scriptura* denied the concept of the corpus Christianum and
shattered the entire monolithic structure of the Roman Catholic
Church. Yet even though the Protestant reformers were sufficiently radical in the sixteenth century to make many needed
reforms, they still retained many mediaeval traditions.

(a) Martin Luther (1483–1546)

In order to understand Luther's views on evangelism and social
responsibility, one has to grasp his concept of two kingdoms—
the kingdom of God and the kingdom of this world. The
Christian, as a child of God, belongs to the former, and as a
citizen of this world he belongs to the latter. He, therefore, is
responsible to God as well as to the civil authority.

Since God is in control of both kingdoms, Luther believed that
God does not want the Christian to compartmentalize his life into
sacred and secular categories. The Christian is to live his life in
this world in order to show forth the love of the kingdom of God.

Luther had a deep concern for evangelism. Most of his letters
carried this phrase: 'By the grace of God, Evangelist at Witten-
berg'. Luther's preaching on the 'Law and Gospel' explained

clearly the way of salvation to the people of the sixteenth century.

In regard to social responsibility Luther taught two important truths. First, he rejected the mediaeval notion that good works bring pardon for sins. In his *Ninety-five Theses* (1517) Luther declared:

43. Christians are to be taught that he who gives to the poor or lends to the needy does a better work than buying pardons.
45. Christians are to be taught that he who sees a man in need, and passes him by, and gives (his money) for pardons, purchases not the indulgences of the pope, but the indignation of God.

Second, Luther maintained that spiritual conversion precedes good works:

But where pure faith is taught in the right way, works will come spontaneously.
Good works never produce a good man, but a good man produces good works . . . Accordingly, it is always necessary that the person be good before there can be any good works at all and that good works result and proceed from a good person . . . Just as faith makes a man godly, so it also produces good works.[31]

Luther opposed the Anabaptists' view of separation between church and state, because he believed that God can use the secular government to establish social justice. In 1520 he wrote an *Open Letter to the Christian Nobility* and urged the state to make economic and social reforms for the betterment of the poor.

During the Peasants' War in Germany (1524–25), Luther condemned the peasants' uprising against the government. He called the uprising the work of the 'murdering prophets', meaning Thomas Müntzer, minister in Zwickau, and his followers. Müntzer's teachings about an inner subjective experience of the Spirit made it possible for him to create a movement which was particularly fanatical in ethical matters. With his thinking deeply rooted in the Old Testament, Müntzer preached about the Jehovah God who wanted his subjects to fight against the heathen and against injustices in society. Luther condemned Müntzer's fanaticism.

In spite of the repeated appeals of the peasants, Luther spoke out against them three times. In 1525 he wrote a tract, 'Admonition to Peace: A Reply to the Twelve Articles of the Peasants in Swabia' in which he appealed to the princes to respond in humility and penitence to the demands of the peasants. He then told the peasants that sedition was always unjust and contrary to God's commandments and that they should adopt a passive stance. He also said that the peasants were often just as greedy for money as were the rich.[32]

(b) John Calvin (1509–64)

Calvin's ideas of evangelism and social ethics were also conditioned by the events of his time. In France during the fourteenth and fifteenth centuries, the king's control over the church had been strengthened through the Pragmatic Sanction of Bourges (1438) and the Concordat of Bologna (1516). By the time of King Francis I, France experienced political absolutism. Calvin tried to safeguard the church from the threat of an all-powerful state by writing a personal letter to the king in the preface of his *Institutes* (1535). He believed in the separation of the two powers, temporal and spiritual. He also believed in a close interrelationship between these two realms because of his belief in the absolute sovereignty of God. God is the supreme Ruler over both the temporal and the spiritual authorities. Calvin accepted the basic notion of the mediaeval *corpus Christianum.*[33]

Calvin believed that Christians constitute a small society inside the larger corrupt society. The church 'is the embryo of an entirely new world where the once perverted social relations find anew their original nature'. The conciliar movement further convinced Calvin that the local ecclesiastical authority should govern the church. With the co-operation of the temporal government Calvin tried to establish a theocratic state in Geneva.

He was not satisfied with the mediaeval ecclesiastical attempt to solve social problems through an extensive system of almsgiving for ecclesiastical merits and through the example of mendicant priests. Luther believed that these practices could not solve the more complicated problems of the sixteenth century. God wanted to use the common man, the lay Christian, to transform society.

Calvin tried to impose his theological and moral standards on the state in the *Articles of Confessions for Geneva*. He advocated, for example, the monthly observance of the Lord's Supper and stricter church discipline in order to establish a purity of doctrine and of life. Religious heretics and violators of the Genevan rules and regulations were either executed or severely punished.

(c) Ulrich Zwingli (1484–1531)

Like Calvin in Geneva, Zwingli, another Swiss reformer, made an attempt in Zurich to reform society through the Little and Great Councils. The Great Council abolished street begging in 1524 and transformed the preachers' monastery into a 'poorhouse' where food was served each morning for the poor. The council also converted monasteries and convents into schools, hospitals, and orphanages and established a charity bureau to distribute food for sick and pregnant women.

During the Peasants' War of 1524–25 Zwingli was very sympathetic with the demands of the peasants. Along with other south German Reformers such as Bucer, Capito, Vadian, and Blaurer, Zwingli severely criticized Luther and Melanchthon for their hostility to the peasants.

(d) The Anabaptists

The Anabaptist theology of church and state was quite different from that of Luther and the Swiss reformers. Like the early church, the Anabaptists believed in strict separation between the spiritual and temporal powers. This was because the Anabaptists believed there was an absolute antithesis between the kingdom of Christ and the kingdom of the world. The Swiss Anabaptists delineated this separation of two powers in the *Schleitheim Confession of Faith* (1527).

Although they emphasized a life separated from this world, they also believed that the state was ordained of God and that Christians should obey the civil law as long as it did not contradict God's commandments. Because Anabaptists were the victims of persecution by the state, they withdrew support from the state.

The Anabaptist movement appealed mainly to the poorer element in society. At the grass-roots level, the reformation impulse was expressed more by this simple, though radical, group than by the other reform movements. Unlike other reform movements the Anabaptists were certain that the task of evangelism and social concern did not depend on the combined authority of church and state. Rather, the task depended on the obedience of individual believers. Their concept of a 'brotherhood of believers' was very strong, and in this brotherhood, they cared for each other. The principle of separation of the ecclesiastical and political powers practised today in countries such as the United States of America owes much to the Anabaptists and to their successors, the Mennonites and Quakers.

6. The Evangelical Revival Movements in Europe and North America (Seventeenth to Mid-Nineteenth Centuries)

Many Christian organizations for social reform were born out of the momentum created by pietism on the Continent, the Wesleyan Revival in England, and the First and Second Great

Awakenings in North America. These revivals in the church created major, lasting changes in the societies of Europe and North America.

Intellectually, the Age of Reason marked the beginning of skepticism and natural religion in Europe. The empiricism of John Locke, the deism of Lord Herbert of Cherbury, Voltaire, and J. J. Rousseau, the skepticism of David Hume and Immanuel Kant, and the German idealism of G. W. G. Hegel led to the rationalization of Christianity and challenged the traditional beliefs of the church.

Economically, the guild system in Europe which controlled trade and industry in mediaeval times gradually gave way during the Industrial Revolution of the eighteenth century to a *laissez-faire* economy. Adam Smith in his *Wealth of Nations* (1776) advocated *laissez-faire* capitalism.

In the early stages of the Industrial Revolution, workers laboured long hours for low wages and lived in urban slums worse than their rural homes. Children and women worked long hours for lower wages than men. The mechanization and noise of assembly lines robbed workers of a sense of meaningful community, personal significance, and tranquility which they had enjoyed in rural society.

A. *The Pietistic Movement*

The pietistic movement started with Philip Spener (1635–1705), a German Lutheran, and his disciple, August Francke (1663–1727). The small groups of believers or associations of piety (*collegia pietatis*) stressed Christian perfection because they believed that a Christian's justification is fulfilled by means of sanctification. By sanctification, the pietists did not mean sinlessness; rather they believed in definite progress in the Christian life. Reacting to the emphasis on theological scholasticism in the Protestant churches, the pietists emphasized the living presence of the Holy Spirit in the believer.

One lasting fruit of pietism was the Moravian Church which Count Zinzendorf (1700–60) founded in 1727. Zinzendorf's deep concern for evangelism and missions was exemplified by his own missionary trip to America from 1741 to 1743 to evangelize the Indians. The Moravian Church sent missionaries to all parts of Europe, Greenland, and the West Indies.

The pietists believed in changing society through changing individuals, particularly leaders, by the power of the gospel. By establishing the University of Halle and later the University of Tubigen, the pietists trained people in the Scriptures who later became evangelical leaders in Germany.

The pietists understood the doctrine of perfection to mean that a Christian should not just give intellectual assent to justification but he should also practise his faith by loving others as himself.

August Francke stressed in his *Scriptural Rules* that a man can change society by improving himself through the power of the Spirit. Besides teaching at Halle university as professor of theology, Francke also preached in Glaucha near Halle where degrading beer taverns, dance houses, and other entertainment facilities drew many neglected people. Francke's evangelistic efforts among the underprivileged transformed the whole area. Francke also founded a number of institutions such as an orphanage, a school for poor children, a Latin school for children of the nobility, a publishing house, and a Bible society to distribute cheap Bibles to the poor.

B. *The Wesleyan Revival in England*

It is impossible to overestimate the spiritual and social impact of John Wesley, Charles Wesley, and George Whitfield, evangelists in England in the eighteenth century. Beginning with a small group known as the 'Holy Club of Oxford' in 1729, the Wesley brothers and other evangelicals brought a spiritual revival to England. According to some historians, this Methodist revival saved England from the horrors of a political revolution similar to that which France suffered during 1789–95.

John Wesley often preached at 5:00 am so that people could hear the gospel before they went to work in mines and factories. He also preached at midmorning and midday in markets so that the crowds there would have opportunity to hear the gospel. His passion to help the poor did not, however, stop with preaching. His social concern is described by Howard A. Snyder in *The Problem of Wine Skins,*

> Wesley himself did more than just talk about social reform. Among other things, he agitated for prison, liquor and labour reform; set up loan funds for the poor; campaigned against the slave trade and smuggling; opened a dispensary and gave medicines to the poor; worked to solve unemployment; and personally gave away considerable sums of money to persons in need.[34]

A number of evangelicals who had been influenced by the Wesleyan revival introduced social reforms in Europe and in England through Parliamentary Acts during the eighteenth and nineteenth centuries. Some examples of these reforms are presented here. John Howard brought prison reforms to England and Europe towards the end of the eighteenth century. William Wilberforce's campaign in England against the slave

trade and for the abolition of slavery succeeded in 1833. Shaftes-
bury improved factory conditions for the working classes,
regulated the labour of women and children, and established
slum schools in the second half of the nineteenth century. George
Williams founded the Young Men's Christian Association
(YMCA) in 1844 and the Young Women's Christian Association
(YWCA) in 1855. William and Catherine Booth founded the
Salvation Army in 1859.

The close association between evangelism and social concern
practised in the Wesleyan tradition has yielded innumerable
social benefits, especially in the Third World. Here Protestant
mission societies, started at the end of the eighteenth century,
spread the message of God's love in word and deed around the
world. Such societies include the London Missionary Society
(1795), the Scottish Missionary Society (1796), the Baptist
Missionary Society (1793), the Church Missionary Society
(1798), the Wesleyan Methodist Missionary Society (1817).

William Carey, David Livingstone, Robert Morrison, Hudson
Taylor, and many others from England pioneered the foreign
missionary endeavour. These missionaries zealously preached
the gospel to the natives in Africa, Asia, and Latin America and
pioneered many needed social reforms in these continents.
Several volumes could be written on the beneficial social impact
of these reforms.

C. *The Great Awakening in North America*

In spite of the rising influence of religious deism, unitarianism,
and universalism, America enjoyed two major spiritual awakenings during the eighteenth and nineteenth centuries. These
awakenings occurred before D. L. Moody's evangelistic movement from 1874 to 1899. The First Awakening began in 1726
through a revival by Frelinghuysen among the Dutch Reformed
in the Middle Colonies. From 1734 on, Jonathan Edwards
carried the revival to New England. The Second Awakening
began with Charles E. Finney through camp meetings in
Kentucky. It spread to Tennessee and then into the Northwest
Territory and to New York State.

During the First Awakening in New England Jonathan
Edwards (1703–58) preached on justification by faith and 'the
Spirit of God began extraordinarily to set in'. George Whitfield's
visit to New England from 1740 to 1743 consummated this
revival which gave birth to some thirty religious societies.

Edwards's concern for social justice was linked with the establishment of the Kingdom of God. In *Pressing into the Kingdom of
God*, Edwards encouraged every Christian 'to press into the

Kingdom of God', firmly believing that the Kingdom of God could be established on the earth with the transforming power of the gospel. Edwards also wrote in his *Obligations to Charity* 'that it is the absolute and indispensable duty of the people of God to give bountifully and willingly for supplying the wants of the needy'.[35]

The Second Awakening was initiated by Lyman Beecher, a Congregational Presbyterian minister, and Timothy Dwight, president of Yale University. The impact of this revival crossed denominational lines, particularly those of the Methodists and Baptists. It emphasized both the importance of man's work in salvation and the sovereignty of God. The emphasis placed on personal encounter with God stressed the democratic nature of Christianity and strengthened democratic institutions in America.

Charles Finney (1792–1875) engaged in revival activities during his years at Oberlin College, Oberlin, Ohio (1835–75). Finney called for spiritual awakening through his teaching, preaching, and writing in publications such as the *Oberlin Evangelist*. He also organized during the 1840s co-operative evangelistic campaigns in the strategic cities of Providence, Boston, Rochester, Cleveland, Cincinnati, and Detroit.

It is interesting to note that a number of important mission societies in America were established during the Second Great Awakening. These include the American Board of Commission for Foreign Missions (1810), the United Foreign Missions Society (1817), the Methodist Missions Society (1819), Missions in Hawaii (1820), and the American Home Missions Society for Western Frontier (1826). Other societies for spiritual ministries were also founded during this time: the American Bible Society (1816), the Sunday School Movement (1824), and the American Tract Society (1825).

The rise and fall in Christian social concern correlates with the ebb and flow of the Second Awakening. The twenty-five years preceding the Civil War in America (1861–65) was a crucial time. Every Protestant denomination was engaged in social services dealing with 'issues such as women's rights, temperance, prison reform, public education, world peace, and the abolition of slavery . . .'[36] Among other benefits, the evangelistic campaigns of Charles Finney led to the founding of hundreds of Christian colleges and elementary and secondary schools.

The awakening of 1858–59 differed significantly from previous revivals in the degree of lay involvement. Bishop Warren Candler points out that the Wesleyan movement in England depended basically on the 'class leaders, exhorters, and local preachers', but 'the revival of 1858 inaugurated in some sense the era of lay work in American Christianity'.[36] Lay businessmen organized most of the daily union prayer meetings and used Christian principles to promote social changes. Among the laymen who were deeply influenced by this revival was D. L. Moody in Chicago. His support for the YMCA as a lay evangelist was typical of the laymen's concern for the welfare of society in his day.

United action for evangelical social concern began to decline after the 1830s. Richard F. Lovelace in his *Dynamics of Spiritual Life* mentions three reasons for this decline. First, some evangelicals, known as 'ultraists', demanded radical solutions such as the redefinition of temperance to mean total abstinence from alcoholic beverages rather than moderation. Many were also afraid of supra-denominational control of the church. In 1838 the first schism occurred in the Presbyterian Church between the Old and New Schools. This division in the General Assembly 'marked the beginning of a gradual dissolution of united evangelical social initiatives'.[37]

Second, the issue of slavery divided American evangelicals into three groups: immediate abolitionist, gradual abolitionist after a period of preparation, and anti-abolitionist. Some evangelicals believed that they should deal only with spiritual matters and ignore political and social issues.

Third, views on eschatology changed in the second half of the nineteenth century. Up to the 1850s premillennialists, post-millennialists, and amillennialists all worked together for spiritual, cultural, and social progress. After the 1850s, Edwardsean post-millennialists became secularized and substituted human effort for the work of the Holy Spirit. Many evangelicals, consequently, lost interest in social reform. This loss of a transcendent basis for Christian social concern led to the development of the social gospel of liberalism in the latter part of the nineteenth and in the 20th centuries.

7. Liberal and Orthodox Polarization of the Church (Mid-Nineteenth—Twentieth Centuries)

The seeds for a major theological polarization in Protestantism were sown in the mid-nineteenth century with the rise of biblical criticism. The humanism and rationalism which predominated in the twentieth century had their roots in the Age of Reason in the mid-seventeenth century. Later, German philosophers such as Kant, Hegel, and Schleiermacher reinterpreted religion and Christianity according to naturalistic presuppositions. Darwin's

The Origin of Species (1859) threw an evolutionary bomb at the biblical account of creation. Theological liberalism captured the mainline denominational seminaries at the beginning of the twentieth century. Since then, evangelical Christians have built their own institutions in order to defend theological orthodoxy against liberalism. Consequently, two models of evangelism and social responsibility, based on radically different theological assumptions, have developed side by side during this century.

A. *From Social Gospel to Salvation Today (1970–present)*

The increased industrialization of Europe and North America, massive immigration from southern and eastern Europe to America, problems of urbanization, recurrent depressions, social tensions, and many other factors aroused the consciences of many Christians to various social issues.

In England the Christian Socialist movement began in 1848 when the 'Communist Manifesto' appeared. Leaders such as F. D. Maurice (theologian), Charles Kingsley (pastor and novelist), and J. M. Ludlow (lawyer) attempted to apply Christian solutions to social problems.

In America the social gospel movement developed at the end of the nineteenth century. The exponents of the social gospel tried to find a theological basis for making social changes which were desperately needed at the time. One of the first two pioneers of the social gospel was Washington Gladden (1836–1918), a Congregational minister in Ohio and author of some forty books, including *Social Salvation*. The other was Walter Rauschenbusch (1816–1918), possibly the best known theologian of the social gospel with his books, *Christianity and Social Crisis* (1907) and *A Theology for Social Gospel* (1917). This theology of the social gospel dominated American Christianity until the Great Depression of the 1930s and World War Two.

Thus, the whole emphasis in evangelism was shifting from the traditional eschatological understanding of the kingdom to a horizontal earthly kingdom attainable here and now through purely secular means. In order to establish this kingdom, Rauschenbusch advocated political democracy, government control, a mild socialism, and unions. He condemned the laissez-faire system of capitalism. His social gospel became the major thrust of the Federal Council of Churches.

After World War Two, when neo-orthodoxy was replacing liberalism, an important neo-orthodox thinker appeared, Reinhold Niebuhr (1893–1971). Niebuhr taught at Union Theological Seminary in New York City for thirty-two years. He attacked both liberal and orthodox Christianity in his book, *The Nature and Destiny of Man* (1941 and 1943). He challenged the ethical system of liberalism because its secular framework prevented it from bringing effective social reforms. Secularism assumes that God is irrelevant and that man is ultimate and self-sufficient. It substitutes man's efforts and situational ethics for God's ethical absolutes.

Niebuhr emphasized the reality of sin and 'the law of love as a basis of even the most minimal social standards'. It was called 'an impossible possibility'.[38] He also criticized evangelical Christians for failing to apply God's love to social problems.

Evangelical mission societies reacted sharply to William E. Hocking's *Rethinking Missions* when it appeared in 1932. Hocking advocated that missions should provide only social services such as medicine, education, and philanthropy. Rather than undertake evangelism, missionaries should seek to accommodate Christianity to other religions. This model of evangelism and social concern dominated the now-dismantled IMC and continues to influence the present Commission of World Missions and Evangelism of the World Council of Churches.

B. *The Evangelical Retreat from the 'Kingdom of God' to 'Soul Saving' (Late nineteenth to mid-twentieth century)*

During the twentieth century, the liberal-orthodox controversy over the Scriptures has greatly affected the way evangelicals understand the relationship between evangelism and social concern. Inevitably, they have defended and sharpened their definitions not only of such concepts as the inspiration of the Bible, the deity of Christ and his virgin birth, but also of evangelism, missions and the social gospel.

Reacting both against the liberal associations of the 'social gospel' and also against a tendency for Edwardsean post-millennialism to become secularized, evangelicals laid increasing emphasis upon preaching the gospel with a view to saving individual souls. This was, perhaps, especially marked among dispensational premillennialists (Cyrus Scofield produced the Scofield Bible with his footnotes in 1909). But between 1919 and 1945 both dispensational and non-dispensationalist groups continued to grow.

Since 1945, the evangelical movement has continued to grow numerically while at the same time mainline denominations have declined in membership. And there have been divisions in the evangelical camp, in spite of their basic agreement. Among the significant factors in these divisions have been past disagreements between fundamentalist and middle of the road evangelicals, the rise of para-church organizations, the spread of the charismatic movement and the increasing influence of evangelicals in mainline denominations.

The Protestant missionary movement which started with the spiritual awakenings in Europe, Britain, and North America in the eighteenth and nineteenth centuries accelerated in the twentieth century particularly among evangelical churches in America. The Inter-Varsity Christian Fellowship (IVCF) which started in 1923 in England and in U.S.A. in 1941 encouraged Christian students to volunteer for foreign missionary service. IVCF began to hold student missionary conferences in Toronto and later in Urbana from 1945.

The shift of emphasis away from social involvement does not mean that evangelicals totally lost their genuine concern for the poor and for social justice at home or abroad. History clearly demonstrates that evangelical missions provided various social services such as medicine, education, relief work, and orphanages for the nationals. However, it is the author's opinion that most evangelicals interpreted social concern as a *fruit* of spiritual conversion and used it as a *means* of evangelism.

All the same, Peter Wagner asserts that 'the kingdom of God theme had been virtually buried by American evangelicals,' until Carl F. H. Henry awakened evangelicals with his book, *The Uneasy Conscience of Modern Fundamentalism*, in 1947. More recently, Ron Sider and others have challenged affluent Christians to help 'a billion hungry neighbours'. These calls to action have awakened many evangelicals in the West and Third World. Although most evangelicals are generally sympathetic to the church's greater social involvement, many theological, hermeneutical, and practical questions remain to be answered.

8. The Rising Tide of Third World Christianity (1950–)

Christianity in Asia, Africa, and Latin America has a short history compared to that of the West. Nevertheless, Latin America claims to be a 'Christian' continent after five centuries of missionary endeavour. With 150 million professing Christians out of 360 million people, Africa may achieve a Christian majority below the Sahara desert by the end of this century. Asia, however, with fifty-six per cent of the world's population is only three per cent Christian.

In the 'Christian' West, the churches are losing 7,600 people each day (2,765,000 each year) to materialism, secularism, and/or unbelief. At the same time, about 16,400 people are added to the church each day in sub-Sahara Africa (about

6,000,000 each year). Churches in East Asia are growing by 360,000 converts each year and in South Asia by 447,000 converts each year. The rapid growth of the charismatic movement in Chile, Brazil, and other Latin American nations has been well publicized.

Six new churches are being planted every day in Korea where Christians represent twenty per cent of the local population. The largest single church in the world with 200,000 members is located in Seoul. The government census in Indonesia in 1981 showed that the Christian population had grown from nine per cent in 1971 to seventeen per cent in 1981. This statistic alarmed the government because of the tension it might create in this largest Muslim country in the world. Certainly, God's pendulum is swinging once again from the West to the East and to Africa and Latin America.

The establishment of the Protestant church in the Third World was basically the fruit of Protestant mission from the West which grew out of the spiritual awakenings in Europe, Britain and North America, in the nineteenth and twentieth centuries. Consequently, the churches in the West and in the Third World have close ties in many areas. It was difficult for national churches in the Third World to break away from the paternalistic missionary pressure of the West until the new concept of 'Partnership in Obedience' was introduced in 1947 at the International Missionary Council's conference at Whitby, Canada.

There are three basic factors which we must consider in the relationship between evangelism and social responsibility in the Third World.

A. *Implementation of Missionary Models in the Third World*

Both the western model of the liberal social gospel and the model of the evangelical soul saving of the twentieth century have been copied in the Third World. Liberal missionaries did their best to introduce the social gospel through education, medicine, relief work, and other philanthropic ministries, while evangelical missionaries concentrated on evangelism, church planting, factory work, student work, theological education, relief efforts, and social reform. It was imperative for evangelical missionaries in heathen Africa, Asia, and Latin America not only to bring spiritual deliverance but also to utilize medicine, education, and orphanages for social reform.

For example, the China Inland Mission (CIM), which Hudson Taylor founded in 1865, concentrated its missionary work on the interior of China. According to the *China Mission Hand Book* produced by the American Presbyterian Mission in Shanghai in 1896, the CIM engaged in church planting and social services at the same time. After working for twenty-seven years from 1867 to 1893 in eight provinces in China, CIM had eleven boarding schools with 113 children, twenty-nine day schools with 416 boys and girls, seven hospitals, sixteen dispensaries, and twenty-eight shelters for the cure of opium smokers. Although it was difficult to separate social concern from evangelism, the ultimate purpose of CIM's social service was conversion. As the handbook points out,

> The aim to win the soul while caring for the body, has not been infrequently rewarded with success . . . Still a foundation has been laid, thousands have learned the plan of salvation; and the number who have destroyed their idols, and attend the worship of God is ever increasing.

A similar example of the relationship of evangelism to social concern is found in Japan. The editor of the *Christian Movement* reported in 1916 that forty-two out of forty-eight missions in Japan had some form of social work. Later, national church leaders initiated their own social service ministry. For example, Rev. Toyohiko Kagawa, an evangelist as well as social reformer, headed the 'Million Souls Movement' for evangelism in 1928 and introduced 'occupational evangelism' for the five million factory workers and millions of fishing folk, miners, and transportation workers. He combined evangelism and social concern and started the 'Kingdom of God Movement' with his *Kingdom of God Weekly* magazine. He thus became the driving force for Christian social action in Japan in the 1930s. No doubt, similar examples of nationals who have combined evangelism with social action can be found by the thousands in other Third World countries.

Dr. Bruce Nicholls, a veteran missionary in India where he has served for more than twenty-eight years, declared the importance of close interaction between evangelism and social responsibility at the All India Congress on Mission and Evangelization (AICOME) at Devlali in 1977:

> This subject is crucial for our evangelical witness in India today. Because if we fail to relate our evangelism to our social responsibility at all, or fail to keep a balance between them, we will progressively fail in discipling this nation for Jesus Christ. If we turn a blind eye to the suffering, to the social oppression, the alienation and loneliness of people, let us not be surprised if people turn a deaf ear to our message of eternal salvation.[39]

B. *Development of 'Selfhood': Spirit of Independence from the West*

Since 1945 more than one hundred nations have received their
national independence. This spirit of nationalism has penetrated
every area of thought in the Third World. And this spirit has
greatly affected the national church in its strategy of evangelism
and social concern.

Rev. Tite Tiénou, executive secretary of the AEAM Theological Commission, when asked 'In your opinion, what are some
of the most urgent needs of the churches in Africa?', replied:

> 'In one word: selfhood. To attain this, African leaders must be
> trained by Africans . . . This process has begun, and I hope it will be
> accelerated.'[40]

Consequently, national church leaders have given serious
thought as to how to promote evangelism and social concern in
their own countries according to their respective situations. A
model imported from the West may not fit the cultural context
of another continent. In fact, a model which may be
appropriate in one country may not be appropriate in another
country on the same continent.

C. *Practical Problems of Evangelical Social Concern
in the Third World*

Each continent and each nation within the continent has its
own peculiar ethos. Many Latin American Christians, for
example, have been influenced by the Roman Catholic
practices in their society. Consequently, their understanding
of evangelism and social concern is shaped by liberation
theology which emphasizes the *doing* part of the gospel.
African Christians, on the other hand, have given much
consideration to their animistic cultural background in order
to relate evangelism and social concern to the people's world
view.

In Asia where major non-Christian religions have shaped
national cultural values for several millennia, Christians have
paid special attention to the world view of these religions and to
other dominant values in the culture. Although Asia does not
have a uniform culture, the continent does share certain common
characteristics.

The historical background of most Asian churches is much
closer to that of the early church than to that of Western
churches. There are a number of similarities as well as
differences in historical background between the early church in
the Roman Empire and the church in Asia. They are similar in
that both the early church and the Asian church represent a very

small minority, have no Christian heritage, and are persecuted. They are different in that the early church did not have liberal Christians promoting a humanistic social gospel and syncretistic theology as the church in Asia has today. Nor did the early church have a large number of professional foreign missionaries with their mission dollars. Nor could the early church be accused of representing a wealthy foreign religion because early Christianity sprang from the indigenous roots of Judaism which were already present in Bible lands.

Asia contains the largest number of starving people in the world. Because of the great number of unevangelized peoples and because of gross social injustice in Asia, both evangelism and social action are imperative. This is true not just because Asia needs both but also because, historically, Christians have built their social responsibility upon the foundation of evangelism.

However evangelical social activity in Asia encounters two serious problems. First, the type of social activity which ecumenical leaders advocate and practise often provokes government opposition. Few people will oppose Christians who engage in charity for the poor and other philanthropic assistance. But if Christians attempt to change existing social structures, they will meet opposition. Problems such as poverty, the ever increasing gap between the rich and the poor, crime, and social injustice are deeply rooted in the religious and social structure of the people.

Corruption is another moral plague which has brought misery to millions. For instance, one Asian Christian magazine recently reported that, 'In Indonesia, the cynics like to say, the best way to tip the scales of justice is to first tip the judge who is trying your case. Bribes of $50,000 are not uncommon in important cases.'[41]

Ecumenical leaders are very critical of South Korea, Taiwan, and the Philippines because they suppress human rights. (These leaders ignore flagrant injustices in Red China, North Korea, Vietnam, Cambodia, and other communist-dominated countries.) Where they have the liberty to do so, ecumenical leaders take the issue of human rights to the streets in protest. But many evangelical Christians question whether protest is the best way to achieve social justice. These Christians may agree on *what* needs to be done, but they disagree on *how* to do it.

Repressive governments have often expelled missionaries and have imprisoned national believers who have challenged official social and economic policies. These governments have curtailed religious freedom because in their eyes Christians are meddling in government affairs. In such cases, the fundamental concern of Christians should be to maintain religious freedom for worship and evangelism. Christian social activity which may provoke repression of religious freedom must be subordinated to the church's need to meet for worship.

A Chinese proverb says, 'You cannot have both fish and bear claw [that is, delicacies from both sea and forest] at the same time.' Like the Christians in the early church, we who are in such situations may have to wait patiently and pray for the day when the Righteous Judge will bring social justice to our countries.

Conclusion

Summarizing the foregoing analysis, I suggest the following findings:

1. From the early church to the present, God's people have an intimate and inseparable relationship between evangelism and social responsibility. Most Christians agree on their responsibility in the areas of philanthropic actions.

2. The issue of the priority of evangelism or social responsibility arose in the mid-nineteenth and twentieth centuries when the liberal social gospel became a dominant force in the church.

3. This paper raises a number of theological, hermeneutical, and practical questions related to the issue at hand. The following are examples of such questions. How do we define terms such as 'evangelism', 'mission', 'the Kingdom of God', 'salvation', and 'the gospel'? How do we interpret passages such as 'Blessed are the poor' (Luke 6:20) and 'He has anointed me to bring good news to the poor' (Luke 6:20)? Should a Christian participate in street demonstrations for social justice in repressive societies? What is the extent and nature of Christian social responsibility for changing social structures?

4. Three important questions still remain: (a) How can we reach millions of unreached Chinese in Asia, Africa, Latin America, and the West with the gospel? (b) How can we address the problem of starvation around the world? (c) Is there a limit to Christian social action as Christians try to intervene in politics, economics, society, religion, and culture?

5. Finally, this author's view on the subject is well expressed by Dr. Michael Green when he said,

> Look down Christian history. Is it not true that the great forward movements of the church have been through the proclamation of the good news? Peter, Paul, Origen, Savonarola, Luther, Wesley, Whitfield, J. Edwards, William Temple, Martin Luther King moved the hearts of people through telling them of Jesus. But in each case there was an inescapable social implication in their

proclamation. It is a matter of *root* and *fruit*. The only gospel worth having is rooted in an encounter with the living God which has as its necessary fruit and stamp of authenticity a passionate concern for people's needs.[42]

TO GOD BE THE GLORY!

Notes

1. Arthur P. Johnston and Ronald J. Sider, 'What is the Church's Mandate?' *Asia Theological News*, VIII, No.2 (April-June, 1982), 4–6, 16–18.
2. John R. W. Stott, *Christian Mission in the Modern World* (Downers Grove, Illinois: Inter-Varsity Press, 1975), p.37, and Michael Green, *Evangelism, Now and Then* (Leicester, England: Inter-Varsity Press), pp.13–14.
3. John Foxe, *Foxe's Christian Martyrs of the World* (Chicago: Moody Press, n.d.) pp.36–128. John Foxe lived in England between 1517 and 1587.
4. George W. Forell, *History of Christian Ethics* (Minneapolis: Augsburg Pub. House, 1979), Vol I, p.46.
5. Michael Green, *Evangelism in the Early Church* (Grand Rapids: Eerdmans Pub. Co., 1970), pp.144–165.
6. *ibid.*, p.47. See Green, *Evangelism, Now and Then*, p.26, and Tadataka Maruyama, 'Simple Life Style from the Perspective of Church History', in R. Sider (Ed.), *Lifestyle in the Eighties*, (Exeter/Philadelphia: Paternoster/ Westminster, 1982).
7. Kenneth Scott Latourette, *A History of Christianity* (N.Y.: Harper & Brothers, 1953), p.65.
8. *1 Clement of Rome*, 33:4; 34:1; 38:2. Several chapters are on good works of the Christian, Chs. 33–39.
9. *The Epistle of Barnabas*, 19:8. See *Didache*, 1:5.
10. *The Shepherd of Hermas*, sim. II, 5–7 and sim. I, 6.
11. Earle E. Cairns, *Christianity Through the Centuries* (Grand Rapids: Zondervan, 1981), p.105.
12. *ibid.*, p.109.
13. Kenneth Scott Latourette, *A History of the Expansion of Christianity*, Vol. I, (Grand Rapids: Zondervan, 1970), p.266. Maruyama, (as note 6, p.144). See Eusebius, *Ecclesiastical History*, Book VI, p.43.
14. Chrysostom, Homily on Matthew, No. 66, section 3 quoted by Latourette, *A History of the Expansion of Christianity*, Vol. I, p.266.
15. *The First Apology of Justin Martyr*, 13–17. See George Forell ed., *Christian Social Teachings* (Minneapolis: Augsburg Pub. House, 1966), p.35. Green, *Evangelism, Now and Then*, pp.24–25.
16. *The First Apology of Justin Martyr*, 27–29. See Forell ed., *Christian Social Teachings*, p.38.
17. Tertullian, *The Apology*, 39:5–6 quoted by Forell, *History of Christian Ethics*, pp.47, 50.
18. Kenneth Scott Latourette, *A History of the Expansion of Christianity*, Vol. 1, p.266.
19. Cairns, pp.125–129.

20. Robert E. Webber, *The Secular Saint* (Grand Rapids, Zondervan, 1979), p.113.
21. *ibid.*, pp.111–113.
22. Augustine, *City of God*, 14:28 quoted by Forell, *History of Christian Ethics*, p.172. See Webber, pp.138–144.
23. Augustine, *Enarrationes in Psalmos*, 103:3, 16; cf. 4:2 and 103:16–17 in Meer p.137.
24. *Augustine Sermones* 159:4–5 in Meer pp.135–136.
25. Basil, Homily on Luke 12 in *Patrologiae Cursus Completus*, in Forell, *History of Christian Ethics*, p.120.
26. The Morals, 70:22 in *Ascetic Works of St. Basil*, p.131 in Forell, *ibid.*, p.119.
27. Forell, *ibid.*, p.128.
28. P. Boissonnade, *Life and Work in Medieval Europe* (N.Y.: Harper Torchbooks, 1964), p.203.
29. James W. Thompson and Edgar N. Johnston, *An Introduction to Medieval Europe* (N.Y.: W. W. Norton & Co., 1937), p.679.
30. Michael de Labedoyère, *St. Francis* (Garden City, N.Y.: Image Books, 1964), p.52.
31. Luther, *Works* (Weimar Edition), VII, 31ff. in Taylor, p.153.
32. Forell, *Christian Social Teaching*, pp.157–161.
33. Bong Rin Ro, 'The Church and State in Calvin' (unpublished S.T.M. thesis, Concordia Lutheran Seminary, St. Louis, Mo., 1967), pp.25–26.
34. Howard A. Snyder, *The Problems of Wineskins* (Downers Grove, Ill., Inter-Varsity Press, 1975), p.172.
35. Jonathan Edwards, *Obligations to Charity*, quoted by Forell in *Christian Social Teaching*, pp.301, 301–305.
36. Tim Dowley, ed. *The History of Christianity* (Tring, Herts., England: Lion Pub. 1977), p.535.
37. Richard F. Lovelace, *Dynamics of Spiritual Life* (Downers Grove, Illinois: Inter-Varsity Press, 1979), p.375.
38. Forell, *Christian Social Teaching*, pp.380–405.
39. M. R. Matthews, 'EFICOR: A Channel of Blessing', *AIM*, Vol. VIII, No. 8 (August 1977), p.7.
40. 'Researcher's Profile', *Forwarding the Missionary Task*, published by the Fuller School of World Mission as a Newsletter (Spring 1982), p.4.
41. Bong Rin Ro, 'Problems of Evangelical Social Concern in Asia', *Asia Theological News*, Vol. 8, No. 2 (April–June 1982), 2.
42. Michael Green, *Evangelism Now and Then* (Leicester, I.V.P., 1979), p.57.

2

A Critical Evaluation
of Contemporary Perspectives

TOKUNBOH ADEYEMO*

Synopsis   Dr. Tokunboh Adeyemo surveys the different ways in which evangelicals attempt to relate evangelism to social responsibility.

He traces some of the strategic regional and international interdenominational conferences that have shaped or influenced the direction of evangelical theologies of mission during the past twenty years. He includes Wheaton 1966, Berlin 1966, Frankfurt 1970 and Lausanne 1974. Among the gatherings that he does not survey we might mention the following: CLADE I & II in Latin America, PACLA, SACLA and AEAM conferences in Africa, ACOME, ATA conferences, CCOME, Madras and COWE in Asia, Basel and High Leigh, Nîmes and Edinburgh in Europe and Green Lake and Kansas City in the U.S.A.

Dr. Adeyemo then distinguishes no fewer than nine schools of thought among evangelicals alone, though recognizing the overlapping between them. He notes that many contemporary evangelical leaders cannot be limited to just one position. Some hold that social action is a distraction from or betrayal of evangelism; others see it as either a means or a consequence or as a partner of evangelism; yet others hardly distinguish one from the

*Dr. Adeyemo is General Secretary of the Association of Evangelicals of Africa and Madagascar (AEAM), Nairobi, Kenya.

41

other or perhaps see both as necessary to the life and witness of
the Church.

His own 'undogmatic conclusion' offers some insights on the
witness of John the Baptist.

Introduction

Our assignment in this chapter is not to engage in a definition of
terms such as evangelism, social concern and mission, good as
that exercise may be. Neither is it our intention to delve into the
controversy between Ecumenicals and Evangelicals in respect of
our topic, profitable as that may prove. We are committed to
understanding one another better; appreciating one another's
points of view more fully; promoting a greater unity of mind on
our subject as we are led by God's Spirit to a better understanding of the Scriptures; and, hopefully, mobilizing ourselves and
other believers (as the Lord enables us) to reach the whole world
with the whole gospel of our Lord Jesus Christ. In the light of
this, we have limited ourselves in this chapter to a consideration
of perspectives on evangelism and social responsibility as
expressed primarily by evangelicals within the past three
decades.

1. Brief Survey of Some Evangelical Consultations

In this section we take a quick look at important or strategic
regional and international interdenominational evangelical meetings since 1960 which have shaped or influenced the theology of
mission. We recognize that evangelicals do not live in isolation
from the rest of Christendom, let alone the world in general.
Since the crucial issue before us is: What does it mean to be '*in*
the world, but not *of* it?', it is necessary to examine what
evangelicals are either responding to or reacting against as they
do their missiology. However, we must leave this for another
paper and concentrate on the evangelicals.[1]

The nineteen sixties were very eventful: at its Third General
Assembly in New Delhi (1961), the World Council of Churches
received into its membership the Eastern Orthodox churches; at
the same meeting, the International Missionary Council which
had developed out of the Edinburgh (1910) vision was integrated
into the WCC. In the same decade four other meetings were held

by WCC and its off-shoots: Commission of World Mission and Evangelism, Mexico (1963); Faith and Order, Montreal (1963); World Conference on Church and Society (1966) and the Fourth General Assembly, Uppsala (1968). During the same period, the Second Vatican Council (1962-65) met, with interruptions, and turned out volumes of material. David Bosch has rightly remarked: 'Vatican II is not conceivable without the stimulus of Protestant theology and Protestant missionary thinking in particular.'[2] Several of the sixteen official Council documents deal directly or indirectly with our subject. At the risk of over-simplification it can be said that the Ecumenicals secularized the sacred during this decade so that at Uppsala, mission was largely humanization. On the other hand, Rome called for the Church's involvement in the sociopolitical issues of the world as well as for world evangelization.

The same period witnessed political independence for tens of Third World nations with new waves of ideologies. The old relationship of mission agencies and the national churches they have helped to found was being called to question and clarification. With all these currents and under-currents, a survey of evangelical gatherings becomes helpful.

A. *Wheaton (1966): Congress on the Church's Worldwide Mission*

A predominantly North American meeting, but with a spread that is far-reaching: 938 accredited delegates from 71 countries. The breakdown looks like this:

   100 boards affiliated with IFMA and EFMA were represented.[3]
   50 mission agencies not affiliated with IFMA and EFMA.
   39 special mission interest groups.
   14 non-North American agencies.
   55 theological schools.

The Congress, which met from April 9–16, and discussed ten crucial contemporary issues affecting missions and the Church, releasing a comprehensive document, the 'Wheaton Declaration', has been styled as 'an attempt to consolidate evangelical forces'. On the issue before us, the Congress upheld the *priority* of preaching the gospel of individual salvation. It declared specifically:

> THAT we affirm unreservedly the primacy of preaching the gospel to every creature, and we will demonstrate anew God's concern for social justice and human welfare.

> THAT evangelical social action will include, wherever possible, a verbal witness to Jesus Christ.

THAT evangelical social action must avoid wasteful and unnecessary competition . . .

THAT we urge all evangelicals to stand openly and firmly for racial equality, human freedom, and all forms of social justice throughout the world.[4]

Maintaining the priority of verbal proclamation, the declaration on social concern shows a departure from the reaction of evangelicals in the early twenties against the 'social gospel'. Then came

B. Berlin (November 1966): The World Congress on Evangelism

Convened by the Billy Graham Evangelistic Association and Christianity Today, the Congress which lasted for 10 days drew together 1,200 participants from 100 countries. The central message of the Congress could be summed up by the closing statement which reads: 'We proclaim this day our unswerving determination to carry out the *supreme mission* of the church'.

What is this supreme mission of the church? This is identified as: 'bearing the Good News of God's saving Grace to sinful and lost humanity; calling upon men and nations everywhere to repent and turn to works of righteousness, and bringing the word of salvation to mankind in spiritual revolt and moral chaos'.[5]

The Congress addressed itself to some social problems under its section dealing with One Race. It upheld the equality of all men as in creation and common need of divine redemption offered in Jesus Christ; condemned strongly racialism wherever it appears; and pledged to 'seek by God's grace to eradicate from our lives and from our witness whatever is displeasing to Him (Jesus Christ) in our relations with one another'.[6]

After rejecting all theology and criticism that refuses to submit to the divine authority of the Holy Scriptures, and after denouncing all traditionalism which weakens that authority by adding to the Word of God, the Congress defined Evangelism as: '. . . the proclamation of the Gospel of the crucified and risen Christ, the oniy Redeemer of men, according to the Scriptures, with the purpose of persuading condemned and lost sinners to put their trust in God by receiving and accepting Christ as Saviour through the power of the Holy Spirit, and to serve Christ as Lord in every calling of life and in the fellowship of his church, looking toward the day of his coming in glory'.[7]

Explicit in the Congress statement and papers is the concensus of the participants that Evangelism is the supreme mission of the church.

Implicit in the same documents is the lordship of Jesus Christ over the believers who, because of their encounter with him, are expected to get involved in socio-economic and political demands bearing witness for him. Paul Rees's paper on 'Evangelism and Social Concern' puts it in this way:

> We have failed to see—and to show—that if the mission of the church is narrow, the witness of the believing community is broad. The evangelistic mission is to proclaim Christ crucified as the one mediator of our salvation. But the confirming witness of believers is one in which they stand related to the whole of life and to the total fabric of society. Here they bear witness both to the mercy of God's forgiveness and the judgments of God's justice. Nothing human is alien to their interest and, so far as their testimony and influence are concerned, Jesus Christ is Lord of all.[8]

In the same year, the Association of Evangelicals of Africa and Madagascar (AEAM) was formed at Limuru, Kenya, and its first General Secretary, Kenneth Downing, a veteran missionary of the Africa Inland Mission, was appointed. A majority of the founding member churches and missions were affiliated to either IFMA or EFMA. In its purpose commitment, the subject of our concern is expressed as follows: 'To promote evangelism and church growth; and, to render special services for all men, but especially for those of the household of faith'[9] (Gal. 6:10).

In 1967, the issues and results of Wheaton and Berlin were discussed by Indian Evangelicals at the Evangelical Fellowship of India (EFI) Leaders' Conference at Nasik. In that year, EFICOR, the EFI Committee on Relief, was formed. The point we are trying to establish is that somehow big meetings—be it ecumenical or evangelical—held in the West find their expression in the Third World.

C. *Frankfurt (1970): Frankfurt Theological Convention*

At this meeting, German evangelical theologians and missiologists who were dissatisfied with the Uppsala (1968) theology of humanization examined the fundamental crisis in mission and produced in tabular form, '7 Indispensable Basic Elements of Mission'. To this caucus, 'Mission is the witness and presentation of eternal salvation performed in the name of Jesus Christ by His Church and fully authorized messengers by means of *preaching*, the *sacraments* and *service* (Jn. 3:16; 2 Cor. 5:20).' If service in this statement is taken for social concern which the group regarded as humanization and we were to ask how this relates to evangelism, we may receive the answer that: 'Humanization is not the primary goal of mission. It is rather a *product* of our new birth through God's saving activity in Christ within us, or an *indirect* result of the Christian proclamation in its power to perform a leavening activity in the course of world history (Ezek. 38:23).'[10]

D. *Devlali (1970): All India Congress on Evangelism*

At this strategic meeting the relationship between *Kerygma* (proclamation) and *diakonia* (service) was grappled with. Robin Thomson assessed that various congresses and consultations called by Indian Evangelicals on our subject were prompted, to some extent, by ecumenical thinking and action on the one hand, and by natural disasters within the nation which called for practical response and reflection on the other hand. At this congress the priority of evangelism was clearly affirmed though the participants were challenged to get involved in social action.

E. *Chicago (1973): Evangelical Social Action*

During one weekend in November, 1973, fifty influential (mainly North American) evangelicals gathered to consider the issue of evangelical social concern in North America in particular and the world at large. The origin of the meeting goes back to a reaction against insufficient inclusion of social emphasis in the programme of Campus Crusade's Explo '72 at Dallas. The aim of the meeting was 'to arouse America's millions of evangelicals to a greater degree of social concern and action'. At the close of the meeting, the participants, who included men like theologian Carl F. H. Henry, former editor of *Christianity Today*, California Baptist Seminary professor Bernard Ramm, President William Bentley of the National Black Evangelical Association and Professor Ronald J. Sider, then of Messiah College, signed a 473-word social action statement, 'A Declaration of Evangelical Social Concern'. The thrust of the document is confession mixed with repentance and a call for change of attitude and action. One commentator says: 'Reading this declaration one gets the impression that he is reading the Stuttgart Confession of Guilt of 1954.' Evangelicals were challenged to emphasize social sins and institutionalized evils as vigorously as they do personal sins.[11]

F. *Lausanne (1974):*
International Congress on World Evangelization

In terms of the spread of its participants—2,700 from more than 150 nations; the range of viewpoints represented—all the six different evangelical groups identified by professor Peter Beyerhaus were represented; the time of meeting—following the CWME theological confusion of 'Salvation Today', Bangkok (1973); and the thoroughness with which the Congress issues were dealt with, it can be said that Lausanne (1974) has been the most strategic evangelical gathering in contemporary history. Paragraphs 4 and 5 of *The Lausanne Covenant*, the official Congress document, deal specifically, though separately, with the subject of our concern. Lausanne was unequivocal as to the content of the gospel and what it means to evangelize: the good news is Jesus, the historical, biblical Christ; his vicarious death and glorious resurrection as recorded in the Scriptures; his exalted Lordship and offer of forgiveness and gift of the Holy Spirit to anyone who repents and believes. Evangelization is the verbal proclamation of the said good news with results which include obedience to Christ, incorporation into his church and responsible service in the world.

Turning to Christian social responsibility, the Covenant states: 'Although reconciliation with man is not reconciliation with God, nor is social action evangelism, nor is political libera-tion salvation, nevertheless we affirm that evangelism and socio-political involvement are both part of our Christian duty.'

Did Lausanne (1974) say anything new which had not been said before e.g. by Wheaton (1966), Berlin (1966), Frankfurt (1970), Devlali (1970) or Chicago (1973)? Did it show more concern for social action than these other meetings? I don't think these questions can be answered in the affirmative. One thing, however, makes Lausanne (1974) stand out: the Covenant positively expresses socio-political involvement as a Christian duty and places it on the same level as evangelism. For the advocates of 'radical discipleship' this is considered to be a giant step forward for the Evangelicals. For the conservative Evange-licals at Lausanne this marriage of evangelism and social action can in no way be called an advancement; if anything it is a retreat. They feel that evangelism is being dethroned. Notwith-standing, they were pacified and kept in the fold by another statement in paragraph 6 of the Covenant. It says: 'In the church's mission of sacrificial service evangelism is *primary*.' The primacy of evangelism soothes the conservatives but angers the radical discipleship advocates. The latter argue that it is mislead-ing to label any task of the church as primary. In the middle of this spectrum are those who advance the 'partnership concept', that social action is a partner of evangelism. No party was completely satisfied. This matter needs further clarification.

Subsequent meetings that can be considered include: PACLA, Nairobi (1976); 'Church and Nationhood', Basel (1976); 'Rhode-sian Congress on Evangelism in Context', Bulawayo (1976); 'All India Conference on Evangelical Social Action', Madras (1979); SACLA, Pretoria (1979); 'Consultation on Development', High Leigh (1980); 'Consultation on Simple Lifestyle', High Leigh

(1980); and COWE, Pattaya (1980). In no significant way has any of these said or done anything that has not been said or done before. The debate which has continued has brought us to where we are today.

How does (or should) social action relate to evangelism?

2. Conflicting Options for Evangelicals

At least nine schools of thought can be identified in this exercise with over-lappings here and there between the views.

A. *That Social Action is a* distraction *from Evangelism*

Some conservative Christians holding an extreme view of dispensationalism consider evangelism as the exclusive mission of the Church. Before the era of the modern 'tent-making missionary movement' as typified by Campus Crusade for Christ's Agape movement, the majority of missionaries went out as soul-winners and church planters alone. They have good theological reasons for this position. Doesn't the 'any moment return of Christ' belief impel an urgency to reach the world with the Gospel before it is too late? Both the movie, 'A Thief at Night' and the song, 'The King is Coming' have contributed in no small measure to this idea of getting the job done in earnest.

Together with this is the apocalyptic dissolution of the heavens which impresses upon us that the whole frame of this world is passing away. It makes sense missiologically to rescue the perishing. By and large, this is where Third World missions are at. Though it may not be verbally articulated, the pre-occupation of indigenous missions of India, Korea and Nigeria (to name just a few) is verbal proclamation of the gospel resulting in church planting.[12]

This does not mean or imply that the adherents of this view disregard education, medical work and compassion. In actual fact, they are often involved in social activities which are considered as secondary. In some way, our theological institutions inadvertently prepare missionaries for this viewpoint. Rather than taking the students to the market-places, the highways and by-ways, the chambers and parliaments, and giving them opportunities of interacting with people in real life situations as Jesus did with his disciples, we confine them to walled-classroom cum library settings, and dose them with principles of evangelism.[13]

B. *That Social Action is a* betrayal *of Evangelism*

This takes the first viewpoint to an extreme. With a dualistic presupposition of conflict between spirit and body, sacred and secular, eternal and temporal, and an almost gnostic type of personal pietism coupled with the hopelessness of the world (with wars and rumours of war, pestilence, drought, famine, earthquakes etc.), most adherents of this view consider social involvement as an undue shift from the legitimate to the illegitimate. The world to them is wicked and irredeemably corrupt. Believers should get away from it so as to avoid contamination. Christians' mission in the world is basically two-fold: personal holiness and winning the lost. It is not uncommon to hear its proponents say: 'Why shift furniture when the house is burning?' or, 'Forget about improving conditions on the sinking ship! Man the life-boats and save as many as possible!'

Leighton Ford has traced the root of this view to the early twentieth century evangelicals' reaction against the widespread 'social gospel' advocated by liberals.[14] This is not far enough unless we are dealing with its recent reappearance. Since the underlying worldview of the position is dialectic dualism one can go as far back as New Testament times and investigate the teaching and practice of the mystics taken to task by the Apostle Paul in his letter to the Colossian believers.

John Stott has rightly identified the modern day 'Jesus movement' and its near-monastic establishments with this camp.[15] Many of the apocalyptic sectarian movements like the Jehovah's Witnesses fit comfortably into this category.

Forgotten is the fact that the God of redemption is also the God of creation, who sits upon the circle of the earth and holds all things together. God has not willed any part of his entire creation to any malevolent force; and though the whole creation may groan and travail in pain until now, its redemption draws nigh. Forgotten as well is the principle that 'salt and light' can have functional meaning not in isolation but only in loving encounter with the tasteless dark world.

C. *That Social Action is Evangelism*

'Some (non-evangelicals) might even see social responsibility as the equivalent of evangelism', writes Leighton Ford.[16] That isn't true. There are evangelicals whose line of distinction between social responsibility and evangelism is so thin that it can be neglected. In his book, *Social Action vs. Evangelism*, an essay on the contemporary crisis, William J. Richardson contends that evangelism is social action. Avoiding the pitfalls of separation and assimilation, and modifying the popular understanding of social action, Richardson submits that since evangelism takes place in a social context—at the temple, in a chariot, before a mixed audience of races and sexes; and since the message proclaimed is the lordship of Christ with a claim upon the world; and since the church, as an aspect of evangelism receives into its fellowship the despised, the weak, the foolish, the slave, the man of another race, along with the noble, the strong, the wise, the free, and the native born, thus confronting a given culture with a new norm of obedience to God, a new norm of what it means to be human—this is social action; it stands to reason that 'Social involvement is not merely a legitimate addendum to evangelism.' Understood in this sense, Richardson concludes his thesis by asserting: 'Social action is hardly a by-product of evangelism because [since] it occurs at the moment someone heeds the call to discipleship.'[17]

Emilio Castro rejects as artificial any attempt to construct a distinction between evangelism and social involvement. He sees both existing 'as parts only, and [which] can only be discovered or recognized separately within the framework of their inter-relatedness'.[18] In another article he states categorically: 'Evangelism only exists where there is social concern. Without it there may be propaganda, proselytism, but hardly good news.'[19]

In his article, 'Relationship Between Evangelism and Social Responsibility', published in *AIM*, Robin Thomson of Union Biblical Seminary, Yavatmal, submits the thesis that 'social action is evangelism'. Though he claims that to accept social action as a partner of evangelism (the position to be considered later) is the most satisfactory, because of the complexity of the relationship and because of the fluidity of situations, he would insist on making no preferential choice. In his own words, 'the issue is not priority, it is obedience'.[20]

The basic weakness of this position is the dangerous blurring of biblical distinction between evangelism and social involvement. The fact that Jesus Christ dealt with situations according to specific needs (social, therapeutic, or spiritual) does not mean that he obliterated what could be called 'divine distinctions'. Jesus would not consider feeding the multitude with bread and fish as one and the same as proclaiming the gospel with authority with the intent of conversion (cf. Jn. 6:15–29). Neither will Paul substitute the preaching of the Word with anything (see 1 Cor. 9:16) nor the apostles confuse the ministry of the Word with the waiting upon tables (Acts 6:1–8). If that cutting edge is lost the church with all its various agencies might as well pack up and turn its assets over to the Red Cross or any other humanitarian charity organization.

David Bosch in his response to Dr. Adeyemo's paper has suggested

*that this viewpoint would be better described as follows: 'Evangelism
and social action are indistinguishable from one another.'* He adds
that two other distinct options might be considered, namely, 'Social
action is more important than evangelism', 'Evangelism is social
action', or, as Sider puts it, 'Evangelism is politics because salvation
is social justice.'* (Evangelism, Salvation and Social Justice, *p.6*).
It is assumed that evangelicals will reject both these positions. Bosch
agrees with Sider that the WCC Uppsala Statement that 'humanization is the goal of missions' belongs to the latter view. Further, he
thinks that these two views logically follow on from viewpoint three.*

D. That Social Action is a means to Evangelism

Synonymous with the word 'means' in this context are words like
'bridge', and 'preparation'. A popular proverb in Upper Volta
goes like this: 'An empty sack cannot stand.' In Sierra Leone the
same idea is conveyed like this: 'An empty belly has no ears.'
The Yoruba people of Nigeria say it differently: 'A hungry man
has no ears for words.' Expressed in many different ways, the
message is one, namely: 'Hungry people cannot listen to
sermons.' Any form of social concern therefore, be it feeding the
hungry, medicine for the sick, education for the illiterate or
rehabilitating the refugees, is regarded as a means to an end—the
end being evangelism and conversion.

This posture has been variously criticized. 'It makes our social
response a dubious decoy for some unutterable intention', writes
Ken R. Gnanakan.[21] According to John Stott, 'In its most
blatant form this makes social work (whether food, medicine or
education) the sugar on the pill, the bait on the hook, while in its
best form it gives to the gospel a credibility it would otherwise
lack. In either case, the smell of hypocrisy hangs round our
philanthropy.'[22] Stott further hints at the danger of producing
so-called 'rice Christians'.

Viewed from another angle however, one wonders if such
criticisms are not too harsh. Consider, for example, the principle
of moving from the known to the unknown, from felt need to
real need, from the material to the spiritual. Think of a
husbandman who digs his vineyard, gathers out the stones, and
plants it with the choicest vine, and builds a tower in the midst of
it, and also makes a wine-press in it. Are all these wrong? Are
they an end in themselves? Not according to the prophet Isaiah.
Similarly, the teaching of our Lord Jesus Christ concerning
himself as the true bread of life on the heels of his feeding five
thousand people with material bread cautions one against dismis-
sing this viewpoint too readily (cf. Jn. 6:1–29).

The history of modern missions reveals what can be called 'the 3 x C presuppositions' of the missionaries as they approached the heathen: to change, to civilize and to Christianize. It was the construction of dams by the Basel missionaries in northern Ghana that opened the way for the gospel. This is also being done today among the Maasai people of Kenya. During the colonial days the majority of conversions which happened in African countries (south of the Sahara) took place in mission schools. Though the practice was resented by some, the majority of the recipients were appreciative and thankful.

The more serious weakness of this viewpoint in my opinion is not the fear of breeding 'rice Christians' but of ceasing to be compassionate, kind and good once the conversion goal has been realized. To what Harold Lindsell has said, namely, 'As long as service makes it possible to confront men with the Gospel, it is useful',[23] I will add that for the sake of credibility such service should not be discontinued.

E. *That Social Action is a* manifestation *of Evangelism*

Proponents of this view, including J. H. Bavinck and John V. Taylor, see social involvement as a demonstration of the gospel. The former gives visibility to the latter. The analogy of faith and work in the epistle of James is often used to explain this viewpoint. John Stott, though himself not a supporter, calls social action in this view the 'sacrament' of evangelism, for it makes the message significantly visible. He locates a strong precedent for the view in the ministry of Jesus Christ whose words and deeds were like twin sisters. He expresses uneasiness however, since the view 'makes service a subdivision of evangelism, an aspect of the proclamation'.[24] It may be added also that the difference between this viewpoint and the fourth is just one of degree and not of kind since both expect the same result.

F. *That Social Action is a* result or consequence *of Evangelism*

Sociopolitical action was always part of teaching them 'to observe all things whatsoever I have commanded you' (Matt. 28:20). The mission of the Church was evangelism by its members at home and abroad. Expressions of love and compassion in evangelism at home and abroad are evident in dispensaries, hospitals, schools, and orphanages, which contribute to that mission of evangelism.'[25]

With these words and many more expressing the same conviction, missiologist-theologian Arthur P. Johnston champions the views of those who believe that changing people through verbal proclamation of the gospel is primary and that, secondarily, the transformed lives will become socially involved simply as a matter of course. The analogy of seed and fruit is often used in this connection. Proclamation with resultant conversion is the seed while sociopolitical involvement is the fruit. The advocates of this viewpoint strongly uphold the priority of evangelism. Elton Trueblood is quoted as saying: 'If we do not start with what is primary, we are not likely to achieve what is secondary, for this is a resultant . . . The call to become fishers of men precedes the call to wash one another's feet.'[26]

This viewpoint takes seriously the creation mandate and the great commandment to love seriously but since the fall, the exponents argue, redemption through the cross and proclamation of that good news has become the mission of God and of his church. Jesus did not come into the world to improve economic order—that is part of the result of his coming—he came at the fullness of time to redeem them that were under the law, that they might receive the adoption of sons (Gal. 4:5 cf. Gen. 3:15). Indeed, he came also to destroy the works of the devil, but this is primarily in the lives of individuals who believe on him rather than the structures which still lie in the hands of the evil one. Social action and social improvements are valuable only where the new birth has preceded and prepared society to accept and sustain them. To reverse the order or parallel it—through the partnership concept—will be like putting new wine in an old wineskin or dethroning evangelism. Michael Cassidy, whose personal view calls for solidarity and greater sociopolitical involvement, cautions that the horizontal should depend upon the vertical and not precede it.[27] Many reputable evangelical leaders adhere to this viewpoint. David Bosch cites Martin Luther as adopting this attitude with regard to the state.

This position has been criticized as supporting the status quo; maximizing personal sins while minimizing structural evils; isolating individuals for salvation from the communities of their relatives, friends, colleagues and governments; and failing to produce a just society (even within the Church) which is a direct result of regenerated lives. Christians' participation in the inhuman slave trade and today's racism are among the examples often cited.

G. *That Social Action is a* partner *of Evangelism*

The foremost advocate of this view is John Stott. He articulates his thesis in the following words:

> As partners the two belong to each other and yet are independent of each other. Each stands on its own feet in its own right alongside the other. Neither is a means to the other, or even a manifestation of the

other. For each is an end in itself. Both are expressions of unfeigned love.[18]

In support of his position, Stott draws our attention to the 'seeing and having' analogy of the Apostle John (cf. I Jn. 3:17, 18) which he regards as two prongs of the same 'fork of unfeigned love'. He argues: 'If I do not relate what I "have" to what I "see", I cannot claim to be indwelt by the love of God.' In practice, the action taken in any given situation will depend on the need 'seen'—spiritual, social, medical or political—and the resources 'had'—gospel knowledge, social expertise, medicine or political action. He hastens to add that the two—evangelism and social action—need not always go together since situations vary as well as Christian callings. He contends that one should not normally have to choose, but should one have to, 'eternal salvation is more important than temporal welfare'.

This view has received criticisms in two major forms. One claims that it has created unnecessary dichotomy which, at the end of the day, 'blunts the verbal witness of the Church in evangelism. This view not only hinders the growth of the church, but proves self-defeating in that the potential children of the Kingdom are not gathered in to produce their fruit of the spirit in the world.'[29] If Stott could respond he would probably say: 'Certainly the "words" and "works" of Jesus belonged indissolubly to one another. In one sense his works made his words visible, were a visual proclamation of the Gospel of the Kingdom, and elicited faith. Christian good works of love have the same nature and effect.'[30] Secondly, the position has been criticized for retaining the phrase 'the primary task . . .' for evangelism which, in turn, has been interpreted by its critics as making social concern subordinate to evangelism. To this Stott has responded by consenting to the expression 'distinct yet equal' partners as long as both ministries (evangelistic and social) are 'qualified not only in theory by the greater importance of the eternal (cf. II Cor. 4:17, 18) but in practice both by existential situations and specialist callings'.[31]

Personally I find that the 'either or' inference of this position (depending on what I 'see' and what I 'have') raises some questions about the alliance in the light of the 'both and' existential realities in which we live and to which the gospel addresses itself. Also, isn't it true that people (including Christians) see what they want to see?

H. *That Social Action and Evangelism are equally important but genuinely distinct aspects of the total mission of the church*

In this camp are men like Ronald J. Sider, Vinay Samuel, Chris

Sugden, Waldron Scott, Samuel Escobar, David Gitari, David Bosch, and Jim Wallis to name a few.[32] Simply put, the main argument of this position has been stated in Sider's words: 'The time has come for all biblical Christians to refuse to use the sentence: The primary task of the church is . . . I do not care if you complete the sentence with evangelism or social action. Either way it is unbiblical and misleading.' The logic is that the mission of the church cannot be subsumed under one ministerial category. If any word can be regarded as adequate to convey the mission of the church, according to Bosch, it will be the 'biblical concept *martyria* (witness) which can be subdivided into *kerygma* (proclamation) *koinonia* (fellowship), *diakonia* (service) . . . and *leitourgia* (liturgy)'.[33]

On the question of where social concern and evangelism meet, Bosch answers: 'They resemble the two blades of a pair of scissors, which operate in unison, held together by the *koinonia*, the fellowship, which likewise is not a separate "part" of the church's task, but rather the "cement" which keeps *kerygma* and *diakonia* together, the "axle" on which the two blades operate . . . Both dimensions are indissolubly bound together. If you lose the one, you lose the other.'[34] Bosch immediately underscores a recognition of a variety of gifts, meaning that different Christians perform different roles, and more importantly, varying situations which demand diversification of forms of Christian witness. In this respect Bosch and Stott agree.

In his 'distinct yet equal' option, Sider, however, sees an inseparable interrelationship. After advancing that: (i) the proclamation of the biblical gospel necessarily includes a call to repentance and turning away from all forms of sin—personal and structural; (ii) giving the full New Testament reality of the church frequently constitutes a challenge to the status quo; (iii) seeking justice sometimes facilitates the task of evangelism; and (iv) it is not helpful to use the words 'the Great Commission' to connote evangelism and 'the Great Commandment' to connote social concern; he concludes by saying 'that evangelism often leads to increased social justice and vice versa and also that biblical Christians will, precisely to the extent that they are faithful followers of Jesus, always seek liberty for the oppressed (Lk. 4:18)'.[35] To substantiate his claim, Sider cites the roles of William Wilberforce and Charles Finney in Britain and America respectively in the abolitionist movement. Equally he argues:

> The Gospels provide no indication, either theoretically or by the space devoted to each, that Jesus considered preaching the Good News more important than healing sick people. He commanded us both to feed the hungry and to preach the Gospel without adding

that the latter was primary and the former could be done when and if spare time and money were available.[36]

This viewpoint is not without criticisms. It has been faulted for seeming to de-emphasize the vertical for the sake of the horizontal. In answer to this for example, Waldron Scott writes: 'It is not my intention to assign an ultimate priority to the horizontal at the expense of the vertical. Like a weaver's loom, it takes both to make the whole. If this book (*Bring Forth Justice*) appears to attach more importance to the horizontal, it does so simply in order to redress a current imbalance.'[37] This is not safe for an extremity can never be corrected by another extremity. For other cogent criticisms including: indiscriminate application of the Kingdom of God and the lordship of Jesus to 'society at large' rather than where Christ rules by bestowing salvation and receiving homage; the apparent depersonalization of Paul's 'principalities and powers'; and inadequate recognition of variety of gifts as well as situations which demand specialization, attention can be drawn to Stott's response to Sider's essay.

I. *That Social Action is* part *of the Good News—Evangelism*

To its advocates, social concern is larger than just feeding the hungry and healing the sick. It is bringing Christ's righteousness to bear on every aspect of life—social, economic, religious, political etc. It is, as it were, defending the truth or standing for the right, the just, and the equitable. 'The task of the Church remains the preaching of the gospel and winning the world for Christ. But this task of preaching the gospel of the Kingdom includes everything, even the socio-political responsibility of the church and its members.' In his thought-provoking book, *A Christian Manifesto*, Francis A. Schaeffer argues vehemently that 'true spirituality covers all of reality and that the Lordship of Christ covers *all* of life and *all* of life equally'. Applying this to our subject he recalls that the old revivals 'did call, without any question and with tremendous clarity, for personal salvation. But they also called for a resulting social action.' Sounding the names of men like Lord Shaftesbury (1801–1855), who stood for justice for the poor in the midst of the Industrial Revolution, and William Wilberforce (1759–1833), he drives home his point, namely: 'These men did not do these things incidentally, but because they saw it as a part of the Christian good news. God uses those involved in the revivals to bring forth the results not only of individual salvation, but also social action.'[39] According to the statements adopted by the Reformed Ecumenical Synod, Nimes 1980, 'The Gospel of the Kingdom is a Gospel of salvation and liberation. This means that the Church cannot be silent when it sees men, women and children in bondage and slavery, spiritual, social, economic, political, etc. either by their own sins or those of others.'[40]

Criticisms of the present form of the Kingdom and the extent and scope of the lordship of Christ as directed against the eighth viewpoint are equally relevant here. It is also asked whether this viewpoint will endorse the use of force or an organized resistance, and the answer rings in the affirmative. This has been criticized as a denial of the church's call to suffering, an essential part of cross bearing.

3. Undogmatic Conclusion

Can there be an evangelical consensus on this subject? Looking again at the options presented, in my opinion the last four have a lot more in common than appears on the surface. As a matter of fact, if we could get over the semantic problem, they may be even closer to one another in the long run. For instance, the 'partnership' concept of Stott, and the 'part of' concept of Schaeffer will both retain the primacy of evangelism which is the main emphasis of Johnston's 'consequence' concept. Similarly, as long as the primacy of evangelism is maintained, the advocates of the 'consequence' concept will not deny the important necessity of socio-political involvement in the name of Christ. If granted, this leaves us with only two vital options and one question. The options:

1. That social action is distinct from, yet equal to evangelism.
2. That social action is a part of/or, is a partner of/or, is included in/or, is a consequence of/or, proceeds from evangelism.

The one question: Which comes first?

Of the two options, I personally feel more comfortable with number 2 which I would like to word differently: Social Action is *implied* in Evangelism. If I were to develop this, my main texts would be Luke 3:1–20; 4:16–30. Let us take the case of John, popularly called 'the Baptist' as recorded in Luke 3:1–20.

Here was a man sent for a witness, to bear witness to the Light, that all men through him might believe. He wasn't that Light, but was sent to bear witness to that Light (Jn. 1:7, 8). The catalogue of names given in verses 1 and 2 of Luke 3 reveals the political, cultural, religious and civil situations under which John (and Jesus) lived and ministered. The Holy Land was under Roman imperialism, a domination of a pagan power. Tiberius' reign was marked by severity and cruelty. Culturally the people were dislocated by imposition of a foreign language and value

systems and a sophisticated life-style. In addition to Emperor
worship, legalism and dead formalism, the highly revered office
of the high priest had become a political tool with high priests
deposed by governors at will. The civil service was corrupt and
administration poor. On the whole, it was a dark picture of moral
degeneration, hopelessness and chaos. Not any different from
the picture of our world today!

John did not need any consultation on 'simple life-style'
(neither did Jesus). His was the simplest of the simple! His commission was: 'to make the crooked straight'—all human deviation
from God must be corrected; 'to fill the valley'—all human
emptiness must be filled; and 'to bring low the mountain and hill'
—all human pride and self-satisfaction must be broken down.
To this end, 'the ϱημα (word) of God came unto John'! and he
responded with a *voice*! So, like a courier sent ahead of the King,
John cried, 'Mend your lives for the King is here!'

And here is social action implied in evangelism: In verse 7, he
demonstrates an intimate knowledge of his audience—they are
the type who want to go to heaven without believing that there is
a hell; in verse 8 he denounces their false security—racial, tribal,
etc.; and summons them to whole-hearted repentance—'Bring
forth fruits worthy of repentance.' In verse 11, he calls for
compassion—meeting the needs of one's neighbours (neigh-
bourly love). In verses 12 and 13, he demands honesty and
justice; and in verse 14, he condemns violence and oppression.

John spoke against both personal sins and structural evil. He
addressed the rich as well as the poor. As the rich need to be
liberated from their greed, selfishness, pride and self-satisfaction, so do the poor from fear, poverty, ignorance and disease.
John was socially involved with his people. He confronted the
dispossessed and the powerless in the same strong terms as he
did the privileged and powerful bureaucrats. His gospel knows
no colour or class or sex.

Whenever a social action—implied—evangel like John's is
preached, it is like light coming against darkness; truth against
error; and righteousness against wickedness. Almost invariably,
the result is predictable as in the case of John. In Luke 7:30 we
read that the Pharisees and lawyers rejected the counsel of God
against them. And in verses 19 and 20 of our text, Herod, who
had been condemned for his sins of divorce, adultery and incest
laid his wicked hands on him, put him in prison and subsequently killed him. The price of true and righteous witness is
high. It is often martyrdom! But it is also comforting to know
that among the first disciples of Jesus Christ were those prepared
by John.

Chapter 4 of Luke follows chapter 3 not by accident. After

Jesus had declared his manifesto in verses 18 and 19 we read in verses 28 and 30 that: the people were filled with wrath; they rose up and thrust him out of the city and dragged him to the brow of the hill that they might cast him down headlong.

Social Action is implied *in Evangelism*

To answer the question, 'Which comes first?' I will say that the reality of life doesn't usually present itself to us in either/or. More often we are engaged in both/and. And like our Lord Jesus Christ our witness must be in words and deeds. However, if a hair-splitting choice of priority has to be made, the Holy Spirit, our paracletos will guide us. In my opinion the eternal is far more important than the temporal.[41]

Notes

1. Several authors have dealt with this subject. Among them are: David J. Bosch, *Witness to the World* (London: Marshall, Morgan and Scott, 1980); Harvey T. Hoekstra, *The World Council of Churches and the Demise of Evangelism* (Wheaton: Tyndale House Publishers Inc., 1979, also published by The Paternoster Press, Exeter, as *Evangelism in Eclipse*); Byang Kato, *Theological Pitfalls in Africa* (Nairobi: Evangel Publishing House, 1975).
2. David Bosch, *ibid.*, p.183.
3. The Wheaton Congress was sponsored jointly by the Evangelical Foreign Missions Association (EFMA) and the Interdenominational Foreign Mission Association (IFMA). At that time the two bodies represented over 13,000 missionaries.
4. *Wheaton Declaration* (Washington, D.C., Evangelical Missions Information Service, 1966), p.24.
5. Carl F. H. Henry and W. Stanley Mooneyham (eds.), *One Race, One Gospel, One Task* (Minneapolis: World Wide Publications, 1967), Vol. I, p.5.
6. *ibid.*
7. *ibid.*, p.6.
8. *ibid.*, p.308.
9. Association of Evangelicals of Africa and Madagascar, *Brochure*, p.3.
10. Prof. Dr. Peter Beyerhaus championed this movement. The full text of the Declaration is contained in *The Conciliar—Evangelical Debate: The Crucial Documents 1964–1976* edited by Donald McGavran. The quotation here is taken from p.289.
11. For the full text of Chicago Declaration of Evangelical Social Concern see *Christianity Today* (December 21, 1973) XVIII: 6, p.38.
12. To my knowledge the 240 missionary families of the Evangelical Missionary Society of Evangelical Churches of West Africa (ECWA), Nigeria working in five African countries are purely engaged in church planting.

Probably the same could be said of the indigenous India missionaries. See R. E. Hedlund and F. Hrangkhuma, eds. *Indigenous Missions of India* Madras: Church Growth Research Centre, 1980).

13. See author's article, 'The Renewal of Evangelical Theological Education', *Perception*, No. 19 (January 1982).
14. Leighton Ford, 'Evangelism and Social Responsibility', *World Evangelization Information Service* (published by LCWE, Nov. 9, 1980), p.1.
15. John R. W. Stott, *Christian Mission in the Modern World* (Downers Grove: Inter-Varsity Press, 1977), p.16.
16. Leighton Ford, *ibid.*, p.2.
17. William J. Richardson, *Social Action vs. Evangelism* an essay on the contemporary crisis (Pasadena: William Carey Library, 1977), pp.26–37.
18. Emilio Castro, 'Liberation, Development and Evangelism: Must We choose in Mission?' *Occasional Bulletin of Missionary Research*, Vol. 2, No. 3 (July 1978), p.88.
19. *ibid.*, 'Evangelism and Social Justice', *The Ecumenical Review* (Geneva), 20, no. 2 (April 1968), p.148.
20. Robin Thomson, 'Relationship Between Evangelism and Social Responsibility', *AIM* (New Delhi) vol. 13, no. 2 (February 1982), pp.8–14, 19–23.
21. Ken R. Gnanakan, 'The Christian Response to Human Need', *AIM* (New Delhi) vol. 13, no. 3 (March 1982), p.22.
22. John Stott, *ibid.*, p.26.
23. Harold Lindsell, 'A Rejoinder", *International Review of Mission* (Geneva) no. 216 (October 1965), p.439.
24. John Stott, *ibid.*, pp.26–27.
25. Arthur Johnston, *The Battle for World Evangelism* (Wheaton: Tyndale House Publishers, Inc. 1978), p.360.
26. Quoted by David Bosch, *ibid.*, p.203.
27. Michael Cassidy, 'The Third Way', *International Review of Mission*, LXIII: 249 (January 1974), pp.9–23.
28. John Stott, *ibid.*, p.27.
29. Arthur Johnston, 'The Kingdom in Relation to The Church and the World' (Grand Rapids) paper prepared for CRESR, June 1982, p.1.
30. John Stott, 'An Open Response to Arthur Johnston', *Christianity Today* (January 5, 1979), p.35.
31. John Stott in his response to Ron Sider in *Evangelism, Salvation and Social Justice* (Bramcote Notts: Grove Books, 1979), p.22.
32. Some of the literature espousing this viewpoint includes Ron Sider's *Evangelism, Salvation and Social Justice; Rich Christians in an age of Hunger* (London: Hodder and Stoughton, 1979); Vinay Kumar Samuel's *The Meaning and Cost of Discipleship* (Bombay: Bombay Urban Industrial League for Development, 1981); Christopher Sugden's *Radical Discipleship* (London: Marshall Morgan and Stott, 1981); Waldron Scott's *Bring Forth Justice* (Grand Rapids: William B. Eerdmans Publishing Company, 1980); Samuel Escobar's *Christian Mission and Social Justice* (Scottdale: Herald Press, 1978); David Gitari's 'The Claims of Christ in the African Context' *International Review of Mission* (Geneva) LXXI: 281 (Jan. 1982), pp.12–19; David Bosch *ibid*; and Jim Wallis' *The Call to Conversion* (San Francisco: Harper and Row, Publishers, 1981).
33. Bosch, *ibid.*, p.227.
34. *ibid.*, pp.227, 228.

35. Ronald J. Sider, 'Words and Deeds', *Journal of Theology for Southern Africa*, SACLA Edition (December 1979) no. 29, pp.47, 48.
36. Sider, *Evangelism, Salvation and Social Justice* (Bramcote, Grove Booklets, 1979), p.17.
37. Waldron Scott, *Bring Forth Justice*, p.259.
38. *The Church and its Social Calling* (Grand Rapids: Reformed Ecumenical Synod, November, 1980, p.105.
39. Francis A. Schaeffer, *A Christian Manifesto* (Westchester: Crossway Books, 1981), pp.63–71.
40. *The Church and its Social Calling*, November 1980, p.105.
41. Statistics reveal that Evangelical Relief and Development agencies from North America, Europe, Canada and Australia spent hundreds of millions of US Dollars on humanitarian projects all around the world last year. This is encouraging. In the words of John Wesley, we are to 'do all the good we can, by all the means we can, in all the ways we can, in all the places we can, at all the times we can, to all the people we can, as long as ever we can'. *But* may I plead that we Evangelicals must never forget or compromise that cutting edge of the gospel—the salvation of man's soul which naturally places unparalleled emphasis on verbal proclamation.

3

In Search of a New Evangelical Understanding

DAVID J. BOSCH*

Synopsis Responding to Dr. Tokunboh Adeyemo, Dr. David Bosch suggests that recent developments in evangelical understanding of the relationship between evangelism and social responsibility were in part precipitated by the evolution of ecumenical Christianity. In his statement he outlines this development from after World War Two to the present day.

1. Recent Ecumenical Developments

It would, I believe, be appropriate to take the year 1960 as the *terminus a quo* of the period to be surveyed. Let me try to explain why.

(a) The post-1945 years were a period of feverish re-building after the destruction of the war, but to a certain extent people in the West were still optimistic: once we have finished our work of reconstruction, the world will be right side up again and we can move forward creatively! Increasingly, however, in the course of

*Dr Bosch is Professor of Missions at the University of South Africa in Pretoria, South Africa.

the 1950s it became clear that nothing would be the same again, and that World War II was a watershed in human history. Instead of problems being solved, new problems kept cropping up. As time went on, the dream of a truly lasting world order went up in smoke. The cold war between the Marxist world and the West had come to stay. In addition to that, the rise of the Third World as a factor to be taken into account—more, as a force which would, for the first time in world history, have a say in the control of its own destiny and that of the world—meant that the already uncertain balance in the world became more precarious still.

By 1960 this uncertainty had become particularly noticeable in the West, the traditional home of Christianity. The West became increasingly conscious of its blunders, mistakes and short-comings. Where it did not realize this of its own accord, the Third World was only too ready to point it out, in and out of season. Western colonialism, civilization, and attitudes of superiority came under fire, as did 'Western religion'. This resulted in the West, and Western Christianity, adopting an apologetic attitude. And as Christianity became more timid, other religions became more aggressive.

Another factor was the growing success of Marxism. There was a time, after World War II, when the West believed that it could eliminate Marxism as a political factor. It gradually became clear, however, that this was a vain hope. Marxism had come to stay. Contrary to expectations, the new Marxist governments in Eastern Europe stayed in power; their countries became more and more estranged from the West and Western Christianity. By 1960 it was clear that the West—and Christianity—had to learn to live with Marxism.

(b) The shift in the political realm was paralleled by a comparable shift in the ecclesiastical sphere. Consciously oversimplifying, one might say that in the period 1945–1960 the dominant thought was the vocation of the Church *towards* the world, while in the early 1960s it shifted to the vocation of the Church *in* and *for* the world. In the words of H. Berkhof: the *apostolic* commitment to the world of the 1950s changed during the subsequent decade into a *diaconal* commitment (Berkhof 1973:432).

The shift was, of course, gradual. It had its roots in the 1952 conference of the International Missionary Council in Willingen (Hoekendijk) and reached its climax in the 1966 Geneva Conference on Church and Society. The shift included a transition from a deductivist to an inductivist theological method and from the Church to the world as the central *locus* of salvation history.

The latter of these two elements is of particular importance. The long battle to put the *Church* in the centre of ecumenical and missionary concern was finally achieved in Tambaram (1938) and re-affirmed in Willingen 1952 (despite Hoekendijk). By the end of the 1950s, however, the line pursued by Hoekendijk, Lehmann and Shaull was beginning to predominate. An important figure in this respect was Dietrich Bonhoeffer, whose influence reached its zenith by the year 1960. Bonhoeffer's own pilgrimage—from an introverted emphasis on the Church as such to an emphasis on the Church as the servant of the world—was regarded as a model and followed by many. His first major theological treatise, published in 1927 at the age of 21, was entitled *Sanctorum Communio* and dealt almost exclusively with the Church. By 1944, however, shortly before his death at the hand of the Nazis, he regarded the Church only in terms of its servant ministry to the world.

Bonhoeffer was only one of several theologians in whom this change in basic approach was discernible. Typical of this period was a book published in 1961 and written by Hanfried Müller, a young theologian from the German Democratic Republic: *Von der Kirche zur Welt*—From the Church to the world.

The very period during which this shift from the Church to the world was in progress was—perhaps anomalously—also the period in which the churchification of the missionary enterprise was realized. A process that had been under way at least since Tambaram 1938 eventually culminated in the 1958 decision of the International Missionary Council to integrate the Council into the WCC. This integration was to be accomplished in New Delhi in 1961. The WCC, because of its organizational structure, can admit only *churches* to its membership. This meant that a large number of *missionary agencies* which had been members of the IMC were now left virtually in the cold. As most of these agencies were evangelical in outlook, the decisions of 1958 and 1961 meant that evangelicals were now for all practical purposes left without any international forum. This would be one of the contributory factors to the budding of the evangelical ecumene in the mid-sixties.

What Berkhof described as a swing away from an 'apostolic commitment' to the world towards a 'diaconal commitment' was given a clear profile at the New Delhi meeting of the WCC (1961). The swing away from a preoccupation with the Church was two-pronged: towards the (secular) *world*, and towards a new evaluation of non-Christian *religions*. It was the *latter* that was uppermost at New Delhi, particularly because of Joseph Sittler's introduction of the concept of the 'cosmic Christ' into the ecumenical discussion. The *former* would surface more clearly at the Conference on Church and Society (Geneva 1966) and the Uppsala Assembly of the WCC (1968).

Whereas the late 1950s were a period of growing malaise among Western nations and churches, the early 1960s were characterized by euphoria among Third World nations and churches. This was closely related to the frequently almost simultaneous 'granting' of independence to Third World nations *and* churches. The process of political independence for the Third World, beginning with India in 1947 (when 'Vasco da Gama' finally returned to Europe), gradually gained momentum, first in the rest of Asia and then in Africa, and reached a crescendo in 1960—the year in which no fewer than seventeen African countries gained independence. The shackles of political and ecclesiastical colonialism were finally shaken off and there was an almost euphoric conviction that all would now go well and that, in due time, the Third World would catch up with the West, both socio-politically and ecclesiastically.

In this atmosphere, evangelism in the sense of winning individual converts to Christ and the Church became less and less of a priority. The Church's task was, rather the *missio Dei*, increasingly understood in terms of the Church's involvement in the world. The report *The Church for Others*, written in preparation for the Uppsala meeting, states *inter alia:*

> Participation in God's mission is therefore entering into partnership with God in history, because our knowledge of God compels us to affirm that God is working out his purpose in the midst of the world and its historical processes . . . Christians therefore understand the changes in history in the perspective of the mission of God (p.14). The churches serve the *missio Dei* in the world when, on the basis of revelation, they point to God at work in world history (p.16). What else can the churches do than recognize and proclaim what God is doing in the world? (p.15).

Similarly, in a key passage in the North American report written in preparation for Uppsala, *humanization* was

> lifted up as the goal of mission because we believe that more than others it communicates in our period of history the meaning of the messianic goal (p.78).

The mood at the main WCC meetings of the 1960s—particularly those of Mexico City (1963), Geneva (1966) and Uppsala (1968)—was typical of the general optimism (if not euphoria) of the period—notably in Third World circles—in the wake of the attainment of independence by almost every country in Asia and Africa. By the end of the decade the mood began to change. Independence did not bring utopia. In fact, in many newly independent Third World countries the people were worse off than they had been previously. Development did not usher in the kingdom of God. As a matter of fact, development aid came to be regarded, in some instances, as an expression of neo-colonialism. So, by the beginning of the 1970s, much of the optimism had disappeared. The new watchword was no longer *development*, but rather *liberation*. People are poor, not because they need development, but because they are oppressed and exploited. 'There is poverty, because there is wealth' (Guttierez). Thus what is needed is not a theology of development but a theology of liberation. In North America and South Africa liberation theology took the form of Black Theology where it—like its counterpart in Latin America—emphasized liberation in socio-political categories. In the rest of Africa and in Asia, on the other hand, liberation in the *cultural* sphere was emphasized.

We would do well, however, to take cognisance of the fact that these and similar Third World theologies were not operating solely in the area of 'social action', to the exclusion of 'evangelism'. The point is that Third World Christians, not sharing the Greek heritage of dualistic thinking to the same degree that Westerners do, have a far more holistic understanding of the gospel than do Western Christians.

I believe (and I know that many do not agree with me here) that there has been something of a change in ecumenical theological circles in the general area of the relationship between evangelism and social responsibility since the beginning of the 1970s. The change was, in fact, already discernible at the Bangkok meeting of CWME (1973) and was developed further at the WCC Fifth Assembly at Nairobi (1975) and the CWME gathering at Melbourne (1980).

The change, in my view, consists of a growing rediscovery of the 'evangelistic mandate' in WEC circles. This, it should be noted, goes hand in hand with a steadily increasing emphasis on the social responsibility of the Church. There is, undoubtedly, a tension between these two elements in the ecumenical movement, but it is a tension that, at least in the circles of the Third World, has not reached breaking point.

I am not trying to whitewash the ecumenical movement. I have criticized it in several recent publications. And yet I believe that there are honest attempts in many ecumenically minded churches and church leaders to reintegrate evangelism into the ecumenical mandate—just as there are honest attempts among many evangelicals to reinject social responsibility into the evangelical bloodstream. I am, moreover, convinced that the ecumenical movement has listened to and benefited from developments in the evangelical ecumene since the middle 'sixties. Lausanne (1974) in particular has had a far-reaching influence on ecumenical thinking and action.

2. The Roots of Contemporary Evangelism

*This section covers some of the ground covered by Dr. Bong Rin
Ro in his historical survey. However, important additional
insights on this key topic are sufficient justification for printing it.*

Evangelicalism can trace its roots chiefly to two post-Reforma-
tion movements: *Pietism* on the European continent, and the
Evangelical Awakening in the Anglo-Saxon world. Other contributory movements include Anabaptism, the 'Second Reformation' (Nadere Reformatie) in the Netherlands, and Moravianism.

Early Pietism, in particular, managed to integrate social
responsibility into the evangelistic enterprise—naturally within
the limits of the society of their time—and gave rise to many
works of mercy. This integrated view of the Church's calling was
even more characteristic of the British and North American
world of the Awakenings. At a time when the liberal Christianity
of Europe and North America was blind to the needs of the less-
privileged and the oppressed—both at home *and* in what was
later to be called the Third World—pietists and evangelicals
exerted themselves on behalf of the needy. We may think here of
people such as William Wilberforce, Lord Shaftesbury, John
Newton, and, particularly, William Carey, who, in addition to
being the true pioneer of modern missions, also protested against
slavery in Britain and the caste system in India, in addition to
organizing a boycott against sugar imports from West Indian
plantations cultivated by slaves. His work in India in the area of
education, agriculture, etc. is too well-known to be elaborated
upon. And none of these activities was regarded as irreconcilable
with evangelism.

This was still the general spirit half a century later, when the
Evangelical Alliance—in a very real sense the precursor of the
modern ecumenical era—was founded (1846). Rouse and Neill
say that, in that age, 'three features appeared wherever the
Evangelical Awakening spread: international Christian inter-
course and action; a missionary awakening showing itself in the
formation of missionary societies; and efforts directed to social
reform (Rouse-Neill 1954:310).

It was not very different in North America. In his study on
The Social Ideas of the Northern Evangelists, dealing with the
period 1790 to 1830, C. C. Cole detects five phases that regularly
followed in the wake of the grass-roots evangelism of the Second
Great Awakening: (1) the organization of home and foreign
mission societies; (2) the production and distribution of Christian literature; (3) the renewal and extension of Christian educational institutions; (4) attempts at 'the reformation of Manners'

—i.e. the reassertion of Christian moral standards in a decadent society; and, significantly, (5) the great humanitarian crusades against social evils like slavery, war and intemperance (reference in Lovelace 1981:297).

An important name to be mentioned in this respect is that of Charles Finney, the lawyer-educator-abolitionist-evangelist of Oberlin, who was also one of the early Calvinist holiness teachers (an emphasis, incidentally, that was also to be found among the Dutch 'Second Reformation' theologians of the 17th century).

In this entire period, as George Marsden puts it in his excellent study on *Fundamentalism and American Culture*, 'the evangelical commitment to social reform was a corollary of the inherited enthusiasm for revival' (Marsden 1980:12).

One of the reasons why these early evangelicals did not experience an unbearable tension between commitment to both evangelism and social justice lies in the fact that practically all of them were *postmillennianists*, who believed that they had to do their share in the reforming of society in preparation for the return of Christ.

All of this changed, as far as North America was concerned, after the Civil War and the final abolition of slavery. The ending of the war had not ushered in a golden age of the reign of righteousness, as some had predicted. The evangelical unity forged by the Awakenings was about to disintegrate: 'The broad river of classical evangelicalism divided into a delta, with shallower streams emphasizing ecumenism and social renewal on the left and confessional orthodoxy and evangelism on the right' (Lovelace 1981:298). The first developed into the Social Gospel movement, the second into conservative evangelicalism and revivalism. Christianity turned outwards on the one hand, and inwards on the other.

The Social Gospel stream upheld the postmillennialism of earlier evangelicalism and in the course of time increasingly made common cause with theological liberalism. Sin became identified with ignorance and the conviction grew that knowledge and compassion would bring uplift as people rose to meet their potentials. The famous Laymen's Foreign Missions Enquiry report, *Re-Thinking Missions*, published in 1932, is an excellent example of the outcome of this theological line of thinking. The emphasis was on mutual understanding and on furnishing the less advanced nations with the amenities made available by Western technology. The language of the Kingdom of God was used 'to effect a quiet transfer from the gospel about Jesus to a programme based on the ideology of the progressive capitalism of the United States at that point in time' (Newbigin 1981:33). The ultimate theological yield of the movement was

aptly summarized in Niebuhr's classic description: 'A God
without wrath brought men without sin into a Kingdom without
judgment through the ministrations of a Christ without a cross'
(Niebuhr 1959:193).

The other stream in North American evangelicalism turned in
the direction of *premillennialism* after the Civil War. Pre- and
post-millennialism had both existed within Protestantism until
then, but the differences between the two were not exceptionally
great (Marsden 1980:51). Now, however, premillennialism
developed a very distinct profile: the world was doomed to
become increasingly worse and the best one could hope for was
to contain some of the evil. The supreme—if not the only—task
of the Church was to save people from the world. Typical of the
spirit of premillennialism was Moody's most quoted statement
from his sermons: 'I look upon this world as a wrecked vessel.
God has given me a lifeboat and said to me, "Moody, save all you
can." ' (Marsden 1980:38).

For some decades after the Civil War the evangelistic wing
continued to support social causes to some degree. These
included protests against unequal taxation, justice denied to the
poor, and in some instances, even women's and children's labour
and the unequal treatment of immigrants and blacks (Marsden
1980:84f., 88f.)

Gradually, however, the scope of social concern was narrowed
down to attacks on sins such as Sabbath-breaking, Free-
Masonry, strong drink, tobacco, card-playing, dancing, the
theatre and other worldly amusements, and the teaching of
evolution. All these sins featured prominently in Moody's evangelistic sermons. 'The sins he stressed were personal sins, not
involving victims besides oneself and members of one's family'
(Marsden 1980:37). In the course of time he dropped all other
direct social involvement from his ministry, not because he
condoned a lack of compassion for the poor, but because 'he was
convinced that the most compassionate possible care was for a
person's eternal soul' (Marsden 1980:37), and that nothing
should interfere with that.

There are several reasons for the disappearance of social
concerns other than those enumerated above. However, the
single most important reason was probably the evangelicals'
reaction to the Social Gospel. Liberal theology became closely
identified—even synonymous— with social concern; so, if you
rejected the one, you also had to reject the other. These remnants
of social concern gradually receded after the year 1900 among
evangelicals who had now come to be called fundamentalists. By
the 1920s all forms of progressive social involvement had
disappeared. The 'Great Reversal' (Timothy Smith) had been

completed. The polarization between the two main positions had become absolute. The position that one could have *both* evangelism and social action became virtually untenable. Not that evangelicals (or fundamentalists) had become entirely 'private' in their outlook. Rather, as Marsden put it, it was a case of their social views having 'frozen at a point that had been the prevailing political opinion around 1890' (Marsden 1980:93). So they indeed had political views, and strong ones at that, but these were dictated by middle-class prejudices. Their major campaigns were against communism, evolutionism, and the like.

3. A Critical Self-Evaluation: Some Negative Influences in our Social Involvement

This all-too-brief historical survey has a purpose. The point is that much of contemporary evangelicalism, particularly the North American version, stems from these roots. The historical sequence—dangerously over-simplified—may be described as the development from Puritanism to postmillennial evangelicalism to (dispensational) premillennialism to fundamentalism to contemporary evangelicalism. Not that present-day evangelicalism is monolithic. Adeyemo has clearly shown that it is not. It presents, in fact, 'a whirlpool of . . . confusion' (Henry 1980:1228), with some using religious arguments to bolster radical social involvement, and others to attack it. The fairly homogeneous profile of the 1920s and 1930s (in the USA) is no longer in evidence.

Many factors have contributed to this. One such factor was the publication of Carl Henry's *The Uneasy Conscience of Modern Fundamentalism* in 1947. This and other publications, together with the increase in communications after World War II, helped to 'unfreeze' the rigid fundamentalist position of previous decades. Relationships with evangelicals elsewhere, e.g. through the International Missionary Council, the 'coming of age' of Third World churches, and the entry into the mainstream of American evangelicalism of groups such as the Mennonites, helped to shape the contemporary evangelical constituency, and—of major importance to our subject—to break the deadlock in the area of social concern.

Trends That Have Hindered Our Understanding

(a) Premillennialism

First, contemporary evangelicalism is still predominantly *pre-*

millennialist. It has moved—over the past couple of centuries—
from a position which saw politics as a significant means to
advance the Kingdom to one which views political action as
being no more than a means to restrain evil. It has learnt to
tolerate corruption and injustice, to expect and even welcome
them as signs of Christ's imminent return. It has become
pessimistic about the world and unable to harmonize any
evidences of progress with our location on the timeline of history
(cf. Lovelace 1981:297).

I am not pleading for a return to the earlier postmillennialist
position, but, rather, for a position beyond the sterile duality of
pre- and postmillennialism, a position where we take seriously
both the present and the future of the kingdom.

Unless each of us clarifies his position in this respect, we will
remain at cross-purposes. Peter Kuzmič's contribution to
CRESR is an excellent aid in this regard.

(b) Individualism

Secondly, evangelicals tend to be very *individualistic.* The
question is whether this is essentially Christian or, rather, an
illegitimate accommodation to the middle-class individualism
which is typical of the contemporary Western world.

This individualism manifests itself particularly in present-day
evangelistic outreach, at least since Moody's time. The *individual*
has come to a decision and has to forsake *personal* sins. Television
evangelists in the U.S.A., we are told, currently buy more than
$600 million in air time every year and are viewed by 15 million
American households each week (Armstrong 1981:4). The
gospel they preach is often entirely individualistic; the listener is
addressed without reference to the relationships in which he is
already involved.

This kind of evangelism in turn fosters pious egocentrism (see
further Bosch 1981:71–73) and often finds support in 'evangelical' Bible translations (compare, e.g. the Living Bible translation of 2 Cor. 5:17 with that of the New English Bible).

This individualistic reading of the Bible (which is usually
unconsciously assumed) often borders on subjectivism in which
the personal experience of the work and guidance of the Holy
Spirit is decisive. This trait often leads to an unresolved tension
between the emphasis on personal experience and submission to
Holy Scripture, for, in spite of evangelicals' avowed confession
that they subject themselves without reservation to the authority
of the Word of God, their insistence on the right of individual
judgment in deciding the precise bearing of the biblical truth
points in another direction. When the Evangelical Alliance was

founded in 1846, one of its stated principles was 'the right and duty of private judgment in the interpretation of the Holy Scriptures'. This clause was subsequently dropped but the underlying sentiment lingers on.

(c) 'Free Enterprise'

Thirdly: a corollary to the evangelical emphasis on individualism is a proclivity towards *free enterprise*. The emphasis is on yet more new initiatives and on inventiveness. The evangelical world is full of independent itinerant evangelists, of different agencies and societies, of magazines and bible schools and fellowships. Uniformity and bureaucracy are rejected in favour of creativeness and adventure.

This attitude is frequently transferred uncritically to the sociopolitical sphere where 'voluntarism' becomes the watchword, capitalism is associated with Christianity, and socialism—in any form—becomes a dirty word.

(d) Ecclesiology

Fourthly, and related to the above: Protestants in general and evangelicals in particular often have a weak *ecclesiology*. Typical of this is the popular evangelical polarization of Bible and Church which flows from the failure to take seriously the nature of the Church as the historical and visible people of God. The television and radio evangelism to which I have referred above is typical of this: individuals are called to Christ as if the *Church* does not really matter, as if the Church is merely 'an aggregate of individuals each possessing a prior relationship to God' (Samuel and Sugden 1982:11).

Because of this weak ecclesiology it is easy to leave one 'church' for another, frequently for very 'untheological' reasons. If I am not mistaken, this tendency is particularly common in North America. New arrivals in a town or city take some time to 'shop around' for a church to their liking. Perhaps this is yet another expression of the free enterprise system: one 'invests' where the dividends show promise of the highest yield. As Marsden puts it: 'Instead of "churches" (in the sense of the official organized religion of a territory) or "sects" (in the sense of separated groups of true believers), America had "denominations", which were sometimes churchly, sometimes sectarian, and usually both. The denominations were the product of a combination of European churchly traditions, ethnic loyalties, pietism, sectarianism, and American free enterprise' (Marsden 1980:70).

Where the free market pattern prevails people do not

experience serious difficulties with church schism or proselytism. This tendency, so it appears to me, also characterizes the Church Growth movement in North America. McGavran, e.g., says, 'Frequently a Church splits and both sections grow' (McGavran 1980:3), and he does not seem to be bothered by this. In a slightly different context, but addressing himself essentially to the same theological problem, he writes, 'The student of church growth . . . cares little whether a Church is credible; he asks how much it has grown' (McGavran 1980:159).

In this reasoning pragmatism tends to reign supreme: we expand more quickly, we communicate more easily, we agree better with one another, we feel more comfortable and at home in each other's company, we share the same fears, suspicions, prejudices and anxieties, etc., etc. The consequences of all this, however, are far-reaching. Our 'church' easily becomes a club for religious folklore where we simply reaffirm each other's sentiments, where there is scant room for differences of opinion and new vistas, and where we therefore willy-nilly conform to a specific socio-religious pattern and hermeneutic.

A more biblical way, or so it appears to me, would be rather to forfeit some of our efficiency and bear with one another even to the point of suffering, in that way creating the opportunity to broaden our horizons and expose ourselves to neglected areas of Christian obedience.

Let me give one example of what I mean. A couple of years ago I became acquainted with the Comunità di S. Egidio in Rome. This is a renewal community consisting mostly of young people. They had a choice of two possibilities: either to establish a new, totally independent community, society or 'denomination', or to remain within the Roman Catholic Church, addressing nominal and other peripheral Catholics from *within*. They deliberately chose the second alternative, with all the restrictions that would bring with it, but they did this because of their high view of the Church.

(e) The 'New Right'

Let us, in the fifth place, take a brief look at the phenomenon called the New Right, which is far from being confined to the United States, though it has the clearest profile here. Perhaps we should have had a separate paper on this subject at our Consultation. I have no idea of the actual support—numerical and otherwise—the movement has, but it is evident that it is a significant factor.

On the surface the New Right appears to be a return to the earlier evangelical position of Jonathan Edwards and the Great

Awakenings, and there are indeed some parallels. As Carl Henry has pointed out, however, it lacks a comprehensive political philosophy or programme and has a notably attenuated range of specifics. Its agenda is narrow and its social vision fragmentary. It concentrates on social issues such as the government funding of abortion, homosexuality, and impositions on private schools. Its main positive contribution appears to be a plea for a revival of voluntarism (Henry 1980:1226–30).

So far, so good. But there are also disturbing elements in the new movement. It appears to wish to introduce a new version of Constantinianism, for it pleads for 'a new theology of dominion'. There must be 'a shift in authority: from the ungodly to the godly, either by *conversion* of the ungodly, or by their *removal* from positions of authority . . .' (North 1981:34, 27).

Equally disturbing is the fact that social justice appears to be excluded from the movement's political agenda, or, rather, that social justice is redefined to mean something completely different. Sider's *Rich Christians in an Age of Hunger* is counteracted by David Chilton's *Productive Christians in an Age of Guilt-Manipulators*. Aid to the less privileged through taxation becomes legalized theft (Rose 1981:61) and programmes such as medicare, aid to mothers with dependent children, welfare payments and tax-supported education are regarded as inherently immoral (Rose 1981:54). To 'condone the civil authority's providing "charity" to the needy' is to be 'guilty of institutionally breaking the Eighth and Tenth Commandment through the collective agency we call government' (Rose 1981:71). In addition, 'it should be of no concern to the political authorities whether prices are high or low, whether employment is high or low . . .' (Rose 1981:70). What is more, we can be confident that 'adhering to God's social laws brings external prosperity' (North 1981:33), and there is nothing wrong in being rich and enjoying it, since you have worked for it and God has blessed you (Rose 1981).

All this is said not in the name of capitalism nor of liberal Christianity, but in the name of conservative evangelicalism. North says that we need 'a social order based on the Bible'. 'All reforms are either consistent with the Bible or inconsistent'; we must strive after 'a uniquely Christian law-order', 'a political order based on the Bible'; 'Only one thing must be preached: that *God's will be done*' (North 1981:19, 22, 22, 19, 27).

In much of this we find evangelicalism linked to right-wing politics and patriotism, and the argument used is that those who disagree are neither Christian nor patriotic. Some of the proponents of the New Right remain premillennialists while at the same time embracing a highly politicized gospel. Perhaps this is so because, incongruously, the New Right has incorporated into its bloodstream elements of the still lingering postmillennialist conviction that God's kingdom may indeed be found in America itself. It therefore combines ultra-conservative hyper-American patriotic anti-communism with old-style liberalism which relieves the anxieties and guilt-feelings of the affluent while preaching a gospel of virtuous wealth as a commendable example to the poor.

4. Beyond Dualism: A Personal Quest

Since Adeyemo has concluded his paper with an explication of his own position I may be pardoned if I attempt a similar—perhaps equally 'undogmatic'—postscript.

My essential problem is that Adeyemo's nine viewpoints plus the two I have added are all, to a greater or lesser degree, fraught with *dualism*. In *all* those options the basic presupposition appears to be that evangelism and social responsibility are intrinsically rivals competing for supremacy.

I shall now, however, endeavour to redefine my own position somewhat, with the aid of a few diagrams.

Diagram 1 portrays the ultra-evangelical position:

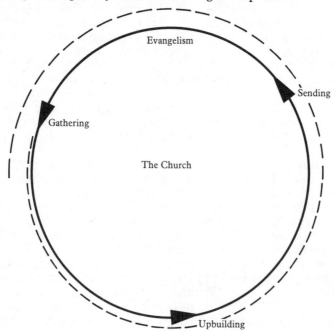

In this diagram the circle represents the *Church*, under the three elements which Barth develops in his *Church Dogmatics* Vols. IV/1, IV/2 and IV/3, which deal successively with the Holy Spirit and the *gathering*, the *upbuilding* and the *sending* of the Church.

In the case of many evangelicals the upbuilding of the Church is almost exclusively for the sake of *evangelism*. Johnston says, 'Historically the mission of the church is evangelism alone' and he chides Stott for having 'dethroned evangelism as *the* only historical aim of mission' (Johnston 1978, 18, 302–3), In similar vein McGavran defines mission as 'bringing unbelievers to saving faith in Christ and membership in his Church', and then, in turn, 'sending them out to find others' (McGavran 1980: 426, cf. 26).

In this definition the *sending* of the Church leads back to its *gathering*, which in turn leads on to *upbuilding*, which again is carried out for the sake of *sending*, understood as *gathering*. As a matter of fact, in this process the circle is not only *completed* each time, but *expanded*. The Church grows. The dotted lines show how successful evangelism guarantees the steady growth of the Church.

Church Growth philosophy, so it appears, corroborates the idea behind this diagram. The purpose of becoming a Christian is to help others become Christians. And 'Christian' is understood exclusively in religious and cultic categories. McGavran quotes with approval Pickett's *Christian Mass Movements in India* in which Pickett measures successful mission in terms of 'attainments' in eleven areas: Knowledge of the Lord's Prayer, Apostle's Creed and Ten Commandments, Sabbath observance, Church membership, Church attendance, frequency of services, support of the Church, freedom from idolatry, charms and sorcery, non-participation in non-Christian festivals, freedom from fear of evil spirits, Christian marriage, and abstinence from use of intoxicating beverages (McGavran 1980:174). Virtually all these criteria relating to being a Christian pertain to areas of religion narrowly defined; none of them indicates any measure of social involvement or responsibility.

In our second diagram on the following page, which illustrates the position with regard to ecumenicals, the situation is rather different. This diagram is basically the same as the first. *Gathering* leads to *upbuilding* which takes place for the sake of *sending*. But sending —mission—is understood differently here.

Mission means, above all, equipping the Church with an eye to its involvement in *the world* (in the form of miscellaneous programmes and actions and development aid projects), in *Third World churches* (in the form of interchurch aid), in *other religions* (in the form of dialogue), and so on. In the case of those who

Diagram 2.

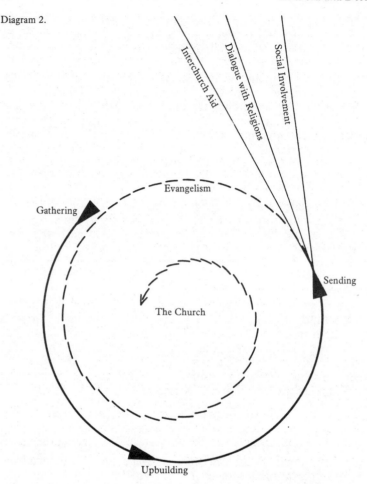

subscribe to Viewpoint 10 (priority of social action), some evangelism—defined in the way evangelicals do—still takes place. The emphasis given to evangelism is, however, very limited; that explains the dotted line from 'sending' to 'gathering'. In the case of adherents of Viewpoint 11 even this dotted line disappears. All we now have, are the solid lines running from 'sending' to various forms of extra-ecclesiastical involvement. Some 'gathering' still takes place, even in the case of Viewpoint 11, but this is due mainly to natural increase. Since, however, the erosion in membership exceeds natural increase, the Church declines numerically—a phenomenon detectable in most ecumenically-minded churches today.

John Stott's suggestion for a way out of this dilemma is to regard evangelism and social action as both being *components* of mission. In other words (perhaps oversimplified): evangelism+ social action=mission. The problem with describing evangelism and social action as two separate segments or components of mission is, however, that this still leaves us—at least potentially —with the battle for supremacy. Stott himself maintains the *primacy* of evangelism; in other words, the battle has been joined! This, in fact, was the reason why some 200 participants at COWE in Thailand signed a 'Statement of Concerns' and criticized COWE for having gone back on Lausanne. The COWE leadership tried to meet this criticism by including, in the Thailand Statement, a reaffirmation of COWE's commitment to both evangelism and social action. The Statement went on to say that 'nothing contained in the Lausanne Covenant is beyond our concern, *so long as it is clearly related to world evangelization*' (my emphasis). The significance of this last statement lies in what it does *not* say; it does not make mention of the need for evangelism *to be clearly related to social responsibility*. Thus the dualism remains, even in John Stott's position!

I agree in essence with Stott's wider definition of mission as the total task which God has set the church for the salvation of the world (Bosch 1980:17). It has to do with the crossing of all kinds of frontiers: geographical, social, political, ethnic, cultural, religious, ideological. Ultimately mission means being involved in the redemption of the universe and the glorification of God. Mission is epiphany: through it the Lord of the universe reveals himself to the world (see further Bosch 1982:24).

Thus far, I believe, John Stott and I are in agreement. He would also agree when I refer to evangelism as being the proclamation of the forgiveness of sins, the call to repentance and faith, and the invitation to become a member of the community called the Church.

Yet I believe that Stott's 'separate but equal' view of the relationship between evangelism and social action, of the 'Great Commission' and the 'Great Commandment' together adding up to 'mission' (Stott 1975:15–34) is misleading. It is too easy, in this definition, for the two components to become detached from each other, to make a Unilateral Declaration of Independence, so to speak. Evangelicals are sufficiently aware of the fatal consequences of such a U.D.I. on the part of social action; they are less prepared to accept that a U.D.I. by evangelism is equally untenable. Evangelism as an isolated and separate activity of the Church does not address the central missionary questions of the world but leads, instead, to the trivialization of God and his salvation.

In the early Church such an understanding of evangelism was impossible—contrary to what many evangelicals believe. The early Church was not called a *thiasos* in the sense of a private religious society worshipping a cult hero but steering clear of any 'political' issues and controversies. It was called *ecclesia*, which was essentially a *civil* concept and which meant that the claims of its Lord went beyond the narrow confines of religious allegiance —not simply as a *consequence* of that allegiance but as part and parcel of it. Christ was both *Redeemer* and *Lord* (Bosch 1981: 72–3). The Church saw itself as a movement launched into the public life of the world. It was, from the beginning, 'on a collision course with the established powers and for three centuries paid the price for this stupendous claim' (Newbigin 1981:47). Not for nothing did it cause the people of Thessalonica to shout, 'Those who have *turned the world upside down* have come to our city . . .' (Acts 17:6).

There are many countries in the world—including my own— where the Church is free to evangelize, provided evangelism deals only with personal salvation and 'religious' activities. However, the moment the Church begins to flesh out its faith it may run into trouble. But then the inescapable question is: Was that other activity evangelism in the first place? I believe not. If our evangelism is not related to the whole context in which we live, the Church itself is suspect.

In a stimulating article Richard B. Cook of the National Farm Worker Ministry in California argues that to translate *euangelizomai* in the New Testament throughout with 'evangelize' or 'preach the gospel' is to ascribe to it modern revivalistic and evangelistic overtones completely foreign to the New Testament. In Paul's Letter to the Galatians, for instance, it should rather be translated 'present the gospel', 'live the gospel', or 'embody the gospel' (Cook 1981:485–498; Bosch 1981:69). In other words, the *way* in which we evangelize, or put differently, the extent to which our evangelism is integrated into the totality of our mission, is decisive. And this, inescapably, introduces the issue of credibility. It is not enough to say that we must evangelize (not in the *modern* understanding of the word 'evangelize' anyway), as though our message is neatly packaged and cut and dried. It is here that my basic problem lies with McGavran's commendable *Understanding Church Growth*. It is, throughout, a call to evangelism but the nature and quality of the Christianity we transmit appears to be completely unproblematical. Only once, in a footnote, does he touch upon the importance of the credibility of our message and our Christianity (McGavran 1980:367). Peter Wagner, explaining why he had written *Church Growth and the Whole Gospel*, admits 'the relative lack of interaction by church growth authors with . . . ethical issues . . .' (Wagner 1982:176). I would add, unless we address ourselves to these issues we are not addressing ourselves to the concept of evangelism, biblically understood.

Therefore, unlike Stott, I would not call evangelism and social action separate components or parts of mission, but dimensions of the one, indivisible mission of the Church. This is more than a matter of semantics. Let me try to explain by means of a third diagram:

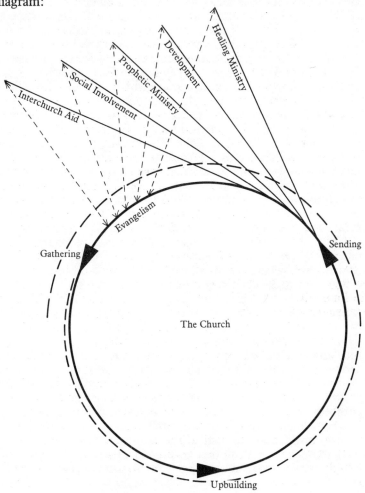

Here evangelism is the inviting and *ingathering dimension of the total mission*, whereas the other involvements represent the serving, self-emptying and humanizing dimension. However, where these different dimensions truly come into their own, relations develop between them. The ingathering dimension supports the serving dimension, while the serving dimension in turn supports the ingathering.

We could also have employed another diagram, namely that of an ellipse with two foci. Ideally the two foci should nearly overlap so that the ellipse becomes almost a circle. I say 'almost' to give expression to the idea of a *creative tension* between the evangelistic and serving dimensions of the Church's involvement. The two are *not* the same (evangelism is not social action nor social action evangelism) but neither can they be separated.

Naturally, different situations may call for different emphases. A church ministering in an 'Old Testament' setting, where it can appeal to a government and a society which, on the whole, share its Christian values, will conduct its total mission in a way that differs from that of a church ministering in a 'New Testament' setting, where government and society are hostile to the Christian faith and world-view. This difference is, however, incidental. It is a difference in the context and not in the concept of mission. But even where a church, because of the context, can do little more than evangelize, that evangelism must maintain the dimension of social responsibility; likewise, where the church, e.g. in a Muslim country, is not able to evangelize, its service should be permeated by a winsome, inviting dimension.

Unless we approach our subject in this spirit, we will not break out of the shackles of dualism which confine us to opposing camps, even where we attempt to work out a balance between evangelism and social responsibility.

Peter Kusmič, in his illuminating contribution to this Consultation has presented us with two tables displaying, in shorthand, the differences between post- and premillennialists (Kusmič 1982:15). I was encouraged to note that, in my tables portray-the differences between 'Melbourne' and 'Pattaya', I have arrived independently at an almost exactly similar delineation of the two camps (Bosch 1981:65–6). My contention has been, and still is, that both positions are indefensible, as both have succumbed to a perhaps not easily detectable but nevertheless insidious dualism in which, ultimately, grace remains opposed to nature, justification to justice, the soul to the body, the individual to society, redemption to creation, heaven to earth, the world to the deed, and evangelism to social responsibility.

BIBLIOGRAPHY

Armstrong, James *From the Underside*. Evangelism from a Third World Vantage Point (Maryknoll: Orbis, 1981).

Berkhof, H. *Christelijkgeloof* (Nijkerk: Callenach, 1973).

Bosch, David J. *Witness to the World. The Christian Mission in Theological Perspective* (Atlanta: John Knox, 1980).

'Evangelism', *Mission Focus* 9:4 (Dec.) 65–74, 1981.

'Theological Education in Missionary Perspective', *Missiology* 10:1 (Jan.) 13–34, 1982.

Cook, Richard, B. 'Paul the Organizer', Missiology 9:4 (Oct.) 485–498, 1981.

Henry, Carl F. H. 'Evangelicals jump on the Political Bandwagon', *Christianity Today* 24:18 (Oct. 24) 1226–1230, 1980.

Johnston, Arthur P. *The Battle for World Evangelism* (Wheaton: Tyndale, 1978).

Kusmič, Peter 'History and Eschatology: Evangelical Views', *CRESR*, 1982.

Lovelace, Richard F. 'Completing an Awakening', *The Christian Century* 98:9 (March 19), 296–300, 1981.

McGavran, Donald A. *Understanding Church Growth* (fully revised) (Grand Rapids: Eerdmans, 1980).

Marsden, George M. *Fundamentalism and American Culture*. The Shaping of Twentieth-Century Evangelicalism: 1870–1925 (New York: O.U.P., 1980).

Newbigin, Lesslie *Sign of the Kingdom* (Grand Rapids: Eerdmans, 1981).

Niebuhr, H.R. *The Kingdom of God in America* (New York: Harper [first edition 1937], 1959).

North, Gary 'Comprehensive Redemption: A Theology for Social Action', *The Journal of Christian Reconstruction* 8:1 (Summer) 9–36, 1981).

Rose, Tom 'Christ's Kingdom: How shall we build?', *The Journal of Christian Reconstruction* 8:1 (Summer) 51–71, 1981.

Rouse, Ruth and Neill, S. C. (eds.) *A History of the Ecumenical Movement 1517–1948* (London, 1954).

Samuel, Vinay and Sugden, Chris 'How would you define the Mission of the Church in Relation to Evangelism and Social Responsibility? A Biblical Study', *CRESR*, 1982.

Sider, Ronald J. *Evangelism, Salvation and Social Justice* (2nd. edit.) (Bramcote: Grove Books, 1979).

Stott, John R. W. *Christian Mission in the Modern World* (London: Falcon, 1975).

Wagner, C. Peter 'Why I wrote "Church Growth and the Whole Gospel" ', *Global Church Growth Bulletin* 19:2 (March-April, 1982).

4

How Broad is Salvation in Scripture?

RONALD J. SIDER and JAMES PARKER III*

Synopsis   In this chapter, Drs. Ronald Sider and James Parker III explore the exegetical and missiological issues of whether we should limit the word *salvation* to the personal and social, vertical and horizontal transformations that occur when persons confess Christ and enter into his Body, the church, or whether we should use the word to refer also to the emergence of justice and wholeness in society beyond the church.

The authors survey the salvation words pronounced in both the Old and New Testaments. In the former they conclude that salvation is clearly social and corporate and covers every aspect of life, including material prosperity, justice for the poor and needy and the continued historical existence of the people of Israel. However, the Old Testament does not speak of God's salvation as present apart from his covenant relationship with chosen people who confess him as Lord.

In the New Testament—the Gospels, Pauline and remaining books—they find that salvation is also individual and corporate, vertical and horizontal, redeeming the whole person but always within the context of Jesus' new community of believers where people personally confess Christ as Lord and Saviour. Sider and Parker then examine and respond to arguments advanced to support the broader view that in some senses, salvation can be used of God's involvement in society beyond the church.

*Dr. Ronald J. Sider is Associate Professor of Theology at Eastern Baptist Seminary in Philadelphia, Penn., U.S.A. and is assisted by Dr. James Parker III.

While accepting the fact that the risen Christ is now sovereign
of history and that in a significant sense his kingly rule is now
present throughout the earth, quite apart from conscious confession of Christ, these writers find little or no biblical evidence to
call this salvation. Christ's kingly reign is present where people
acknowledge Christ. They conclude that there is no warrant in
the New Testament for talking about the coming of the Kingdom
of God via societal change apart from the confession of Christ.
Because we know that God's cosmic plan for justice and peace
will be fulfilled when Christ consummates his reign, we believe
that the church through its work for peace and justice moves
history towards the coming Kingdom and puts into practice its
theology of the Kingdom. They add that though we believe that
reconciliation with God is not the same as reconciliation with
persons, this in no way undermines the importance of the social
responsibility.

---

1. An Introduction to the Central Issue in the Current Debate

The breadth of our topic underlines the difficulty of our task. As
Carl Braaten pointed out in a recent article, there is an important
sense in which one's doctrine of salvation deals with every theological issue:

> The whole of theology is inherently developed from a soteriological
> point of view. Salvation is not one of the many topics, along with the
> doctrine of God, Christ, church, sacraments, eschatology, and the
> like. It is rather the perspective from which all these subjects are
> interpreted.[1]

Fortunately, however, our task is not to offer a comprehensive
overview of the biblical view of salvation. If it were, we would
need to deal comprehensively with the different theories of the
atonement, the debate over pre-destination, the question of universalism, etc. For the purpose of this consultation, however, the
central focus of this paper can be much narrower. As we understand it, our task is to try to develop those aspects of the biblical
understanding of salvation that relate to the question of the
relationship between evangelism and social responsibility. Even
more precisely, we are to attempt to adjudicate the important
current debate between those on the one hand who insist that the
word salvation connotes only what happens when persons consciously confess Christ as Lord and Saviour and those on the
other who argue that salvation includes *both* this *and* the emer-

gence of justice and shalom in the larger society beyond the church quite apart from personal faith in Christ.

The Lausanne Covenant and the documents from the WCC's Bangkok Conference (1973) illustrate the two viewpoints. The Lausanne Covenant affirms the importance of socio-political involvement, but insists that 'reconciliation with man is not reconciliation with God, nor is social action evangelism, nor is political liberation salvation' (Section V). For those at Bangkok, on the other hand, the word salvation refers not only to the forgiveness and regeneration of individuals through faith in Christ, but also to the growth of peace and justice: 'Salvation is the peace of the people in Vietnam, independence in Angola [and] justice and reconciliation in Northern Ireland.'²

In order to be fair to both positions, it is crucial to distinguish a common distortion of each view from the basic viewpoint itself. The first stance which limits the word salvation to where there is conscious confession of Christ is sometimes developed in an individualistic fashion that denies its corporate character. And the second view is sometimes partially or totally secularized. Both distortions merit brief discussion so that we can focus on the central debate without fighting 'straw men'.

Those who argue that the word salvation ought to refer only to what happens when persons consciously confess Christ, sometimes emphasize only the individualistic, vertical aspects of salvation. Salvation is limited to the justification and regeneration of the individual person through a vertical relationship with God. As our paper will show, this is a crucial, indispensable aspect of the biblical concept of salvation. But salvation in the Scriptures has also a profoundly corporate character. At the heart of God's plan of salvation in both testaments is the calling forth of a redeemed people. In the New Testament, those who confess Christ enter his new community, the body of Christ, where all relationships are being redeemed. Being in Christ transforms every aspect of their relationship with other brothers and sisters, even economic relationships. But that does not mean that salvation includes socio-economic changes in secular society. In this view, salvation pertains to both personal and social, both vertical and horizontal relationships but only within the community of believers who personally confess Jesus Christ.

There is also a rather common distortion of the broader view of salvation. Some who use the word salvation with reference to the emergence of peace and justice in secular or non-Christian society emphasize or even limit themselves to the horizontal aspects of salvation. They see sin as largely or exclusively structural, they ignore the distinction between the church and the world (sometimes because of an implicit or explicit universalism), and they focus the bulk of their energy and concern on the transformation of social structures.[3] This approach, we believe, is clearly unbiblical, and therefore to be rejected unequivocally.

It is important, however, to realize that there is no necessary logical connection between the broader definition of salvation and distortions of the sort just outlined. It is possible to insist that everything that the first view asserts is important and central to the Christian understanding of salvation and then add that the word salvation should also be used to refer to the emergence of justice and peace in society beyond the church. As long as one does not deny or de-emphasize the personal, vertical elements of salvation and as long as one is clear that the forgiveness and regeneration of the individual are not the same as the emergence of social justice (limited and imperfect to be sure, but still significant), then it is quite possible to use the broader definition of salvation without denying the central affirmations of the first view. And in fact some evangelicals deeply concerned with evangelism and personal salvation have adopted the broader terminology.[4]

The mere existence of these two definitions, however, does not mean they are equally valid. Our question is this: On the basis of the Scriptures, should we adopt the first or the second definition of salvation? Should we limit the word salvation to the personal and social, vertical and horizontal transformations that occur when persons confess Christ and enter his new body, the church? Or should we use the word also to refer, *in addition to the above* (but *never* in neglect of the above), to the emergence of justice and wholeness in society beyond the church?

How shall we attempt to settle this dispute? First a negative comment. It is crucial that we avoid the genetic fallacy. The fact that the one viewpoint has arisen in evangelical circles and the other in ecumenical circles does not settle the debate. The fact that *some* ecumenical folk who wrongly neglect personal evangelism and the vicarious atonement, tend toward universalism and often use the broader definition of salvation no more proves that the broad definition is wrong than does the fact that some evangelicals who wrongly neglect social concern and tend toward a platonic, unbiblical view of persons as disembodied 'souls', and prefer the narrow conception of salvation prove that the narrow view of salvation is mistaken. We must remember the simple philosophical points that the source of an idea and the mistakes of its proponents do not invalidate a concept.

Positively, we want to listen to all of Scripture for our definition of salvation. A selective listening only, say, to the Old Testament theme of Exodus, or the Pauline theme of justification is not adequate. We must try to hear the whole witness of Scripture on our question. We will try to do that via word studies of the key words in both testaments and also examination of central (or disputed) passages in a few instances.

2. Salvation in the Old Testament

Five basic Hebrew words are used in the Old Testament to express salvation.[5]

(i) *Hayah* used in the causative (pi'el and hiph'il) means 'to give a full and prosperous life' or 'to preserve, to keep alive'. The non-religious meaning of 'to spare the life of' predominates, but the word is used also to speak of the way God grants life and material prosperity to his people.

(ii) *Go'el*[6] is a familiar word used to refer to the performance of the duties of a kinsman. The kinsman purchases a family member from slavery as in Lev. 25:48f., or redeems property by a payment (Lev. 25:26, 32) or avenges his blood (Josh. 20:3, 9). As the kinsman of his people God is seen as the archtypical *Go'el* in the Old Testament.[7]

(iii) *Padah*[8] means basically to get something by returning something in exchange. In Exodus 13:13 it is applied to the redemption of a life where one life is substituted for another. Substitution is a fundamental idea in *padah*. The Septuagint almost always translated *padah* by *lutroo* (ransom). The costliness of salvation is conveyed by *padah*.

(iv) *Kopher* means 'ransom price'. In Exodus 21:28ff., and Job 36:18, etc., the word is used to indicate what a person must pay in order to be set free, rather than die. The word is used corporately of Israel in describing God's salvific activity in Isaiah 43:1-4.

The three words, *go'el*, *padah*, and *kopher* all convey in the strongest possible terms the costliness of God's grace.

(v) *Yasha'*, *yeshu'a*, and *yesha'* are by far the most commonly used group of words to convey the idea of salvation in the Old Testament. These words convey the idea of 'being at one's ease, free to develop without hindrance' and 'bringing into a spacious environment'.

In the *Meaning of Salvation*, Michael Green lists six aspects of the context of salvation conveyed by this word-group (*yasha'*, etc.) in the Old Testament.[9]

(a) *Salvation is the work of God.* God is always seen as the author of salvation. The people are rescued by God (Hos. 1:7), who alone can save the flock (Ezek. 34:22), for there is none other who can do it (Isa. 43:1). While God may use human deliverers (I Sam. 9:16), he is not dependent upon them. He alone is entitled to the accolade 'the Lord God of our Salvation' (Ps. 68:19; 88:1; 118–14).

(b) *Salvation is historic.* Exodus 14:30 is paradigmatic: 'There the Lord saved Isarel that day out of the hand of the Egyptians.' Green comments: 'It is no exaggeration to say that this rescue from Egypt, the land of bitter bondage under the threat of imminent death at the hand of harsh taskmasters determined the whole future understanding of salvation by the people of Israel.'[10] For Israel, God's single most important act of salvation was a concrete historical event.

The people of Israel remembered this act of salvation in the three great feasts of Unleavened Bread (Ex, 23:5; 34:18; Lev. 23:9; 23:15), Weeks of Pentecost (Lev. 23:17 and Deut. 16:12), and Tabernacles (Lev. 23:43). The Israelites are reminded at all of these great feasts that they are a 'delivered' or 'saved' people. The God who brought them into being is a saviour God. The communal, historical event of the Exodus is the confirming seal of their salvation.

(c) *Salvation from enemies.* The Psalms portray God as continuing his activity of salvation in delivering the people from a host of physical ills and human enemies and even death itself (Ps. 6:4–5; Ps. 22:21; Deut. 20:4; Ps. 59:2; 69:1–2; Isa. 38:20; Jer. 30:7).

(d) *Salvation 'unto the Lord'.* There is an object to Yahweh's work of deliverance in the Old Testament. The point of it all is rescue for a specific purpose—for the praise, honour and obedience of the Lord. 'Save us . . . that we may give thanks to thy Holy Name, and glory in thy praise. Blessed be the Lord God of Israel for ever and ever. And all the people said "Amen", and praised the Lord' (I Chron. 16:35–6).[11]

(e) *Conditions of Salvation.* In both the personal and national sphere the prime condition of salvation is trusting in God alone, not in oneself or one's natural powers. Foreign alliances will be of no avail (Hos. 5:13–6:3; Isa. 31:1; Ps. 33:16–20) if God is absent. God saves the individual in the same way. Thus it is the humble and weak (Job 5:5; 22:29; 26:2), those of a contrite heart (Ps. 34:6) and those that fear him (Ps. 85–9) who will be saved. Faith is the proper posture towards the saving God: salvation is impossible without faith and can be forfeited by apostasy (Ps. 78:21ff.)

(f) *The Content of Salvation*: Victory, Vindication, Satisfaction, Costliness.

Victory. One important element of salvation in the Old Testament was victory in history over the enemies of the people of Israel.

To save meant to be possessed of the necessary strength, and to act on it so that it became manifest. David gained salvation when he reduced the surrounding peoples to obedience (2 Sam. 8:14). Any chieftain who had sufficient strength to gain victory over the foes of the people could be described as a saviour (Judg. 2:18; 6:14), but as it was God who had raised up the saviour (Ex. 14:30, I Sam. 10:19), he was pre-eminently their saviour . . . To save another is to communicate to him one's own prevailing strength (Job 26:2), to give him and to maintain the necessary strength. Only God is so strong that his own arm obtains salvation (victory, security, freedom) for himself (Ps. 91:1; Job 40:14), and everybody else must rely on a stronger than himself (i.e. God) for salvation.[12]

Vindication. When the elders of Israel met at the gate of the city to hear judicial cases, they were to 'vindicate' or 'save' weak persons (orphans, widows, poor and oppressed) who were being exploited by someone stronger. In a parallel way, God himself vindicates and saves the poor and weak. Justice and salvation are closely linked together. Psalm 76:9 says: 'God arose to establish judgment, to save all the oppressed of the earth.' Psalm 72:4: 'He shall judge the poor of the people, he shall save the children of the needy, and shall break in pieces the oppressor.' The idea of salvation as vindication for the poor and the oppressed runs throughout the passages that deal with the administration of Hebrew justice.[13]

The idea of vindication is closely tied to the covenant idea. Because of his covenant, God makes his people's cause his own. 'God vindicates his own name among the heathen captors of Israel by espousing the cause of this feeble, oppressed nation which trusts him. His salvation is indeed an expression of his righteousness in the sense of faithfulness to his covenant promise.'[14]

Satisfaction. The idea of complete well-being (shalom is perhaps the best word) is present both in the root meaning of *Yasha'* as well as in the context in which it is used in the Old Testament. To experience salvation is to be brought into a 'space' where there is protection from both physical and spiritual assaults on the human being (Ps. 116:13; Mic. 4:10). Salvation involves wholeness of personhood, mind, body and spirit. Ps. 28:9 reads: 'Save your people, and bless your inheritance; feed them also, and lift them up forever.' Similarly Ps. 69:35–6: 'God will save Zion and will build the cities of Judah, that they may dwell there and have it in possession. The seed also of his servants shall inherit it; and they that love his name shall dwell therein.' When Yahweh 'saves' someone or a people, they are brought into a place of freedom and release where they can experience 'abundant life'.

Costliness. God's grace is costly. 'Surely, they are my people, children that will not lie. So he was their Saviour. In all their affliction he was afflicted and the angel of his presence saved them; in his love and in his pity he redeemed them, and he bare them and carried them all the days of old' (Is. 63:8–9).[15] God identifies so completely with his people that he too suffers in a costly way in bringing them salvation.

In the Old Testament, salvation is clearly social and corporate and includes every aspect of life. God's salvation pertains to material prosperity, justice for the poor and needy in the judicial system, and the continued historical existence of the people of Israel. The very centre of God's saving activity in the Old Testament was the calling forth of a redeemed community, the people of Israel. At the same time the vertical dimension is everywhere present. God himself is the author of salvation. He took the initiative to effect salvation at the exodus. Both persons and the people of Israel continue to enjoy salvation only as they trust in Yahweh.

In fact, the Old Testament rarely, if ever, talks about the presence of God's salvation except in the context of the covenant community who trust in Yahweh. Certainly Yahweh is Lord of all nations. And he works there as well as in Israel to accomplish his will including justice for the poor (eg. Dan. 4:27). But the Old Testament does not speak of God's salvation as present apart from his covenant with his chosen people where he is consciously confessed as Lord.

3. Salvation in the New Testament

A. *Salvation in the Gospels*

In the teaching of Jesus one finds the idea of salvation inseparably linked with the Kingdom of God that Jesus inaugurated. The Kingdom had dawned in the person of Jesus and was proclaimed in his preaching. When the rich young man asked how to inherit eternal life, Jesus told him to sell all his goods, give to the poor and follow Jesus. And when he left, Jesus explained that it is almost impossible for a rich person to enter the kingdom of God. To that, the disciples said: 'Then who can be saved?' (Mk. 10:17–26). Receiving salvation and entering the kingdom are virtually identical. By a relationship with the One who proclaimed the kingdom, people entered into a submission to God's kingly rule (Lk. 8:10, 12; Mk. 10:15; Lk. 22:20; Matt. 13:41, 43; Mk. 4:30; Lk. 16:16). Michael Green summarizes this relationship of salvation and the kingdom in this way:

[Salvation is] entered on here and now as men enter (Mk. 9:47), or receive (Lk. 8:17) or inherit (Matt. 25:34) the Kingdom. It is to be fulfilled hereafter (Lk. 20:34–36). And for the meantime, life in the Kingdom is characterized by humility (Lk. 6:20), the assurance of answered prayer (Matt. 7:7), the confidence of forgiven sin (Matt. 6:10–12), the experience of God's power (Lk. 11:20), the understanding of God's plan (Lk. 8:10), single-hearted obedience to God's will (Matt. 6:23, 24) and an implicit trust in his protection (Matt. 6:31–34). It is a foretaste of the life in heaven.[16]

Just as a new redeemed community was central to God's salvation in the Old Testament, so too Jesus called out a new community of disciples who received the salvation of the dawning kingdom and began to live out the kingdom values of the new age. Experiencing the salvation of the kingdom Jesus announced meant a total transformation of values, actions and relationships. Sometimes, as in the case of the rich young man, people rejected the kingdom's salvation because they were unwilling to abandon wealth and give to the poor. Sometimes, as in the case of Zaccheus, they repented of sin (dishonesty, official corruption and injustice) and righted those unjust relationships by returning unjustly obtained money and giving to the poor. 'Today,' Jesus said, 'salvation has come to this house' (Lk. 19:9). The text does not say explicitly that Jesus announced forgiveness to the sinful Zaccheus, although the context makes it abundantly clear that Jesus' whole action of visiting the home of this public sinner was an act of forgiving acceptance. But the salvation that happened was not just some vertical forgiveness of sin although it certainly included also that important component. Salvation in the story of Zaccheus included the new social relationships that grace made possible in the life of the repentant, forgiven Zaccheus. The salvation of Jesus' dawning kingdom is corporate and social as well as personal and individual.

We saw in the Old Testament that the word salvation connoted shalom in every area of life. The same is true in the Gospels. The concept of salvation in the Gospels includes the forgiveness of sins—and more. The language about salvation in the Gospels is applied to more than what we normally think of as 'spiritual concerns'. In almost one out of four times where Jesus' healings are recorded in the synoptics, the word 'save' is used to describe the physical healings (*sozo* is used 16 times this way; therapeuo—33 times; laomai—15 times).[17] 'As many as touched him were saved' (Mk. 6:56; Matt. 14:36, etc.). The Samaritan leper was 'saved' (Lk. 17:19) as was blind Bartimaeus (Mk. 10:52), as was the man whose withered hand was restored (Mk. 3: 4, 5) and the liberated demon-possessed man (Lk. 8:36). The word 'save' is used also to describe physical rescues from danger

which might have resulted in harm or death to the parties
involved. Jesus saves disciples from a storm (Matt. 8:25) and
Jesus rescues Peter from sinking in water (Matt. 14:30).
At times the Gospels seem to play on the ambiguity of the
word *sozein* ('heal' or 'save'). Mk. 5:34 (and parallels) is one such
instance where we read the story of the woman with the haemorr-
hage; Mk. 10:52 (and parallels) where blind Bartimaeus received
physical sight from Jesus and 'followed the way' is another.
Salvation then includes the transformation of broken, physical
bodies when the Messianic kingdom breaks into history in the
person of Jesus.

We would be distorting the Gospels, however, if we focused
exclusively or even primarily on the horizontal aspects of salvation. Salvation is accomplished at the cross by the Son of Man
who had come to suffer for others. The Son of Man, whom Jesus
identified as none other than himself, had to suffer. Jesus
combined the tasks of the Suffering Servant (Isa. 53) with this
heavenly Son of Man (Dan. 7) when he spoke of the necessity of
his coming suffering (Mk. 8:31; 9:31; 10:33, 45; 14:21) and
return in glory (Mk. 8:38; 13:26; 14:62). He came to serve and
give his life a ransom (*lutron*) for many (*anti pollon*). J. Jeremias
has shown[18] that Jesus' mention of 'body given' and 'blood shed'
in the institution of the Lord's supper (Mk. 14:21–24; Matt. 26:
24–28; Lk. 22:20; I Cor. 11:24) indicates a violent death—almost
certainly a sacrifice which avails 'for many'. The background is
Isa. 53 and this heightens the reference to the 'new covenant'
sealed with blood—his own blood which achieved the forgiveness of sins and established the new covenant for which the
prophet Jeremiah had longed (Jer. 31:31–34). So the Son of Man
sought and saved sinners (the lost). He bore vicariously the
wrath of God upon sin; in him wrath and mercy were resolved.
That is absolutely central to the gospel's portrayal of salvation.

The Gospel of Luke offers a powerful integration of the
various inter-related aspects of salvation we have been discuss-
ing. Luke uses the language of salvation to an astonishing
degree.[19] It has been argued strongly that the purpose of Luke-
Acts is none other than to record just how the world came to see
the salvation of God. In the body of his gospel Luke shows what
salvation means. The healing of a Gentile soldier's servant (7:3),
the forgiveness of a fallen woman (7:50), the restoration to
wholeness of a demented man (8:36), and the provision of new
life for a dead girl (8:50) are all described in the language of
salvation by Luke, and are clearly intended to be paraenetic. He
wants us to understand that this is what salvation is like—new
life, wholeness, forgiveness and healing. Physical amelioration
can be called 'salvation' in the context of the presence and

acknowledgment of Christ. But the mighty acts of Jesus were not merely acts of compassion but also signs of the presence of the kingdom of God in his person. Salvation is the response of believing hearts to the kerygma (8:12), and this kerygma is nothing other than the proclamation of a person, Jesus the Messiah and the announcement of his dawning kingdom. Salvation is '. . . inextricably linked by Luke with the person of Jesus'.[20]

B. *Salvation in Pauline Thought*

For Paul, salvation refers to the past, present and future activity of God in Christ for humanity. It includes the sacrifice of the cross, the experience of justification, regeneration and sanctification, the reality of Jesus' new community and the ultimate cosmic restoration of all things in Christ. As in the Gospels, then, salvation in Paul is individual and corporate, vertical and horizontal. And it is virtually always related to conscious confession of Christ.

Salvation as a *past event* focuses on the redeeming act of Christ on the cross. Paul uses three different key words [*soteria* (salvation), *apolutrosis* (redemption), and *katallage* (reconciliation)] to refer to the salvation effected at the cross where Christ died vicariously for our sins. We obtain *soteria* as we hear the gospel, are justified by faith rather than works (Rom. 1:16–17), and are freed from the wrath of God because of the cross (Rom. 5:9). *Apolutrosis* (redemption) similarly is defined as the forgiveness of sins (Col. 1:13–14; Rom. 8:23) which has been granted to us because of the expiation of the blood of Christ at the cross (Rom. 3:24–25). And *katallage* (reconciliation) which as we shall see, has a powerful horizontal component, is grounded in the cross where Christ was made sin for us so that we could be reconciled to God (2 Cor. 5:18–21).

Salvation as a *present reality* refers to the power available through the Holy Spirit. 'Who shall deliver me from the body of this death?' (Rom. 7:24), Paul asked. Deliverance comes from Jesus who is 'the power of God unto salvation to every one that believeth' (Rom. 1:16). The present tense of salvation includes both the present experience of justification and the opportunity for victorious living. In the words of Eph. 1:19, it is 'the surpassing greatness of his power towards us believers, according to the working of the power of his might which he wrought in Christ when he raised him from the dead'. Salvation as a present reality means that Jesus the Lord now takes care of his disciples. Since Jesus is now at the central and pivotal place of power in the universe (I Cor. 15:24ff; Phil. 2:9–11), the believer is utterly protected: 'Neither life nor death, angels nor powers, nor things present nor things to come can separate us from the love of God' (Rom. 8:38f.).

A corporate dimension is central to salvation as a present reality. In Ephesians 2:11ff., Paul describes the vertical and horizontal dimensions of salvation through the cross. At the cross, God reconciled both Jews and Gentiles to God and therefore also made possible the horizontal reconciliation of the two most hostile social groups in the ancient world. After underlining the way this twofold reconciliation (with God and with other believers) has broken down the dividing wall between Jews and Gentiles in Christ, Paul then proceeds to discuss the 'mystery' of Christ which had been revealed to him and which he preached: 'That is, how the Gentiles are fellow heirs, members of the same body, and partakers of the promise of Christ Jesus through the gospel. Of *this* gospel I was made a minister' (Eph. 3:6–7). The reality of this new redeemed community where two hostile social groups are now, in fact, reconciled in the body of Christ is part of the gospel and thus part of the salvation Paul announced.

The Pauline concept of being 'in Christ' captures all aspects of the present reality of salvation: forgiveness, sanctification; corporate transformation. Richard Longenecker states in *The Ministry and Message of Paul*:

> In speaking of the personal appropriation of the work of Christ, the apostle repeatedly employs the expression 'in Christ'. The phrase, together with its cognates occurs a total of 172 times in Paul's writings . . . it is the major soteriological expression of Paul, being the basis for and incorporating within itself the patristic themes of 'victory' and 'redemption', the Reformation stress on 'justification', the Catholic insistence on 'the body', the more modern emphasis on 'reconciliation' and 'salvation' and all the Pauline ethical imperatives and appeals.[21]

'In Christ' is used to describe the most intimate and personal relationship a person can have with God in Christ. But it 'also has a corporate significance for it means incorporation into a community wherein the members, being intimately related to Jesus Christ, are thereby inextricably related to one another and are therefore described as the "body of Christ" '.[22]

Salvation has also a strong *future aspect* in Pauline thought. God, who has begun a work in us, will continue it in the present and will consummate it in the future (Phil. 1:6). The salvation which we have already experienced is a downpayment of the complete inheritance which will be ours at the return of Christ

(Eph. 1:13–14). At his return, even our bodies will experience *redemption* (Rom. 8:23) in the final resurrection (I Cor. 15). Central to eschatological salvation is St. Paul's cosmic expectation. It is not just 'souls' or individual 'bodies' that will be restored. The whole created order waits eagerly for the eschatological day when it too will be redeemed and 'set free from its bondage to decay and obtain the glorious liberty of the children of God (Rom. 8:18–25). Redemption understood as the forgiveness of sins is just the beginning of God's incredible cosmic plan of salvation. God's grand design in Christ is his cosmic 'plan for the fulness of time to unite all things in him, things in heaven and things in earth' (Eph. 1:7-10). This, of course, is not a universalist assertion that all persons will be saved, but rather a breath-taking claim that God's plan of salvation in Christ includes the eschatological restoration of all parts of the entire created order to wholeness.

C. *Salvation in the Remainder of the New Testament*

In the book of Hebrews the imagery of the Old Testament language of sacrifice is prominent. The one sacrifice of Christ has replaced the oft-repeated sacrifice of animals. Christ constitutes himself both the Victim and Priest. Atonement is effected by the pouring out of his life-blood so men and women can enter into God's presence because of the new covenant ratified by him (Heb. 9:51; 12:24). Stress is laid on Christ's death which deals with sin, and on his return, which will consummate that salvation (9:28).

James uses the word 'save' to indicate both physical healing (5:15) and escape from divine punishment at the final judgment (5:19). I Peter stresses the future aspect of salvation 'ready to be revealed in the last time' (1:5). In 2 Peter salvation involves deliverance from worldly corruption and lust by partaking in the divine nature (1:4). While the words for salvation are little used in the Johannine epistles, the sacredotal language of Hebrews is congenial to I John. Salvation involves knowing God, possessing eternal life, and dwelling in God (as in the fourth Gospel). In the epistle of Jude, 'common salvation' (v.3) involves the experience common to his readers where the church holds on to those saving truths and experiences the demands and privileges of believers. He urges his readers to hold fast to this salvation (v.22f.). In the *Revelation* of St. John salvation is depicted in Hebraic sacerdotal terms as cleansing from sin by the blood of Christ and being a royal priesthood of believers (1:5–6). Salvation is seen in terms of forgiveness of sins (7:10), the universal victory of God over all enemies (12:10) and the vindication of God's just judgment

(19:1ff.). As in every other part of the Bible, salvation is seen as from and by God (5:9; 14:3).

D. Summary

In the important article on the word salvation in Kittel's *Theological Dictionary of the New Testament*, the author summarizes his findings as follows:

> New Testament soteria does not refer to earthly relationships. Its content is not, as in the Greek understanding, well-being, health of body and soul. Nor is it the earthly liberation of the people of God from the heathen yoke as in Judaism . . . It has to do solely with man's relationship with God . . . In the New Testament . . . only the events of the historical coming, suffering, and resurrection of Jesus of Nazareth bring salvation from God's wrath by the forgiveness of sins.[23]

Although basically correct, this is obviously overstated. We have seen the important corporate aspects of the present reality of redeemed relationships in the body of Christ. And we have seen also how, particularly in the Gospel material—and closely related to Jesus himself—the 'salvation' word-group is used to describe physical healing where Christ brings persons to physical wholeness and well-being. *This, however, is always in a specifically Christological context.* In order to use the word 'salvation' in a biblical way, we must use it in a specifically and distinctively Christological/Christocentric context. As in the Old Testament, *Yasha'*, etc., was in the context of a common confession of Yahweh, so in the New Testament 'salvation' is in the context of the presence and/or confession of Jesus as Saviour and Lord.

The conclusion would seem to be that the biblical usage points us away from the broader definition of salvation. Salvation certainly is individual and corporate, 'spiritual' and physical. Salvation in Christ does redeem the whole person. But all of this takes place within Jesus' new community of believers where people personally confess Christ as Lord and Saviour.

That is not to deny that redeemed persons and redeemed Christian communities have a profound impact as preserving salt and prophetic critics in the larger society. When the church truly obeys all God's revealed word, extremely important, sweeping structural changes in secular society inevitably occur. But these changes even at their best are always so imperfect, partial and temporary that it is not appropriate to use the word salvation with reference to them.

Some people may reply that the church likewise continues in equally tragic imperfection and sin. Therefore it is no more (or less) appropriate to speak of salvation in an imperfect church than in an imperfect secular society. But that is to overlook the fact that there are three factors present in the church that are not present in the world: justification through faith in Christ's cross; regeneration and sanctification through the Holy Spirit; and the presence of Jesus' new redeemed, supportive community of Christians where all relationships are already in the process of redemption. As a result, the church should be dramatically and visibly different from the world. It should be empirically obvious that salvation is a present reality in the church in a way that it is not in the world. Too often, tragically, the church has conformed to the world to such a degree that it is no different from (or even occasionally behind) the world. But this practical disobedient failure does not change the theological fact that the church ought to be a visible demonstration of God's mighty salvation in a way the world will never be until Christ returns.

Arguments Advanced in Support of a Broader View of Salvation

Before concluding our paper, however, we need to face directly several major ways in which the broader view of salvation is advanced and supported. Some of these arguments are exegetical; and some are of a more general theological nature. A careful examination of each of the following arguments will be necessary.

A. *An Interpretation of Principalities and Powers in Col. 2:15*

Paul asserts that at the cross Christ disarmed the principalities and powers. If, as is widely assumed,[24] the principalities and powers in Paul's thought are both supernatural, fallen spiritual beings and also present socio-political, economic political structures of society, then this passage means that at the cross, Christ in some important way has already begun his victory over the corrupt, unjust structures of human society. Certainly the victory will be completed only at his return, but it has begun at the cross. Since this crucial victory happened at the cross, it must be linked with redemption and salvation. How could something that was accomplished at the cross not be a part of salvation? Therefore, the limited peace and justice in society that emerges today results from Christ's disarming of the principalities and powers at the cross and is a part of Christ's saving activity. Therefore we must use the word salvation to describe it, even though we do not mean that improvement in social conditions in society by itself brings a person into a personal saving relationship with God.

B. *An Argument Based on the Kingdom of God*

The crucial question is: Is the Kingdom of God that comes in Christ present only where persons consciously confess Christ as Lord and Saviour or is the Kingdom present beyond the circle of believers?[25]

The Kingdom is the reign of God that broke most decisively into history in the work and person of Christ. Obviously the reign of Christ is most visibly present in the church. But the New Testament repeatedly asserts that Christ is Lord of the world as well as the church (Eph. 1:22; Col. 1:15–20). The Great Commission makes the sweeping assertion that 'all authority in heaven and earth' has been given to Christ (Matt. 28:18). And Revelation 1:5 states boldly that Jesus Christ is *now* 'ruler of kings on earth'. If Christ is Lord of the world as well as the church, is there not an important sense in which his reign is present in the world as well as the church?

Obviously, there is a crucial difference. His reign is *not* present in the unbelieving world in the sense that persons are forgiven for their sins, regenerated through the Spirit and thus on their way to eternal life. Only a personal relationship with God in Christ brings salvation in that sense.

But that does not mean that the reign of Christ is not present in the entire world. And if Christ's Good News of the Kingdom is good news both about that salvation that leads to eternal life and also about the fact that Christ's transforming reign is now at work in all of society, should we not speak of salvation (although *always* with an important qualification that we do not mean forgiveness, regeneration and eternal life) when the reign of Christ produces greater justice and peace via socio-political transformation of societal structures?

C. *An Argument based on Christ's Cosmic Plan of Salvation*

Howard Snyder and others have pointed out that evangelicals too often ignore the cosmic character of the plan of salvation revealed in Christ. It is not just 'souls' or isolated individuals who are and will be saved. God's plan of salvation is intended to counter the consequences of the fall in every area in which sin has corrupted the good creation. Certainly that includes individuals, but it also includes society and nature too.

As we have already seen, *Revelation* speaks of the way the cultures and nations of the world will bring their glory into the New Jerusalem (Rev. 21:1ff, 24–26). Romans 8:18–25 shows that even nature itself will be freed from the bondage and decay resulting from the fall. At the return of Christ, every area of the

7252

creation—persons, cultures and nature—will experience God's cosmic salvation.

Obviously that salvation will come in its fullness only at Christ's return. But if God's plan of salvation is cosmic, why should we not believe that all aspects of that cosmic plan have already begun? If that salvation that comes with conscious confession of Christ has already begun but is not yet complete, why cannot we say the same about the transformation of society and nature? To be sure, the transformation in the latter two areas is less complete because society and nature do not experience the forgiveness of sins or the presence of the Holy Spirit the way persons do. But the Scriptures speak of redemption and salvation with regard to the ultimate eschatological transformation of all things, including cultures and nature. Why then should we not use the language of salvation to refer to very imperfect beginnings of that transformation in society and nature that happen before the eschaton?

D. *Full Humanization is Impossible Apart from Changed Social Structures*

The biblical view of persons is that we are social beings who exist in community, i.e., in socio-economic structures that profoundly shape our lives. Certainly one can be justified and regenerated, no matter how oppressed one is. But the full wholeness God wills for us is not possible if we are starving, discriminated against and oppressed. Only if discriminatory, oppressive social structures are changed can persons experience the full humanity God intends. But is not salvation the word for the total transformed wholeness God wills? Is not therefore salvation in its totality impossible apart from justice and peace in society? (Again, let us not confuse the argument with a straw man and suppose that means that a personal saving relationship with God in justification and regeneration and the promise of eternal life is impossible apart from social justice. That is *not* being asserted. A hungry, oppressed person about to die of starvation can experience forgiveness and the promise of eternal life.) If therefore the fullness of salvation God wills is possible only when social justice is present, should we not speak of partial salvation when greater (albeit still imperfect) forms of social justice emerge in the larger society?

We will examine each of these, starting with the last.

Certainly the word salvation is the right word to use when full humanization is truly present. But that will happen only in the final kingdom. Whether or not the significant but imperfect movements toward that full humanization in human history should be called salvation depends on biblical usage (and perhaps in part as well on whether such usage is generally helpful or confusing). But the mere fact that final eschatological humanization is salvation does not decide for us whether it is appropriate to use salvation language today for the emergence of partial, imperfect manifestations of peace and justice in secular society.

Does the New Testament (especially Pauline) discussion of God's cosmic plan of salvation help us? In Romans 8:18ff, both persons and the whole created order groan in anticipation of the final redemption of all things. But there is an important difference in the present between believers and creation. Paul says that Christians already have the 'first fruits' of the Spirit and indeed *have been saved* in the hope of the final eschaton (vv.23, 24). But he does not say either of these things about creation. There is no hint that the created order apart from persons has already in some partial sense been so redeemed or saved. Paul merely says that it will be fully redeemed at the eschatological revealing of God's glory and that meantime it stands on tip-toe in eager anticipation of that eschatological deliverance. Romans 8:18ff. then offers no support at all for using salvation language today to refer to environmental or socio-economic improvements in secular society.

The situation, however, is not the same in Col. 1:20. This passage says that 'God was pleased [aorist] . . . to reconcile [aorist infinitive] to himself all things, whether on earth or in heaven; having made peace [aorist participle] by the blood of his cross.'[26] In v.16, Paul had talked of the fact that all things in heaven and earth had been created through Christ. Now he says that all things have been reconciled through Christ's cross. In the context of this discussion of God's cosmic plan of salvation, surely we must take all things to refer to much more than just persons. Every part of the created order has both been created by and reconciled in Christ. (Of course that does not mean that every single person will be saved. Paul was not a universalist. But it does mean that every area of creation has been affected by the cross.)

The word reconciliation is one of the important terms in Paul's salvation word group. Since this text places this act of reconciliation in the past tense, it seems appropriate to speak of reconciliation and therefore salvation having already begun to impact all things in heaven and earth. Obviously the mopping up operations will not be complete until the end of history (I Cor. 15:20–26), but the decisive victory has been fought and won. But since this text says that the reconciliation of all things has already begun, this text seems to warrant the use of salvation language for the partial emergence of shalom in the larger society.

Col. 2:15 needs to be discussed in conjunction with Col. 1:20. In the RSV, the text says that Christ disarmed the principalities and powers at the cross. But there is a problem. A recent (1981) dissertation of Wesley Carr published by Cambridge University Press challenges the entire viewpoint summarized above which sees the principalities and powers as both supernatural, fallen beings and related socio-cultural structures of human society. Carr argues that the principalities and powers are a part of the *good* heavenly host of angels and archangels that surround the throne of Yahweh.[27] Thus, Col. 2:15 means not that Christ won a victory over the fallen principalities and powers, but rather that at the cross, Christ led a triumphal procession of good angels and archangels celebrating his victory.[28] Obviously, we cannot try to settle this question here. It will take extended scholarly debate to evaluate this bold, well argued thesis.[29] If Carr is correct, then this text has nothing to say on our topic.

On the other hand, if he is not, then the text does seem to say that an important victory was won at the cross over evil societal structures and the fallen supernatural beings that lie behind them. One might argue that Col. 2:15 speaks of disarming, not redeeming, the principalities and powers. Nowhere else, in fact, does Paul use salvation language with reference to the present condition of the principalities and powers, except quite possibly Col. 1:20.[30] Perhaps then Paul means that at the cross, Christ has disarmed the principalities and powers to the point where they can no longer dominate the lives of Christians even though their transformation is far too incomplete to talk of redemption. On the other hand, this text does seem to offer some basis for using the language of salvation for all aspects of Christ's victory over evil at the cross. If Carr is not correct, then Col. 2:15 provides at least a modest basis for the broader usage of salvation language.

Finally, what about the argument based on the view that since Christ is Lord of the world as well as the church, the kingdom of God comes both where there is conscious confession of Christ and also (albeit in a different way) wherever peace and justice emerge irregardless of any acknowledgment of God or Christ? As Calvin puts it, civil government 'in some measure begins the heavenly kingdom in us'.[31] Surely no one would want to deny that the risen Lord is now sovereign of history and that therefore there is a significant sense in which his kingly rule is not present throughout the earth quite apart from conscious confession of Christ. But that does not mean that God's salvation is equally present everywhere. The church has always believed that the sovereign rule of the one God extends everywhere even though rebellious humanity rejects his salvation. Therefore his kingly reign is present where his salvation is not.

Is there not some necessary distinction between God's overall sovereign rule of history and the kingdom of God understood as that saving reality that broke into history so decisively in the person and work of Jesus Christ? God's creative and sustaining activity cannot simply be equated with his redemptive work. It is important to note that *absolutely none* of the scores of New Testament texts on the Kingdom of God speak of the presence of the Kingdom apart from conscious confession of Jesus Christ. In the New Testament, the Kingdom of God comes only where people acknowledge Christ. New Testament usage does not seem to support the view that the Kingdom of God comes both where there is conscious confession of Christ and also where non-Christians unconsciously do God's will by creating greater peace and justice.

Certainly there is a sense in which it is true to say that wherever greater peace and justice emerge, there God's will is more nearly approximated. Therefore his reign is present in some sense. When Christians like Wilberforce and Finney, moved by salvation in Christ, transform secular social structures—and Christians ought to be doing this all the time—we can even speak of the power and influence of the kingdom invading society at large. In some important sense the Kingdom of God is at that point present in the larger society. But the fact that the New Testament does not use the language of the Kingdom in this way makes us hesitate. There seems to be no warrant in the New Testament for talking about the coming of the Kingdom of God via societal change apart from confession of Christ.[32] Therefore the burden of proof still seems to rest on those who want to argue that we should speak of the salvation of the Kingdom of God emerging where non-Christians foster peace and justice. New Testament usage points the other way.

This in no way means that one cannot ground one's social responsibility in a theology of the Kingdom. We know that the Messianic Age that has already broken into history in Jesus Christ will come in its fullness at his return. In that final Kingdom, peace and justice will prevail. Hunger, tears, injustice and violence will have fled away. It is precisely that coming Kingdom which has already invaded this old sinful age. The church (while not identical with the Kingdom) is the visible expression now of that coming Kingdom.

Since we know the cosmic plan of justice and peace that will surely come, since we know that is where history will eventually go, we know what God's will is. It would be obvious nonsense to suppose that God does not desire the peace and justice now that he will bring in its fullness at the Eschaton. Therefore, our work for peace and justice now moves history, however imperfectly, toward the coming Kingdom. That is not to deny discontinuity between what we do now and the final consummation. But it is to insist that we know where history is going. And the church is —or ought to be—a visible demonstration that the powers of the New Age are already present in history today. When the church, through its silent example, prophetic word, and political deed, succeeds in moving the larger society in the direction of that peace and justice which we know is surely coming, it puts into practice its theology of the Kingdom. We do not call the imperfect peace and justice which results 'salvation' or 'the Kingdom of God' because reconciliation with God is not the same as reconciliation with persons. But that in no way undermines the importance of social responsibility. Nor does it detach it from our theology of the Kingdom.

Conclusion

The overwhelming volume of biblical usage points towards the narrower usage of salvation language. Col. 1:20 (and perhaps 2:15) seems to be the only textual basis warranting the broader connotation. If biblical usage is decisive, then we should use salvation language to refer only to what happens when persons confess Christ, experience the salvation he offers, and begin to live out the radical demands of his new kingdom. Certainly that salvation is vertical and horizontal, personal and social. But it is all within the context of conscious confession of Christ. Salvation language should probably not be used to refer to the imperfect emergence of justice and peace in society at large before the return of Christ.

Even those who adopt the broader usage are forced to distinguish between two or more kinds of salvation (unless of course they simply equate salvation with societal change). Thus even Gustavo Gutierrez speaks of three levels of liberation.[33] Rather than reintroducing the same distinctions between two or three levels of liberation, we find it less confusing and more faithful to biblical usage to restrict salvation language to the sphere of conscious confession of faith in Christ.

That of course in no way weakens the demand for Christians to seek justice in society at large. It merely means that we should not use salvation language for the very significant although always partial results the Sovereign of history enables us to achieve. At the same time, we acknowledge that there is some limited warrant for the broader usage. As long as those aspects of salvation that relate to justification, regeneration and sanctification, and the new community of Christ's body, remain central and are not equated with societal peace and justice, the broader use of terms seems to be a possible, legitimate usage for Christians. But our inclination—until better instructed by God's Word and God's people!—is to stay with the more narrow biblical usage.

Notes

1. Carl E. Braaten, 'The Christian Doctrine of Salvation', *Interpretation*, XXV (1981), p.117.
2. *Bangkok Assembly 1973* (Geneva: WCC, n.d.), p.90. See similarly liberation theologian Gustavo Gutierrez, *A Theology of Liberation* (Maryknoll: Orbis, 1973), pp.145ff.
3. See Braaten's summary and rejection of the approach in 'The Christian Doctrine of Salvation', pp.120–29.
4. E.g., Richard J. Mouw, *Political Evangelism* (Grand Rapids: Eerdmans, 1973), p.13; and Orlando Costas, *From the Periphery: Missiology in Context*, (Maryknoll: Orbis, 1982).
5. For the following, see. E. M. B. Green, *The Meaning of Salvation* (London: Hodder and Stoughton, 1965), pp.13–33; *Theological Dictionary of the New Testament*, ed. G. Kittel and G. Friedrich and trans. G. W. Bromiley (10 Vols; Grand Rapids: Eerdmans, 1964–1976), IV, 329ff. [hereinafter cited as *TDNT*].
6. *ibid.*, p.330.
7. E.g. in the book of Hosea.
8. *TDNT*, IV, 330–31.
9. pp.15–29.
10. *ibid.*, p.16.
11. Also, Isa. 43:11–12; 49:3, 6, 7.
12. A. J. Taylor, 'Save, Salvation' in *Theological Word Book of the Bible*, Alan Richardson, ed. (New York: Macmillan, 1951), p.219.
13. See further Isa. 51:4–5; 59:15–17.
14. Green, *Salvation*, p.27.
15. See also Isa. 49:26; 60:16; 49:7, 8.
16. Green, *Salvation*, p.102.
17. *TDNT*, VII, 990. Similarly Acts 4:9; 14:9 and James 5:15.
18. *The Eucharistic Words of Jesus* (1955), p.140ff.
19. This has been noted by W. C. Van Unnik 'The Book of Acts, True Confirmation of the Gospel' in *Novum Testamentum*, IV (1960); I. H. Marshall, *Luke: Historian and Theologian* (Exeter and Grand Rapids: Paternoster and Zondervan, 1971), and many others.
20. Green, *Salvation*, p.126.
21. Richard Longenecker, *The Ministry and Message of Paul* (Grand Rapids: Zondervan, 1971), p.98.
22. *ibid.*, p.99.
23. *TDNT*, VII, 1102.
24. See the bibliography cited in Ronald J. Sider, *Evangelism, Salvation and Social Justice* (Bramcote Notts: Grove Books, 1977), p.10, n.2. See also the

recent important refutation in Wesley Carr, *Angels and Principalities: The Background, Meaning and Development of the Pauline Phrase Hai Archai kai hai exousai* (Cambridge: Cambridge University Press, 1981).

25. Sider argued (briefly) the latter view and John Stott objected, defending the former; in Sider, *Evangelism, Salvation and Social Justice*, pp. 11, 23.
26. The aorist infinitive refers to particular action at a particular time. Since the passage speaks explicitly of the cross, the natural meaning is that the reconciliation occurred at the cross.
27. Carr, *Angels and Principalities* (see n.24), pp.43, 122–3.
28. *ibid.*, p.65.
29. There are, however, clear weaknesses. He argues (with very little textual evidence!) that Eph. 6:12 is a second century interpolation (*ibid.*, pp.104–110); he argues that I Cor. 15:24 is irrelevant to the discussion of the principalities and powers because it uses the singular (*ibid.*, p.91).
30. Col. 1:20 is probably an exception because of the probable reference to Col. 1:16. See Ronald J. Sider, *Christ and Violence* (Scottdale: Herald Press, 1979), pp.53–55 for the argument that they will be redeemed at the eschaton.
31. John Calvin, *Institutes of the Christian Religion* (2 Vols; Grand Rapids: Eerdmans, 1957), II, 652.
32. I therefore am inclined to modify the language I used in *Evangelism, Salvation and Social Justice*, p.11 and would no longer speak of the coming of the kingdom when justice emerges in secular society.
33. Gutierrez, *A Theology of Liberation*, p.176.

RESPONSE

In a short response, Dr. Ludvig Munthe states that he basically agrees with Sider and Parker, but he would like to see in addition to exegetical exposition of the relevant soteriological terms a systematic reflection on the relationship between creation and salvation within a trinitarian theological framework. Dr. Munthe adds: 'The main question is namely whether God counteracts sin and evil with one or two arms. That is: only with his redeeming arm or also with his sustaining arm. If you choose the first alternative you must call every political social change for the better in society a means to the coming of God's Kingdom or for salvation. If you choose the second alternative, the discussion on our social responsibility must be considerably broadened. We are then co-operating with God for a just society in our capacity as God's stewards given a cultural mandate and motivated by our citizenship in the Kingdom of God.'

The respondent then raises another important issue. He writes: 'I would also like a clarification about the relationship between the view of salvation in the Old Testament and in the

New Testament. It is quite evident that the Old Testament represents a broad multi-dimensional view of salvation. In the New
Testament however, the picture seems to be more complex.
Jesus and Paul represent a more narrow view of salvation.
Concepts like "Kingdom of God", "peace" do not seem to have
the same broad connotation in the Synoptics and in Paul's letters
as they do in the Old Testament, at least not the "Kingdom-
already-come", but "the peace experience here and now". At
the same time the "Kingdom not yet arrived" encompasses all
the dimensions of human life, or better, encompasses and transcends the broad connotations of the Kingdom concept in the
Old Testament.'

He concludes by doubting that the broader view of salvation
has any exegetical or general theological arguments in its
support. While it is true that the whole world is in God's hands,
Dr. Munthe adds, 'But his work in society at large today is to be
understood as an act of creation, an act of upholding creation for
all mankind (even when he punishes) and not as Salvation.'

Dr. Ludvig Munthe is Professor of Missions at Det Teologiske Menighets fakultet, Oslo,
Norway.

5

The Kingdom in Relation to the Church and the World

ARTHUR P. JOHNSTON*

Synopsis Recent theologies of the Kingdom have significantly modified biblical teaching about the mission of the church in and to the world. Contrary to some modern views, Dr. Johnston emphasizes that the Kingdom of God is at present manifested as an inner rule within believers. Although the citizens of the Kingdom do produce changes in society as a fruit of redeemed lives, the Kingdom is not to be equated with progressive social improvement. The Kingdom of God, while identified with the church, is not embodied in it: it represents a wider and deeper conception. Nor is it to be associated with any form of political or cultural grouping. Certainly the Kingdom of God is not to be relegated to the sphere of what will happen after a believer dies or after the Judgement. It is not beyond history but is already present within history. It has come in Jesus; people enter it now by faith and will one day see an earthly fulfilment of what they now experience as an inner reality. At the present moment the Kingdom is experienced as a divine activity calling out a people from the world in order that, as an optimistic new humanity within the world, they may await a future consummation in accordance with God's plan and direction. It is important to dis-

*Dr. Arthur P. Johnston is Professor of Missions, Trinity Evangelical Divinity School, Deerfield, Illinois, USA.

tinguish between Israel's theocratic institution and mission and that of Jesus and the church.

There are several levels at which God relates to the church and to the world. He is sovereign king and nothing can thwart his purposes for creation. In addition, he has given all authority to the crucified and resurrected Christ, whose present reign is administered by the Holy Spirit. Third, Christ the king is to be obeyed and served in the fellowship of the church which is his body. The church will equip members of the body for ministry and service in the world and to the world. Fourth, only those who have been born again will inherit the future Kingdom now being prepared by Christ. The present task of disciples is to make disciples, to baptise and then to teach the commandments of the King, who is with them wherever they go.

Introduction

> 'I am a king. For this I have been born, and for this I have come into the world to bear witness to the truth. Everyone who is of the truth hears my voice' (Jn. 18:37).

This study endeavours to come to grips with the nature of the mission of the Church as this nature relates to the biblical teaching concerning the Kingdom. Contemporary evangelical and non-evangelical theologies of the Kingdom influence, modify or even change one's understanding of the mission of the Church in and to the world.

The debate centres around the consequence of this exegetical and theological question whereby the historical view of the mission of the Church as evangelism is now understood by many evangelicals to include social action as a coequal partner to evangelism. That is, both evangelism and social action are necessary for mission and both of them are an end in themselves.[1] This study contends that such a view deflects our attention from world evangelism and blunts the verbal witness of the Church in evangelism.[2] This view not only hinders the growth of the church, but proves self-defeating in that the potential children of the Kingdom are not gathered in to produce their fruit of the Spirit in the world.

A subsidiary issue has arisen which seems to reintroduce the Kingdom either into the temporal sphere by placing its focus in the Church and applying Kingdom ethics in the Church, or by identifying the entire world as presently in the process of becoming the consummated Kingdom without the second coming of

Christ. In some cases Satan has been demythologized to the 'demonic' in politics, economics, oppressor societies and racism. In both cases the moral, economic and social responsibility of the world has been shifted to the Christians. Salvation is often seen more in terms of God's ultimate decree in reconciling the world under his present or future cosmic lordship than in the unique redemptive gathering of believing individuals into the visible fellowship of the Church. Horizontal and humanitarian concerns, as a Kingdom responsibility, seem to have equalled, or, in some cases, even eclipsed the task of proclamation evangelism.

Attention must be called to two misunderstandings. First, the evangelistic mission of the Church should *not* be seen as entailing a lack of social concern, action or responsibility. These fruits of the gospel are biblically seen as an essential *part* of the Christian's service in addition to worship, glorification of God, verbal witness and biblical teaching. Second, the good works of the Christian are not to be used as *bribes* to make 'rice Christians', but as bridges of love leading toward a Spirit-led verbal witness.

Evangelism must be understood again as *the* biblical mission of the church. For the personal eternal destiny of the individual created in the image of God is the mandate of Old as well as New Testament mission; evangelism as the mission of the Church represents the highest vindication of the reconciling work of the Cross and the greatest benefit to the world's poor and oppressed flows from multiple individual lives made new in Christ Jesus. It must also be understood that the imminent return of the King to establish his Kingdom on the earth was the motivating hope of the early Church.

In any final consideration of this subject, the extensively researched papers of Lausanne 1974 should be mentioned, especially Peter Beyerhaus's 'World Evangelization and the Kingdom of God', René Padilla's 'Evangelism and the World' and Howard Snyder's, 'The Church as God's Agent in Evangelism'. The use of the term, 'Kingdom' in the Lausanne Covenant should also be noted.

This study will first attempt to summarize the biblical view of the Kingdom from an evangelical perspective. Then the relationship of the Kingdom to the Church will be discussed, and finally, pertinent issues regarding the Kingdom and the world will be examined. Each section attempts to deal with the questions of evangelism, the mission of the church and the kingdom responsibility toward the world.

1. A Biblical View of the Kingdom

The Kingdom of God is a term of central importance in the

synoptic gospels and it stands in contrast with the kingdoms of this earth and their earthly kings. As human kings reign over an earthly human kingdom so 'the god of this world' is explicitly mentioned as the devil and Satan (Matt. 4:8; 12:26).

Repent, for the Kingdom of Heaven is at hand (Matt. 3:2). These words by John the Baptist announced the fulfilment of Old Testament prophecies as found in Isaiah 4:3. The person of Jesus and the presence of God's Kingdom are inseparably connected. The earthly authority or rule of God (Heb. *malkuth*) as the heavenly king has been initiated (Ps. 145:11, 13) and the Old Testament promise of the enthronement of God as King is anticipated in prophecy (Ps. 96:10–13). Now in the birth and baptism of Jesus the King himself was present in their midst and the Kingdom of heaven was at hand. After the centuries of silence which followed the Old Testament revelation, the Spirit of God had resumed his messianic activity and the great blessings of the messianic promises appeared.[3] He had been drawing near and was now at hand.

First, Jesus brought the Kingdom with him. 'The New Testament locates the Kingdom in Jesus' person and ministry.'[4] Second, Jesus preached about this Kingdom (Matt. 4:17) and instructed the twelve also to proclaim that the Kingdom is at hand when he sent them out to the lost sheep of the house of Israel (Matt. 10:6, 7). While both apocalyptic and rabbinic Judaism of Jesus' day anticipated a world-shattering divine visitation, the Kingdom came in an earthly and eschatological manner, 'in the proclamation of good news, in words which in and of themselves are weak and powerless'.[5] Third, the coming of the Kingdom would bring judgment upon the unrepentant.[6]

But if I cast out demons by the Spirit of God, then the Kingdom of God has come upon you (Matt. 12:28). The coming of the Kingdom introduced a present *dynamic* power working among men even before his second coming and the consummation of this age. Yet this does not mean that the Kingdom had come in its fullest expression. By the exorcism of demons, Jesus demonstrated that a greater power was present in his own person. In Jesus, God was present among men—not merely to continue his rule providentially in the world but to establish actively his rule among men. God took the initiative to introduce his dynamic power within history. His reign would not be initiated or fulfilled by men. It is by the divine ministry of the Holy Spirit that spirits are exorcised and the work of the Kingdom is accomplished. This exorcism by Jesus demonstrated that the rule of God was already in their midst.[7]

But seek first his Kingdom, and his righteousness (Matt. 6:33). The question of the Kingdom is not a matter of religious indifference: man is responsible to seek consciously the Kingdom and the King who rules. To seek God's Kingdom is to seek and to receive his accompanying righteousness as the gift of God.[8] But to seek the Kingdom now and its rule over all one's life implies also an understanding of a future eschatological relationship to him in the coming Kingdom.

But God is also the loving Creator who cares about his creation (Matt. 6:26, 28). Consequently the priority of the Kingdom and the subordination of material and physical concerns of life does not mean that they are to be despised. There is the expectation of divine provision now as a first fruit of that redeemed world to come (Matt. 18:28).[9]

For behold, the kingdom of God is in your midst (Lk. 17:21). The mystery of the Kingdom revealed by Jesus was that it had already come into the world in advance of that prophesied by Daniel. Daniel's kingdom would come with mighty power to destroy the godless nations. Rome would be overthrown and the world cleansed of evil and unrighteousness. Jesus' miracle in feeding the five thousand prompted the Jews to try to make him king (Jn. 6:15), but he rejected their political intentions and understanding of the Kingdom. God would exercise that hidden work through the King among men *in* history before carrying out his final redemptive political plan *at the end of* history.[10]

The Kingdom was in their midst but not in the form the Pharisees expected. Before the coming of the Kingdom in glorious power, God purposed to defeat Satan and to begin a work of redemptive power among mankind in history. Christ's presence on earth was both historical and spiritual in his incarnation, life, death, resurrection and ascension.

As in the parable of the soils, the Kingdom is now working quietly and secretly among men. It is not forced upon them, but they receive it willingly and bring forth fruit (Mk. 4:1–20). The parable of the tares indicates the King's secret working in the world. Society should not be disrupted in this age to purify it of unbelievers on behalf of the sons of the Kingdom who have received his reign; the children of the Kingdom will intermingle with a *mixed* society and, yet, inherit its ultimate blessings. Angels will separate the ungodly from the godly of this world (Matt. 13:24–43).

The parable of the leaven reveals the hidden way in which the small band of Jesus' disciples would be the instruments to introduce the final and complete victory of the Kingdom anticipated by the Jews (Matt. 13:33).[11] The evangelistic ministry of the apostles would extend the presence of the Kingdom into all the world in anticipation of the restoration of the literal Kingdom to Israel (Acts 1:2–8).

But woe to you, scribes and Pharisees, hypocrites, because you shut off the kingdom of heaven from men, for you do not enter in yourselves; nor do you allow those who are entering to go in (Matt. 23:13). Jesus taught that the Kingdom is a present fulfilment. Those in Jesus' audience were invited to the Kingdom and were entering in. The present historical reality of the Kingdom remains as certain as its future consummation.

. . . I am a king. For this I have been born, and for this I have come into the world, to bear witness to the truth (Jn. 18:37). In reply to Pilate's question, 'So you are a king?' Jesus openly affirms this title of king ascribed by Pilate. He had already declared that his present kingly power was not related to the political, social or economic sphere as conceived by Pilate when he said, 'My kingdom is not of this world' (Jn. 18:36). Previously he had rejected the mistaken intention of those of the five thousand who would 'take by force, to make him king' (Jn. 6:15). 'It was his prophetic work that was the foundation of His royalty. The truth, the revelation of God, this was the sceptre that He carried on the earth. This method of conquest that Jesus unveiled to Pilate was the opposite of that by which Roman power was established.'[12] The power of Jesus was expressed by the exorcism of demons which represented the invasion of Satan's domain (Matt. 12:28). His unique prophetic mission consisted in the communication of truth. Jesus summarized, therefore, his entire mission upon earth by classifying it as a witness to the truth. He embodied the truth (Jn. 14:6) and this was the purpose of his ministry.

The holistic revelation of truth to which Jesus witnessed was not proclamation alone or his miraculous signs or acts alone, but it was an activity which combined both propositional revelation and deeds.[13] '. . . the words and acts belong together in the unity of the person of the revealer. He Himself is the revelation in all that He says and does . . .'[14] In the Gospel of John the signs are connected with their verbal interpretation. His glory was disclosed and the signs demand faith in the Father who sent him (Jn. 10:32, 37, 38). While faith in Jesus' external signs was considered an inferior faith (4:48; 10:37, 38; 14:11) it is nevertheless a true faith that points to Christ.

Unbelief in the human heart, so morally darkened by sin, prevents acceptance of the evidences communicated by signs and Scripture (Jn. 5:37–40; 45–47). For this reason Jesus adds that 'Everyone who is of the truth hears my voice' (Jn. 18:37). Jesus' witness to the truth was supremely confirmed by his resurrection as the sign surpassing all others in leading people to belief or disbelief.[15] Consequently, the resurrection account of the crucified King dominates the proclamation of the gospel as the central truth used by the Spirit to call men to Christ and his Kingdom (Jn. 20:30, 31).

And this gospel of the kingdom shall be preached in the whole world for a witness to all the nations, and then the end shall come (Matt. 24:14). The apostolic band assembled around Jesus at the Temple heard and received this mandate and this promise. This verse was part of Jesus' reply to their question concerning the sign of his coming again and of the end of the age (Matt. 24:3). They received from him two teachings that remain in tension to our day, the imminence of the Kingdom and the responsibility to proclaim the Good News of the Kingdom in the whole inhabited earth and to all the Gentiles before his second coming.

The message of the apostles was focused upon the Kingdom, then present in Jesus, and upon Jesus the King who would return to reign in the eschatological Kingdom (Matt. 24, 25) The entire world would become their missionary responsibility. The return of the King was intimately connected with the universal proclamation of the Kingdom of God.

Jesus prophesied a kingdom *to come* prepared for those who have favourably received and kindly treated 'the brethren' of Jesus (Matt. 25:34, 40).[16] His present kingship in relation to the future Kingdom is described as 'already' but 'not yet.'[17] Pentecost marked the beginning or inauguration of the 'last days' with *preliminary signs* of the end (Acts 2:16ff.). This present intermediate period will be concluded by *later preliminary signs* addressed to the world as a final call to repentance: cosmic catastrophies, wars, persecutions as described by the apocalyptic passages of the synoptics, Paul and John.[18]

An urgency accompanies those who bear the Good News because of the imminence of his return and his Kingdom (I Thess. 1:10; 2:19; Rom. 15:18–21). The whole world must hear (Rom. 10:12–15). Jesus was concerned about that Kingdom (Acts 1:3) and the gospel of the Kingdom occupied an important place in the apostolic ministry (Acts 28:23, 31) for they did not know when he would return in judgment and to reign upon the earth (Matt. 13:24–37; 14:62; 24:36–44; II Thess. 2:1). It was incumbent, therefore, upon the disciples of Jesus and other future members of the Kingdom to endure tirelessly (Matt. 24:13) and devotedly proclaim the message of the King and his salvation (I Cor. 9:16, 17).

Truly I say to you, I shall never again drink of the fruit of the vine until that day when I drink it new in the Kingdom of God (Mk. 14:25). Jesus' death and the coming of the Kingdom are intimately linked together in the eucharistic meal. This new covenant relationship reminds the disciples of the Old Covenant of the Exodus (Ex. 24:8) and looks forward to the consummation of the Kingdom and its perfected fellowship. Israel will be regenerated, their sins forgiven, and perfect knowledge of God effected (Jer. 31:31–34; II Cor. 11:25–26).[19]

The meal itself is part of that common picture of table fellowship anticipating that day in the Kingdom when men will eat and drink at Jesus' table (Lk. 22:30). People will be gathered from all parts of the earth in communion with the saints of the Old Covenant (Matt. 8:11). It is described as a wedding feast (Matt. 22:1–14; 25:1–12), a final and full restoration of communion broken by the fall of man and consummated by the union of the marriage of the Lamb and the bride who has made herself ready (Rev. 19:7–9).

Areas of General Agreement

Among the many views regarding the Kingdom from the wholly futuristic understanding of the pre-Augustinian church to the wholly present concept expressed by some non-evangelicals in our day, evangelicals may find certain areas of general agreement.

First, the Kingdom teaching of the Old Testament centred primarily upon God's sovereignty over all creation. His providential reign is supreme and he will bring all history to the fulfilment of his purposes in creation. Satan and his demon forces are active and powerful opponents of God's will, but their powers are derived and subordinate to God's authority and rule: there can be no dualism of ultimate being (Job 1:12; 2:6; Lk. 4:6; I Cor. 10:13).

Second, as the moral sovereign of the universe and of mankind God revealed his holiness, law and love in and through an elected people, Israel. She failed to submit to God's theocratic rule (I Sam. 12), failed in her mission and came under God's judgment. Nevertheless, God's covenant and promise to Abraham (Gen. 12) prevailed in and through the lineage of David (II Sam 7), the Son of David. The Old Testament of Israel reveals the ethical righteousness of the Kingdom, individually and corporately, locally and nationally.

Third, the incarnation of Jesus Christ introduced the King himself to the world. His kingship was rejected by Israel and the world (Matt. 21:43; Jn. 1:11). In contrast with the thoroughly political and national popular expectations, Jesus' kingship was affirmed by signs of healing, exorcisms, resurrections from the dead and preaching the gospel to the poor (Matt. 11:5). His disciples represented the faithful remnant in Israel who believed that God had sent him and had given Jesus' words (Jn. 4:25). The kingdom of God was present in a unique way in history as a result of the incarnation; nevertheless, his substitutionary death alone, as the King of the Jews, brought forgiveness of sins and freedom from the bondage of the Law.

Fourth, during the interim period between Jesus' resurrection and ascension the eleven received special instructions regarding the Kingdom to come. Jesus had received all authority in heaven and earth so that the disciples could accomplish their world mission. His imminent return was related to the task of gospel proclamation to every creature, people and nation. Their call to repentance from sin involves an obedience to all Jesus commanded (Matt. 28:19; Jn. 14:21). Belief initiates a life of works.

Fifth, Pentecost initiated the last days and continued the kingship of Christ Jesus through the leadership of the Holy Spirit, but the reign of Christ in and through the lives of those born from above is not to be compared with the fulfilled kingdom inaugurated by the second coming of Jesus to rule as King upon the earth (Zech. 14). This earthly rule will be followed by a new heaven and earth (Rev. 21).

The Kingdom's Relation to the Church

So little is said by Jesus regarding the church. So little is said about the Kingdom in the remaining New Testament books. Many solutions have been suggested and adopted theologically,. Some are now emphasizing the Kingdom and others the Church.

A. *The Kingdom and Israel*

Jesus' ministry was directed to the 'lost sheep of the house of Israel' (Matt. 15:24) and he instructed his disciples to limit their preaching to them (Matt. 10:5, 6). Israel was God's chosen people and the promise of the Kingdom belonged to them. However, 'Jesus did not appeal to Israel in terms of national solidarity but in terms of a personal relationship.'[20]

Israel as a whole rejected both Jesus and his message, making herself the object of God's judgment instead of blessing (Matt. 11:20–24; Lk. 13:34; 21:20–24). Jesus said: 'Therefore I say to you, the kingdom of God will be taken away from you, and be given to a nation producing the fruit of it' (Matt. 21:43). Nevertheless, many in Israel did respond to Jesus by a complete personal commitment to him and his message. They became the people of the Kingdom, the true Israel and the recipients of the Messianic salvation. As in the final restoration of a remnant of

Israel to the coming Kingdom because of their faith (Jer.
23:3–6), so the disciples of Jesus embodied the true Israel, the
little flock who heard the voice of the Shepherd (Lk. 10:10; cf.
Ezek. 34:15ff.). Because of this the disciples will inherit the
Kingdom and will sit on thrones 'judging the twelve tribes of
Israel' (Lk. 12:32; 22:30).

B. *The Kingdom and the Apostles*

The twelve are already recipients of the blessings and powers of
the Kingdom and are destined to rule in the eschatological
Israel.[21] They, and those who are committed to the Messiah, are
not a new Israel but the true Israel, an eschatological communion
of those who will enter the glorious Kingdom prepared for them
(Matt. 7:21; 25:34; Lk. 7:9; Rom. 5:10–13). As recipients of the
Kingdom they have received forgiveness of sins, fellowship with
Jesus and other children of the Kingdom, and a knowledge of
God the Father of Israel (Isa. 64:8; Mal. 2:10). This Kingdom is
perpetuated by salvific faith (Jn. 1:11, 12).

As future custodians of the mission of Jesus (John 20:21) the
twelve were sent to preach repentance and to perform the works
of the Kingdom (Mk. 3:13, 14). What were these works? The
disciples were vested with authority over the unclean spirits and
to heal (Mk. 6:13; Lk. 9:1, 2). Their Kingdom mission was
defined by Jesus' sovereign call to be with him, to preach and to
have authority to cast out demons (Mk. 3:13–15). These specific
spiritual ministries to the moral, spiritual and physical being of
people in Israel signified that the Kingdom had come near in the
apostolic representatives of Jesus. To reject those who are sent
by Jesus is to reject Jesus and his Kingdom for the Kingdom of
God is working in and through his sent ones.[22] They were
prepared and sent to bring others in all nations into the same
relationship with Jesus that they as disciples had experienced
(Matt. 28:19). Those who became disciples attached themselves
to the person of Jesus and were to be taught all that Jesus had
instructed.[23] The true Israel unconditionally accepts the authority and teaching of Jesus.[24] The proclamation of the need to
repent and to do the works of the Kingdom becomes the mission
of the true Israel, the people of God.

C. *The Church is a Society of Redeemed People*

Entrance into the Kingdom is inseparable from the new birth,
that birth from above (Jn. 2:2, 5). To enter the Kingdom is not
the same as entering the church. Even though the Kingdom is
the sphere of God's *rule* and the church is a society into which
one may enter, 'the present sphere of God's rule is invisible, not

a phenomenon of this world, whereas the church is a body of men.'[25] Conversion involves the acknowledgment of the kingly rule of God as well as repentance for sin (Lk. 24:47).

A distinction, therefore, must be made between those who are 'dead professors' of Christ, and who may live in the sphere of the influence of the church, and those who are born again. As the effects and fruits of Christianity are felt in morality, art, culture, law, politics and world history, so dead professors live in the sphere of the church and are influenced by the citizens of the kingdom (Matt. 7:21-23; 13:41; 22:11-14). At any given time in history those living on the earth as redeemed citizens of the Kingdom form that organism which is the biblical church. The church is present only where Christ is acknowledged as Lord by redeemed people.[26]

The church is a society of people in fellowship with Christ, but the presence of the Kingdom of God in the church speaks of God's dynamic reign invading the present age *without the authority or the power of transforming it into the age to come.* This divine power of the Kingdom of God has come and God is at work and his Spirit is active: men are forgiven of their sins and are delivered from the powers of evil, demons are cast out by a power superior to theirs. Certainly God, the eternal King, rules ultimately over all creation as the Old Testament teaches, and he is also a present dynamic God who rules actively and universally for his people in the church through the coming and mission of Jesus on earth. This activity 'between the times' will culminate at the end of the 'last days' in his full and sovereign rule over the nations of the earth. Present evangelization by the people of God in the church prepares for the true and real christianization of the world at his bodily and visible return.

D. *The Church is a 'Called Out' Society*

Some have attempted to equate the Kingdom with the church by an erroneous interpretation of the parable of the tares (Matt. 13:24-30). The Son of Man, it is said, will gather the causes of sin out of the Kingdom, the church (Matt. 13:41, 43). But this parable teaches the invasion of the entire world in history by the Kingdom of God. The Kingdom of God has not disrupted the structures of society, but good and evil have remained mixed together until the return of Christ and the final judgments of Christians, nations and the unbelievers.

The inaugurated Kingdom is a dynamic spiritual rule of God in the world, yet the Kingdom is not the church. His providential design for world history is sovereign. But this kingship must always be distinguished from the dynamic and invisible operation of the Spirit of Christ that calls individuals to redemption in Christ and to the Kingdom. Nevertheless, God's providence, his inaugurated Kingdom, and the Church are all manifestations of the One Spirit on earth.

E. *The Kingdom Enables the Planting and Growth of the Church*

The proclamation of the gospel was not and is not a fruitless exercise because God's reign enables supernatural deliverance of individuals from the captivity of sin, self and demon powers. Missionaries and evangelists go forth knowing that the power of the Kingdom of God and of his Christ is greater than all opposition encountered on the earth.

Those who hear the Word of truth and believe possess redemption, the forgiveness of sins (Col. 1:5, 14). Those believers were identified with one another as 'saints and faithful brethren' and as those who have love for all the saints (Col. 1:3, 4). This visible manifestation of those related to Christ and his Kingdom is called an *ekklēsia*, a church (Acts 8:1; 13:1; I Cor. 1:2; Col. 4:16). Not only are local congregations recognized as churches but the whole community of those redeemed is so identified in a universal sense, the one Church, the body of Christians (Acts 9:31; 15:41).[27]

We speak of the Kingdom as that spiritual and dynamic rule of Jesus in the lives of those that believe on him, and of the church as the assembly of those who are called out of the world to become associated with one another as his Body. As a result of proclamation of the gospel, the church is planted, gathered and grows. Although the church is a living organism nourished by the Word and by the gifts of the Spirit distributed according to the will of God, it also possesses apostolic organizations (characteristics) prescribed by the apostles and suited to every culture.

3. The Church's Witness to the Kingdom

This is the mission of the church, to proclaim reconciliation to God through the redemptive mission of the King who rules now and who will reign in his future Kingdom (II Cor. 5:17–21). Although the church is not the Kingdom, it bears witness to the rule of Christ in the believers as they are dispersed in the hostile world of unbelief.

A. *Israel Was to Bear Witness to the Kingdom*

As the priestly nation of God, Israel was his witness before the nations (Isa. 43:10, 12; 44:8). Israel was to declare God's self-revelation as the content of this witness—Jehovah's uniqueness, reality, deity, and will (Deut. 28:9, 10; I Kgs. 8:41–43; Jer. 4:1, 2). God's mighty acts and their interpretation were divinely given to Israel (II Tim. 3:16, 17). The Scriptures of Israel bear witness to Jesus, the King (Jn. 5:39).

B. *God Bore Witness to the King and His Kingdom in Jesus*

First, the Apostle John records the witness of John the Baptist whose prophetic mission was to reveal the King to Israel (Jn. 1:31). God himself bore a direct witness to Jesus by a voice from heaven at Jesus' baptism by John (Jn. 1:32, 33; 5:32; 8:18).

The works of Jesus likewise further substantiated Jesus' own divine claims and they are to be understood also as the direct witness of the Father to Jesus' claims (I Jn. 5:6–12). God himself was seen in all of Jesus' works, words, and actions. The resurrection of Jesus is the historical sign above all others that excels in its ability to lead people to belief or unbelief for by it God validates before men the substitutionary nature of Christ's death (Acts 3:14–19; Rom. 1:4; 4:25; 10:9).

C. *The Witness to the Kingdom is Given by the Scriptures*

Jesus' revelation of truth enabled the apostles he chose to believe and receive this message (Jn. 17:6–8) and in turn to bear *factual* witness to Jesus (Lk. 24:28; Jn. 15:27; I Jn. 1:3). The mission of the apostles became an extension of Jesus' mission. The apostolic mission was secondary to Jesus' own mission (Jn. 20:21). Jesus did not cease his ministry of revelation because by breathing upon them his Spirit (Jn. 20:22) he united himself to the apostles so that through them his work continues. Now through the New Testament, as well as the Old Testament, *Christ himself* continues to bear witness (Jn. 5:39; 16:12–15).

The apostles' mission involved the preservation and transmission of truth for the extension of Jesus' mission to all the world. They have no successors. Cullman concludes that

> The apostle cannot, therefore, have any successor who can replace him as bearer of the revelation for future generations, but he must continue *himself* to fulfill his function in the Church of today; *in* the Church, not *by* the Church, but by his word, δια του λογου (John 17:20), in other words by his *writings*.[28]

Through the apostolic writings, Jesus and the apostles continue to speak, the Kingdom draws near, and a people is called out from the world.

D. *The Witness to the Kingdom is Intimately Related to the Witness of the Spirit*

Jesus declared that the new birth is intimately related to the activity of the Spirit, who is the subjective counterpart of the historical and objective witness of the apostles to Jesus (Jn. 3:8). The Spirit would lead the disciples into truth (Jn. 14:26; 15:26; 16:12–15). Believers have been anointed by the Holy One who abides in them and witnesses (I Jn. 2:20, 27; 5:7; I Cor. 2:12–15; Eph. 1:16–20). The Spirit works to give the new birth and to provide for the entire growth of the believer in spiritual wisdom and a knowledge of God through the Scripture.

The Spirit alone works on the life and mind of the disciple to authenticate the Scripture. This internal witness of the Holy Spirit has been called the *testimonium Spiritu Sancti internum*. Neither the institutional church, personal experience, nor the witness of the church may fulfil or usurp the mission of the Spirit to exalt and reveal Christ Jesus, his rule and his coming Kingdom.

E. *The Witness to the Kingdom of the Lives of its Citizens*

The mission of the church is best defined in terms of its continuity of Jesus' ministry of reconciliation of man to God. The church is the sign of the Kingdom primarily in the sense that it points people to Jesus' earthly ministry, to his present personal rule as Lord and Saviour and to his coming Kingdom. The church bears witness to Jesus by pointing people to the authority of Christ as recorded in Scripture. Under his rule the people of God in the church endeavour to please him in every sphere of life. This is a fruit of their ministry expressed by doing 'good to all men, and especially to those who are of the household of faith' (Gal. 6:10).

Visible good works are an essential fruit of God's work of justification. People are not saved *by* good works, but *for* good works (Eph. 2:10). To this they have been prepared beforehand, created and appointed. Visible evidences of the inward and invisible work of faith are to be expected and seen as long as we live (Phil. 1:22). The disciples of Jesus Christ are to let others see the righteousness of the Kingdom and give glory to the Father (Matt 5:16).

Christ has wrought supernatural changes in the family, the market place, the community and the nations through the lives of believers. They give a testimony to the power of God's Kingdom and lead the unbeliever to associate the 'fruits' with the 'roots'. Initial awareness and interest in the gospel may be aroused enabling a loving verbal witness to be given and received. Nevertheless, the proclamation of the gospel would be seriously hindered if an effective proclamation was dependent upon *perfect* Christian people, families and nations. There are none. Jesus is to be Lord in the lives of those who believe on him and they are to bring forth the fruits of the Kingdom in all societal relationships.[29]

The more Christians there are, the more fruits of the Kingdom may be expected in all areas of society.

F. *Believers in the Church are Instruments of the King in the World*

Recognizing the present Kingdom as primarily God's rule and, then, the nature and sphere of his rule, we must also understand the church to be the body of Christ, that body which is an instrument of the King in the world. Jesus worked good in response to faith (Mk. 2:5) and his miracles became signs pointing men to faith in his word (Jn. 5:24; 20:30, 31). This word has been preserved, and it remains to see in what way, and in what sense, the church is the instrument of the King.

The works of the Kingdom were performed through the disciples that Jesus sent out preaching the Kingdom. They, like Jesus, healed the sick and cast out demons (Matt. 10:8; Mk. 3:14; Lk. 10:17). This power had been delegated to them by Jesus and they were conscious that these miracles were not accomplished by any power of their own (Matt. 10:7; Lk. 10:17; Acts 3:16). They rejoiced that even demons were exorcised in Jesus' name for Jesus had done this and to this he had called them also (Matt. 9:35ff.).

Second, the ministry of the Scripture through the church is the principal and essential instrument by which people are delivered from their works of sin to works of righteousness. The believer's body was an instrument of sin. Now this same body is to be presented to God as an instrument of righteousness (Rom. 6:12, 13). The fruit of deliverance from sin and demon domination results in righteousness (Rom. 6:19).

The New Testament continues to address the question of personal moral issues that by no means limits the extent to which good works may be practised. The Apostle Paul was primarily concerned about personal ethical issues. He declared that fornicators, idolaters, adulterers, homosexuals, thieves, coveters, drunkards, swindlers, etc. would not inherit the Kingdom (I Cor. 6:9, 10; Gal. 5:17–21; Eph. 5:3–6). Those cleansed, forgiven and transformed by the Spirit are equipped to bring healing and help to society in addition to a verbal witness to others. Holiness of life and good works in society are always the fruit of justification. People see these works, hear the witness to the Kingdom and glorify the Father (Matt. 5:16; Jn. 15:18).

G. *The Future Kingdom of Glory is the Inheritance of the Church*

Those sanctified in Christ will inherit and enter into the Kingdom prepared for them (Acts 14:32; I Thess. 1:6; 9:10). The future Kingdom is the goal of those citizens living under the rule of Christ. They are counted worthy because of what they have suffered in this present conflict (II Thess. 1:4ff.). They will be rewarded for their service to Christ and his own brethren (Matt. 25:40). The glorious nature of the union between Christ and his own 'will not appear until the King declares his identification with his brethren before the whole universe'.

His future Kingdom will be God's divine gift to man's poverty in the nations. This Kingdom will manifest the power of God, for the divine King will solve the political and social problems of mankind by bringing peace to the nations (Isa. 2:2–4), by pronouncing true justice for the poor and the widow, and by redistribution of wealth (Isa. 11:3–5).[30]

The present inauguration of the Kingdom can be only a dim foreshadowing of the final fulfilment. That future Kingdom will reveal the glory of God in all its majesty. The future Kingdom and the blessedness of the redeemed will inexpressibly surpass any human anticipation of it (I Cor. 2:6).[31]

Conclusions

A number of conclusions emerge from this study.

1. The church is seen in Scripture as a divinely ordained institution that is both visible and transcendent. The formal use of the word *ekklēsia* has a local, provincial or national, and universal sense. *Ekklēsia* also transcends this visible usage to speak of the body of which Christ is the Head: all believers of all times are generally included and those who are living now are also often considered to be present members of the Kingdom; all those who are members of a visible church, however, are not necessarily members of the Kingdom (Eph. 5:24, 25; Col. 1:18).

2. The visible church should not be isolated from or identified with the present Kingdom of God. Those who are members of the Kingdom by faith in Jesus Christ are to find a place of fellowship and service of the King in the church. As Christian citizens, they are to serve Christ in every calling of life.

3. The church does not have direct continuity with the theocracy of Israel and her role as a kingdom of priests to the nations (Ex. 19:5, 6). Israel's distinct mission is destined to have an eschatological fulfilment (Rom. 11:11, 12, 25ff.).

4. The church is not portrayed in the New Testament as a prototype and example of a new society. This confuses the church with a new or renewed political and social Israel. For while the church is necessarily social in character, it differs from others in its universal character for it is open to all men in every place. It is a brotherhood giving full recognition to all in society, however degraded or despised. The church will always have an uplifting effect upon society, but the essentially spiritual and invisible nature of the church's transcendence, prohibits that which has been accomplished by personal regeneration through the redemptive work of Christ from being transferred to a world estranged, rebellious and antagonistic to him. In addition, the consummated Kingdom of Christ will be a dominion quite different from that which the suffering, pilgrim church now occupies. While the church resembles the earthly Christ, it is not yet the church victorious. Like Christ, she suffers, is persecuted and yet wins people to Christ.[32]

5. It is biblically untenable to assume that the socio-political impact of the church or the Kingdom will open the door for evangelism, for this presupposes the church of the present Kingdom to be like a 'kingdom' of this world and reduces its ultimate essence to a politico-social goal.[33] Jesus' reference to Isaiah 61:1 in Luke 4:18 most certainly speaks of *spiritually* liberated individuals through faith in him as the Messiah and should not be construed to mean *earthly liberation*. The liberation of which Jesus spoke was illustrated by individual cases, the widow at Zarephath or Naaman, one cleansed among many lepers in Syria.[34] The new relationships of the gospel were not and should not be imposed without the consent of the parties concerned. It seems more biblical for individuals or groups of Christians instructed by the Scripture to undertake rightful socio-political pursuits—and 'let the church be the church' by pointing people to forgiveness and fulness of life in Christ.

The Kingdom and the World

A biblical understanding of the relationship between the Kingdom and the world is founded upon an understanding of the dynamic rule of God in the world where he rules not only providentially in history to call a people for his name from out of the world but where he rules also in the church and through the lives of the believers. Nevertheless, there is a basic biblical distinction between the present Kingdom and the world, between the church and the world and between the Kingdom to come and the world.

A. *Jesus' View of the World*

In the latter part of the first century, the Apostle John seems to have clarified these Kingdom-church-world relationships as the institutional nature of the church arose and as the Messianic hopes of Israel cooled and waned as a result of the conquest of Jerusalem and the destruction of the temple by Titus in 70 A.D. Christians were not only separated from the Messianic institutions of Judaism but had also become a heavily persecuted minority in the Roman Empire.

'World' is one of the distinctive Johannine terms. Wescott summarizes Jesus' view of the world: 'The fundamental idea of *kosmos* in St. John is that of the sum of created being which belongs to the sphere of human life as an ordered whole, considered apart from God (17:5, 24).[35] This world system, John asserts, had no place for Jesus because the world—and even the disciples—misunderstood his words, his personality and his mission (Jn. 1:10). Jesus was not of the world that rejected what it did not appreciate and hated what it rejected. The world was openly and avowedly hostile to Jesus. He said that, 'it hates me, because I testify of it that its deeds are evil'.[36]

Likewise, Jesus warned the disciples of the world's hatred for them. They would be involved actively with a world cultural and religious system opposed to the will and purpose of God. Their known association with Jesus would bring ostracism and contempt, for the disciples were different in nature from the world and their message of Jesus would bring conviction of sin upon the world (Jn. 15:18-27).[37] The chasm between the world and the believer cannot be bridged because the world cannot possess the Spirit of truth and cannot receive, see or know him.

Nevertheless, this same world of condemned people is the object of God's love (Jn. 3:16). He was their light (8:12; 9:5; 12:46), their Saviour (4:42; 12:47), their life-giver (6:33, 51) and their sin-bearer (1:29). Jesus addressed himself universally to the entire world and not to a sect or nation (18:20; 8:26). Into this world Jesus caringly sent his disciples (17:18). Jesus was supremely concerned that this world came to the knowledge of the truth and to faith in himself and to this end he voluntarily surrendered himself (14:31), sent the Holy Spirit to convict the world (16:18), and prayed for the unity of the disciples (17:21).

B. *Incarnation Signs of the Kingdom to the World*

John's Gospel gives a prominent place to the concept of 'seeing and believing' while Paul's epistles stress the importance of preaching and 'hearing and believing' (Rom. 10:14–17). It was necessary for the special mission of the apostles as eyewitnesses to *see* and believe. So Thomas had to see. 'As an apostle he must touch the risen Lord.'[38] Thomas' seeing was followed by the public testimony of belief, 'My Lord and my God' (Acts 20:28). But now the written word only and the Spirit enable the world to 'see' and to appropriate the biblical witness and explanation of these historical acts of messianic identification. He who hears the apostles, by voice or written word, hears Jesus (Jn. 10:27; 8:47; Lk. 10:16).

Seeing does not always result in faith. Jesus' brothers saw him without believing (Jn. 7:3–5). The majority that witnessed the multiplying of the loaves were unbelieving (Jn. 6:36). The Jewish rulers and some of those who witnessed the resurrection of Lazarus disbelieved (Jn. 11:45, 46). The individual reaction to the recorded event is the difference between salvation and judgment. Belief and unbelief hinge far more upon the doctrine of the Spirit, who, like the wind, impenetrably 'blows where it wishes' (Jn. 3:8), and upon the sovereignty of God (Jn. 6:37) than many today—so heavily oriented towards the behavioural sciences and contemporary philosophies of communication—are ready to recognize.

Jesus' signs are revelation pointing to the need for personal faith (Jn. 20:30, 31). Jesus was served by Martha (Jn. 12:2) and believers are to serve him (12:6; Rom. 1:1). As believers live in Christ they serve the King, love one another in the fellowship of the church and bring forth the fruits of the Kingdom by redemptive witness and humanitarian graces in every walk of life.

The destiny of those in the world depends upon the way in which they respond to the representatives of the King incarnate (Lk. 10:16; Matt. 10:40). This final destiny of the righteous and the wicked is described in the dramatic language of Jesus' day picturing the joy of the marriage feast and the horrors of darkness (Matt. 8:12; 22:13; 25:30) and fire (Matt. 13:50; 25:41). The wedding points to the initiation of that new and long-awaited relationship of the King with his bride, while darkness and fire represent the reality of permanent separation from the King and eternal punishment.

This new Kingdom of God stands in total opposition to the world, its sin, its oppressive systems and materialism. Consequently, the demands of the gospel are not minimized and a true repentance is required.

Conclusion

A serious study of the Kingdom reveals a wide spectrum of

interpretations and explanations. Yet this concept of the Kingdom must be reconsidered by each generation as serious biblical
and theological research increases the depth of our knowledge of
the Scripture and as new interpretations require consideration.
This study has concluded:

1. That the Kingdom of God is the present inner rule of God
in the moral and spiritual dispositions of the soul with its seat in
the heart. God does rule as King in the lives of those 'born
again'. He is not present as Saviour and King in the lives of the
'world' which is already condemned because of unbelief
(Jn. 3:18).

2. The Kingdom of God is not to be identified with the
progressive social improvement of mankind in which the task of
the Church is to transform earth like unto heaven and to do it
now. Citizens of the Kingdom do produce changes in society as
the fruit of their redeemed lives. Spiritual revivals and improvements in society may be expected, but there can be no optimistic
prospect of the moral and social well-being of mankind before
the second coming.

3. The Kingdom of God is identified with the church but not
embodied in it.[39] Citizens of the Kingdom normally find their
fellowship in a biblical expression of a local church of which
Christ is the *Head*. As sovereign and providential ruler of the
world, God will make even its wrath to praise him.

4. The Kingdom of God is not to be associated with any form
of political nation or cultural grouping of people. The people of
the Kingdom in a culture or nation are to seek directly the total
evangelization of their own national or cultural group, but they
are to be concerned for the social good and betterment of their
own people. The Kingdom of God represents a wider and deeper
conception than that of the church.[40]

5. The Kingdom of God is more than the perfect reign of God
in a heavenly kingdom to be entered at death by the believer, or
after the last judgment.[41] It is also a Kingdom that has come in
Jesus and in which he now reigns but which finds its covenanted
fulfilment only at his second coming. People enter the Kingdom
now by faith (Col. 1:12) and will see the earthly rule of Christ at
his return (Jn. 3:3).[42]

6. The Kingdom of God is not *beyond* history but 'already' *in*
history and anticipates divinely given resurrection bodies in
history (I Cor. 15:50).

At the end of history the transformation of the whole of human
and cosmic reality will occur, peace will be concluded between
the Creator and the creature and the rule of God will be established over all men and things.

7. The Kingdom of God is not merely a cosmic social process

in world history. It is a divine activity resulting in the calling out of a people *from the world* who constitute God's people to be an optimistic new humanity *in the world* who await the consummation. The future is not 'open' but planned and directed by God according to his sovereign rule over the world.

8. The Kingdom of God and the Gentile church are not an extension of Israel's messianic mission to the world. Some contemporary theologians understand the *parousia* not as Christ's coming to close history, but as a key to history, an end of all things rather than the end of the world. For them Christian eschatology is not eschatology for Christians alone: it is concerned with Israel's hope, the hope of world religions, the hope of human society, and the hope of nature. The present task of missions, then, remains that of Israel's throughout history.[43] Consequently, liberation toward an open future occupies the central eschatological hope in Moltmann's theology.

Moltmann, recognized by many as providing the theological foundation for liberation theology, has failed to distinguish between Israel's theocratic institution and mission and that of Jesus and the church. He rightly sees Israel as God's eschatological people, but he identifies 'hope' with a present sociopolitical progress accomplished by Israel and the community of Christians who have inherited Israel's mission. The present reign of Christ seems to be reinterpreted to include the providential and future earthly reign of Christ because the *parousia*, the second coming, is more an historical perspective of the present age before God becomes all in all.

9. Finally there are several levels of God's relationship to the church and to the world.

First, most evangelicals would agree that God is sovereign King over the world and is providentially reigning over all his creation. He will bring the world, as well as the church, to the fulfilment of his purposes in creation and redemption. Satan and his demon forces are powerful and active opponents of God, his Kingdom, the reign of Christ and the church, but their powers are derived from God (Lk. 4:6) and can be actively exercised only within the limits God permits (I Cor. 10:13; cf. Job. 1:12; 2:6).

Second, *all* authority was given to the crucified and resurrected Christ (Matt. 28:18). Because of this new dynamic and inaugurated reign of Christ, no hostile power of that malignant reality, Satan, can overcome the church he loved and for which he gave up himself (Eph. 5:25). Without this present reign of Christ administered by the Holy Spirit this world of sinners would be impotent and hopelessly lost in their sin; the church would be an historical impossibility.

Third, the Christian church is the body of which Christ is the Head—whether invisible or visible, universal or local (Col. 1:18). Christ the King is to be obeyed and served in the fellowship of his Body. This divinely ordained church is governed by the dynamic reign of Christ, but this reign and the institutional church are not to be confused. The church is to equip the saints for ministry and service in the world and to the world; in the church believers are taught to learn and do all the will of God in every vocation of life.

Fourth, only those who have been born again or from above will inherit the future and fulfilled Kingdom now being prepared by Christ. At the second coming his Messianic rule as Lord and King will be initiated upon the earth and Satan's power, sin, suffering, sickness, injustice and death will be no more.

Finally, because the disciples were committed to Jesus the Messiah and because all power had been given to him in heaven and earth, they were to go, to bring others into a discipleship relationship to him throughout all the world, to baptize, and, *then* to teach them all *he* commanded. This same Jesus would be with them wherever they went, for he is King.

Notes

1. Cf. John R. W. Stott, *Christian Mission in the Modern World* (London: Falcon, 1975), p.27; Waldron Scott and Emilio Castro 'Your Kingdom Come: A Missionary Perspective'. Report on the World Conference on Mission and Evangelism, Melbourne, Australia, 12–15 May 1980 (Geneva: WCC, 1980), pp.26–36; and Philip Potter, 'From Edinburgh to Melbourne', p.17.
2. Arthur P. Johnston, *The Battle for World Evangelism* (Wheaton: Tyndale, 1978) *passim*.
3. George E. Ladd, *Jesus and the Kingdom* (New York: Harper and Row, 1964), pp.25, 109.
4. Ladd, p.152.
5. *ibid.*, p.165.
6. Willoughby C. Allen, *A Critical and Exegetical Commentary on the Gospel According to Matthew*, I.C.C. (Edinburgh: T. & T. Clark, 1912), p.23.
7. Lenski, p.480.
8. Ladd, pp.211, 212.
9. *ibid.*, pp.315, 316.
10. *ibid.*, pp.221, 222.
11. Ladd, pp.225–234.
12. F. Godet, *Evangile de Saint Jean* (Neuchatel: Allinger Frères, N.D.), III, p.416, translation mine.
13. James Montgomery Boice, *Witness and Revelation in the Gospel of John* (Grand Rapids & Exeter: Zondervan & Paternoster, 1970), p.59.
14. *ibid.*, p.65.

15. Boice rightly observes that: 'The signs themselves are revelational, and Jesus performs them, not primarily for the sake of His compassion for suffering humanity, as in the Synoptics, but to demonstrate His divine nature and supernatural power and thereby to provoke faith in the observers' p.94.

16. Ladd, p.250.

17. This view has been set forth as 'inaugurated eschatology' in contrast to 'future eschatology': cf. Anthony A. Hoekema, *The Bible and the Future* (Grand Rapids & Exeter: Eerdmans & Paternoster, 1979).

18. So Cullman also understands the way in which the first Christians looked on these events, Oscar Cullman, *Christ and Time* (Philadelphia: Westminster, 1950), p.156.

19. Ladd, p.321.

20. Ladd, p.243.

21. *ibid.*, p.248.

22. Ladd, p.252.

23. Karl Barth, 'An Exegetical Study of Matthew 29:16–20,' ed. Gerald H. Anderson, *The Theology of the Christian Mission* (New York: McGraw Hill, 1961), p.69.

24. Rengstorf, *TDNT*, IV, 441ff.

25. Ladd, p.260.

26. Erich Sauer, *From Eternity to Eternity* (Grand Rapids & London: Eerdmans & Paternoster, 1954), pp.91–93.

27. L. Schmidt says that the singular and plural in Acts are used indiscriminately. *TDNT*, III, 505.

28. Oscar Cullman, *The Early Church* (London: SCM, 1956), p.80.

29. A significant contribution to a theological understanding of social ethics as expressed in Article 5 of the Lausanne Covenant has been made by Klaus Bockmuehl, *Evangelicals and Social Ethics* (Downers Grove & Exeter: Inter-Varsity & Paternoster, 1979), pp.17-39.

30. Sauer, *From Eternity*, pp.94, 95.

31. Allen, *Diet. Ap. Church* I, p.678.

32. Bockmuehl, p.11.

33. Charles Hodge, *Systematic Theology* (Grand Rapids: Eerdmans, 1946), III, p.857: As to the nature of this kingdom, our Lord Himself teaches us that it is not of this world. It is not analogous to the kingdoms which exist among men. It is not a kingdom of earthly splendour, wealth, or power. It does not concern the civil or political affairs of men, except in moral relations. Its rewards and enjoyments are not the good things of this world.

34. Bockmuehl reacts to Carl F. H. Henry, René Padilla, and Samuel Escobar's use of Isa. 61 and Lk. 4 and says, 'Jesus' sermon in Nazareth proves that the new life presently is realized only very individually, not generally (only one widow in Zarephath and "only Naaman the Syrian," Lk. 4:26–27) and that it requires an acceptance accompanied by the conquest of pride which the population of Nazareth significantly had already declined. A social ethic cannot be based on Luke 4:18–19. The new life takes preliminary shape only in individual cases which certainly then will serve as an example and illumination' (p.11).

35. B. J. Wescott, 'St, John's Gospel,' *The Holy Bible Commentary*, F. C. Cook ed. (New York: Charles Scribner's Sons, n.d.), II, p.31.

36. Merrill C. Tenney, *John the Gospel of Belief* (Grand Rapids: Eerdmans, 1948), pp.67, 68, 131.
37. *ibid.*, pp.230–232.
38. Boice, p.147.
39. Augustine, *De Civitate Dei;* Roman Catholicism in pre-Vatican II perspective and Calvin and Luther to lesser degrees.
40. 'The Church is, as a society, the visible expression of the kingdom in the world; is, indeed, the only society which does formally profess (very imperfectly often) to represent it. Yet the Church is not the outward embodiment of this kingdom in all its aspects, but only in its directly religious and ethical, *i.e.*, in its purely spiritual aspect. It is not the *direct* (emphasis mine) business of the Church, *e.g.*, to take to do with art, science, politics, general literature, etc., but to bear witness for God and His truth to men, to preach and spread the gospel of the kingdom, to maintain God's worship, to administer the sacraments, to provide for the self-edification and religious fellowship of believers. Yet *the Church has a side turned toward all these other matters,* (emphasis mine) especially in all efforts for the social good and bettering of mankind, and cannot but interest herself in these efforts, and lend what aid to them she can . . . social injustice . . . immorality . . . principles of conduct . . . capital and labour, rich and poor, rulers and subjects . . . A wholesome tone in literature, a Christian spirit in art and science, a healthy temper in arguments, wise and beneficient legislation on Christian principles in the councils of the nation . . . the condition of the masses of the people—these are matters in which the Church can never but be interested.' James Orr, *The Christian View of God and the World* (Grand Rapids: Eerdmans, 1948), p.358f.
41. Archibald Robertson, *Regnum Dei* (New York: MacMillan, 1901), p.119.
42. George N. H. Peters, a Lutheran clergyman of the nineteenth century, presents an exhaustive and convincing study asserting the necessity of the restoration of the covenanted theocratic Kingdom upon the earth. '. . . we are logically and irresistibly driven to the conclusion that the future Messianic Kingdom is a visible, external, world–dominion. The covenants and prophecy declare this emphatically, and *the very nature* of a restored Theocracy demands it. What Kingdom is it that was once existing, then withdrawn, and shall again, under the Messiah, be restored? The *same Kingdom* in which God ruled on earth as an earthly king is to be reinstated. To this all the prophets with one voice testify, and this is the one postponed to the Second Advent. Now any other kingdom, not having a visible, world dominion, not having Theocratic rulers, organization, subjects and territory, could be the one thus held up to our faith and hope. A Kingdom, not Theocratic, not one in which God Himself rules, cannot possibly fill the divine portraiture; and so, on the other hand, a Kingdom, without its material aspects, without its subjects and territory, can possibly correspond with the covenants and predictions on the subject.' George N. H. Peters, *The Theocratic Kingdom* (Grand Rapids: Kregel, 1957), Vol. III, p.460, 92ff.
43. '. . . the task of mission . . . is founded, in fact and in time, on the church's relationship to Israel; the church's relationship to the state, and the political commitment of Christians, is determined by their understanding of the Old Testament and their relationship to Jewish messianism; and . . .

the relationship to nature and our hope for this relationship is dependent on the acceptance or suppression of Israelite thinking. Israel is Christianity's original, enduring and final partner in history.' Jürgen Moltmann, *The Church in the Power of the Spirit* (London: SCM, 1977), p.135.

RESPONSE

In his response, Dr. René Padilla of Editorial Caribe, Buenos Aires, Argentina, confesses he has great difficulty in following the thesis of Dr. Johnson's paper. The author seems to mean that social responsibility is a fruit of evangelism and therefore an essential aspect of the Christian life but not an aspect of the Christian mission, lest it sets evangelism aside. Dr. Padilla responds by stating that both evangelism and social responsibility are the fruits of justification, for we cannot expect a non-Christian to evangelize any more than we can expect him or her to do good works for which we are created in Christ Jesus.

Dr. Padilla replies to Dr. Johnson's equation of the Christian Mission with 'the verbal witness of the Church in evangelism' with three theses.

1. That in Jesus Christ the Kingdom has become a present reality, even though its consummation still lies in the future. He fulfils the Old Testament prophecies in his person and work. This simultaneous affirmation of the present and the future gives rise to the eschatological tension that permeates the entire New Testament. It represents a rediscovery of the Old Testament 'prophetic-apocalyptic' eschatology which Judaism had lost by abandoning the present to the dominion of evil and suffering. Jesus affirmed that the last act of drama—the last days—had already begun in him. Thus the Kingdom of God is God's dynamic power made visible through concrete signs pointing to Jesus as the Messiah.

2. That the Church which is called to be the first fruits of the new humanity, reflects the tension between the 'already' and the 'not yet' of the Kingdom of God. The Church is the community of the Kingdom in which Jesus is acknowledged as Lord of the Universe. Through the Church in anticipation of the end, the Kingdom is now concretely manifested in history. Kingdom ethics are inseparable from the revelation of God's will for human life embodied in and taught by Jesus Christ. Conversion which is necessary for entering the Kingdom always has a specific ethical context related to the situation in which it takes place. The fruit of the Spirit is ethical in content. The mission of the church is the extension of the mission of

Jesus and this involves both evangelism and social service and action. But neither verbal proclamation in itself, nor good works necessarily result in faith. No one can say 'Jesus is Lord' except by the Holy Spirit.

3. That God's purpose, which will be consummated according to God's own timetable is that the whole world is placed under the universal lordship of Jesus Christ and looks forward to its full liberation from sin and death in God's Kingdom. Though Christ's sovereignty extends over the whole of creation only those who fulfil his conditions enter the Kingdom. The Cross spells both judgement and grace. The Church is the sign of God's universal Kingdom and therefore his purpose for the Church cannot be separated from his purpose for the world. To speak of the Kingdom of God in relation to the world is not simply to affirm the providence of God, but rather to speak of the Mediator-King whose reign is made visible in the community which confesses his name.

Dr. Padilla ends his response with a number of conclusions. One is that since the gospel is good news concerning the Kingdom, every human need may be used by the Spirit of God as a beachhead for the manifestation of his kingly power. In every concrete situation the needs themselves provide the guidelines for the definition of priorities. As long as evangelism and social responsibility are regarded as essential to mission the question of priorities becomes irrelevant.

6

History and Eschatology: Evangelical Views

PETER KUZMIČ

Synopsis Dr. Kuzmič sets the stage for the discussion of history and eschatology by reminding us that the purpose of the prophetic books of Daniel and Revelation was to provide comfort, hope and strength to those facing opposition and persecution and not to encourage idle speculation on the end times.

He surveys the history and tenets of the three traditional views of the millennial reign (Rev. 20:1-6) namely, post-millennialism, amillennialism and premillennialism. He criticizes premillennialism and with it dispensationalism which dominate contemporary evangelicalism, especially in North America, for their part in the atrophy of the evangelical social conscience. At the same time he notes that premillennialists have a strong record in evangelism and in the missionary expansion of the Church. He criticizes an unhealthy preoccupation with apocalypticism and current sensational books and films on the subject. Hope, he thinks, is essential to a balanced commitment to both evangelism and social service.

Kuzmič outlines some of the tensions in relating eschatology to the Kingdom of God, such as now and not yet, continuity and discontinuity, souls and society, optimism and pessimism. He writes, 'Conservative Christian theology has an inbuilt tendency

---

*Dr. Peter Kuzmič is Director of the Biblijsko Teoloski Institut in Zagreb, Yugoslavia.

to oversimplification of complex issues. Evangelicals seem to find it hard to think in dialectical terms and can hardly endure to live with unresolved questions and amidst tensions.' He sees that belief in the total discontinuity between the present earth and 'the new heaven and earth' without understanding the continuity inherent in the standing Kingdom and in the resurrection leads to an escapist attitude and to minimising the role of culture and social involvement in the witness and service of the Church. Therefore he calls for both responsible participation in the Kingdom already arrived and watchful expectation of the Kingdom still to come.

Finally, in a section on eschatology and ethics, he decries the relegation of the ethics of Jesus to a future millennial rule and the acceptance of a present status quo. Christian ethics should be an ethic of change and Christian hope lead to Christian practice.

Introduction

Eschatology is often treated as a postscript or a kind of appendix to Christian theology. For evangelicals who take God's purposes with man and history seriously, eschatology is a very vital doctrine pointing to both the *finis* (time-end in the sense of chronos), and the *telos* (the goal) of history. One's view of eschatology determines one's views of history. And one's view of the purpose and goal of history as pointing to the eschaton definitely modifies one's attitude toward the this-worldly historical realities. It is with these views and ensuing attitudes that I am primarily concerned. I am concerned with such questions as these: How does one's eschatological view affect one's conception and practice of social responsibility and evangelism? Does one's view of eschatology determine one's behaviour? What significance does eschatology have for social ethics? How do evangelical eschatological views relate to evangelical involvement in society?

A word of caution and warning in handling such a topic is hardly necessary. Eschatology is a 'slippery word'[1] and if not clearly defined from the outset, it entails the risk of misunderstanding and confusion. There are diverse views of the future even among the most sincere and studious Bible-believing evangelicals. As a matter of fact, there is probably no other doctrine on which evangelicals are more divided and even opposed to each other as the doctrine of 'the last things'. In some Western countries, especially the USA, 'end times' are a growing brand of industry and a flourishing business. A whole apocalyptic book-market has developed (Hal Lindsey's *The Late Great Planet Earth* has sold, so I am told, more than 20 million copies), accompanied by a flood of films, specialized 'prophetic' news-letters and magazines. Much of it is marked by extravagances and speculations, exploiting both the biblical theme of the return of the Lord and the prevalent secular moods to such an extent that definite behavioural patterns are created as a result.

One of the curious and saddest features of so much of the evangelical literary output on eschatological themes is its failure to spell out the meaning and implications of the Christian hope for Christian living in the present, here and now. Some evange-licals go to great lengths to examine the 'signs of the time' and some even dare to speculate unscripturally so as even to prognos-ticate the actual date of the return of Christ. The average believer is overwhelmed by a plethora of controversial details about end-time events by those who claim to have *the* inside track on the future of the planet earth, and he is confused by disagreement and division among the 'experts on prophecy'. Many of these 'experts' and expositors seem to ignore the basic fact that Daniel and Revelation were written first of all for people of God who faced opposition and persecution. They overlook the fact that the purpose of these books so popular nowadays, was neither to provide ground for idle speculation and biblical arithmetic nor to show them how to escape the tribulation they had to endure. Rather biblical apocalypses in their original setting provided comfort, hope and strength to the troubled people of God. Because of a lack of this biblical emphasis and because of largely speculative concentration on some peripheral matters pertaining to the 'last things', the credibility of the evangelical witness is seriously undermined and questioned both in Christian and theo-logical circles and in the world at large.

1. Millennial Views and Attitudes

The doctrine of the millennium has been a bone of contention through the centuries. It is one of the most divisive issues in evangelical Christianity in our century. The key scriptural passage, and the only one where a thousand-year rule of Christ is explicitly mentioned, is Rev. 20:1-6. Depending on the hermeneutical principles used in interpreting the Book of Reve-lation, and on the hermeneutics applied to Old Testament prophecies pointing to an era of the restoration of Israel, and an age of peace, progress and prosperity, Christians have decided for or against a millennial Kingdom and have developed elaborate theologies and schemes relating to the parousia, the second coming of Christ. By millennium is meant a distinct end-historical category of certain duration and marked by a special form of Christocracy.

A. *Postmillennialism*

Postmillennialists interpret Rev. 20 figuratively, and in such a way as to place the millennium within history and prior to the parousia. It is defined by one of its better known exponents as 'that view of the last things which holds that the Kingdom of God is now being extended in the world through the preaching of the gospel and the saving work of the Holy Spirit, that the world eventually is to be Christianized, and that the return of Christ will occur at the close of a long period of righteousness and peace, commonly called the millennium'.[2]

Evangelical post-millennialists should not be falsely accused and confused with those holding liberal views of human progress and social improvement by natural means and by evolutionary process. The rise of evangelical post-millennialism is usually associated with the Great Awakening (1740–1743) and with Puritan and Pietistic thinking and practice. They linked the millennial hope with the fulfilment of the Great Commission and thus were actively involved in mission and evangelization of the world.

In the eighteenth and nineteenth century Post-millennialism was the predominant evangelical view. It was first articulated as a distinct view in England in the early eighteenth-century, and became 'by far the prevalent view among American evangelicals between the Revolution and the Civil War'.[3] Some of the leading evangelical postmillennialists were: Philip Spener, Daniel Whitby, John Owen, Samuel Rutherford, John and Charles Wesley, Jonathan Edwards and among later Pietists Johann Christoph Blumhardt. These were followed by Charles Hodge, Benjamin Warfield, A. H. Strong, and James Orr.

The ultimate goal of the Puritan theology of mission and of their strong missionary consciousness was the kingdom of God, the Millennium. Jonathan Edwards (1703–1758), father of the Great Awakening and the first major post-millennial thinker, believed that revival and mission were signs of the progressive development by which the millennium would arrive. Edwards actually taught that the Kingdom of God would most probably be inaugurated in America.[4]

The Evangelical revival in the eighteenth as well as in the nineteenth century had a strong social concern.[5] Sufficient study has been done to justify the thesis that 'it was the evangelical awakening that saved England and America from the woes of the French Revolution, *not* because the revival functioned as "opiate of the people" but precisely because it spawned greater social consciousness and involvement. People such as William Wilberforce, Lord Shaftesbury, John Newton and many others whose names are associated with the abolition of slavery, the upliftment of the poor, and the war against vice, all hailed from the evangelical awakening.'[6]

Postmillennialism is optimistic in its outlook and activistic in its mission. It believes in the gradual improvement and redemption of the world. It believes in a golden age of prosperity, justice and peace as the rule of Christ is extended on this earth prior to his second coming. Postmillennialists insist that we should put greater emphasis on the demands of the Bible and those commands of Christ that require social justice, and the elimination of poverty, exploitation, and disease. Clothing of the naked and feeding of the hungry are taken as part of the mission of the church, which is to share the compassion of Christ for suffering humanity.

The evangelical postmillennialist believes in the present rule of Christ and in the transforming power of the Holy Spirit. He 'takes more seriously, or at least more literally, the socio-political aspects of the biblical prophecies' and 'expects the rule of Christ, exercised by the Holy Spirit and mediated by the word of the gospel, ultimately to transform dramatically men's social, political, and international relations'.[7] Jesus' parables of the leaven and of the mustard seed (Matt. 13:31–33) are interpreted 'as biblical evidence that the kingdom is not ushered in suddenly and cataclysmically but slowly, quietly, and almost imperceptibly'.[8] The conversion of all nations is anticipated along with the advance of civilization. Marsden, in his authoritative study *Fundamentalism and American Culture* points to this dual expectation.

> American evangelical postmillennialists saw signs of the approach of the millennial age not only in the success of revivals and missions, but also in general cultural progress. The golden age would see the culmination of current reform efforts to end slavery, oppression, and war. Moreover, in this wonderful era science, technology, and learning would advance to undreamed of accomplishments.[9]

The weakness of postmillennialism lies in its very strength— optimism. It does not seem to take seriously enough the strength of the forces of evil still operative in the world. It easily lends itself to an evolutionary understanding of history with a this-earthly hope. With its expectations for the church and the world it also undermines the expectancy of the imminent return of Christ.

B. *Amillennialism*

Amillennialism, also called the 'nonmillennial' view, is not a rejection of Rev. 20, as it is sometimes misunderstood to be. Rather it consists of a non-literal and non-temporal interpretation of this disputed passage. The millennium reign of Christ is seen in spiritual, non-earthly, and non-political terms. Amillennialists insist that the Book of Revelation be interpreted in conformity to its nature and message and that the vision of chapter 20, as G. C. Berkouwer puts it, 'is not a narrative account of a future earthly reign of peace at all, but is the apocalyptic unveiling of the reality of salvation in Christ as a backdrop to the reality of the suffering and martyrdom that still continue as long as the dominion of Christ remains hidden'.[10]

The amillennial interpretation dates back to the *Epistle of Barnabas*.[11] Augustine identified the millennial kingdom with the church and it became the prevalent prophetic view for over one thousand years until the Puritans of Old and New England modified it in the seventeenth-century and laid the foundation for postmillennial thinking.[12] All the Reformers were amillennialists.[13] Among today's evangelical theologians who accept this view we find Louis Berkhof, G. C. Berkouwer, Leon Morris, Donald Bloesch, Thomas Torrance, Anthony Hoekema, and others.

Amillennialists do not anticipate, as do the postmillennialists, a 'golden age' of widespread peace and justice on this earth, the result of the preaching of the gospel. Usually, they share the premillennialists' pessimistic outlook. The difference however, is that an amillennialist 'seldom bemoans the deterioration of world conditions or condemns the prevalent culture. He has noticeably less preoccupation with the details and sequence of the last things and less curiosity about "signs of the times".'[14]

Donald Bloesch, who considers that of the three views, the amillennial has the strongest exegetical support,[15] criticizes it however at four significant points, which are especially related to our considerations. Firstly, it 'too easily falls into a church imperialism', especially in cases where (as in Augustine and Calvin) the visible church is identified with the Kingdom of Christ. Secondly, Bloesch states, Amillennialism has the tendency, as we have also noted above, 'to be overpessimistic concerning the course of world history'. Some therefore look at the church 'as a remnant in the world that is still wholly under the spell of the powers of darkness, despite the fact that Revelation 20 depicts Satan as being so bound that he cannot deceive the nations any further'. Thirdly, amillennialists 'are inclined to spiritualize the kingdom and make it primarily other-worldly' thus neglecting the this-worldly dimension of the kingdom of Christ. 'Their focus of attention,' Bloesch writes, 'is usually on the life hereafter rather than the events of the last days, on immortality rather than the harvest of history, on the vision of God rather than the great commission to go into the world with the Gospel.' Fourthly, 'amillennialism tends to take away the expectancy of Christ's second coming by seeing this coming realized, at least in part, in the gift of the Holy Spirit to the church.'[16]

C. Premillennialism

As we have seen, since the time of Augustine and up to the Puritans of the seventeenth century Amillennialism was the most prevalent eschatological position. This was followed by about two centuries of postmillennial emphasis, in which the preaching of the gospel and social work went hand in hand. Premillennialist beliefs which were held by many of the church fathers in pre-Augustinian days and by some of the Anabaptists in the sixteenth century, were becoming once again widely spread in the latter part of the nineteenth century. The basic distinctive of Premillennialism as far as the sequence of expected events is concerned, is a reversal of the postmillennial view: Christ must first return, and then the millennium will follow.

Premillennialism seems to be the most prevalent, popular and aggressively advocated evangelical view in our times. Since there are varieties of premillennialism leading to significantly varied practical and behavioural consequences for both evangelism and social involvement, we have to devote more attention to it than to postmillennialism or amillennialism.

Following the Civil War in America, things instead of getting better were continually getting worse. This brought about increasing disillusionment and pessimism, which seriously undermined the credibility of Postmillennialism with its optimistic outlook for the spiritual and cultural progress of society. Such disappointing developments, preceded by the cataclysmic events at the turn of the nineteenth century and followed by two world wars in the twentieth, provide the framework for at least a partial understanding of reasons for the rapid spread and popularity of premillennial views in modern times. It is a historically observable fact that premillennialism with its apocalyptic assumptions has a special appeal and tends to flourish in times of great crisis and distress.[17] This is due to both its emphasis on the power of evil and resulting despair as far as the present age is concerned, and to the upholding hope of the dramatic inbreaking of divine intervention with its vindication of the righteous—followed by a period of justice, peace, and prosperity under the kingly rule of Christ on this earth.

There was also, however, a somewhat parallel theological development which widened the premillennialist sphere of influence and strengthened its position. It has to do with an unusual tactical alliance between premillennialists with their literalistic interpretation of Scriptures and the 'Old School' Princeton conservatives with their intellectual defence of the authority of the Bible, as they 'faced a common enemy and saw in modernism a threat to the basic assumptions of their world view'.[18] The two movements were coextensive, and the Princeton School influenced the premillennialists' view of the Scriptures.

Although we shall look at it later, we must for the reason of providing a fairly complete picture of historical development mention at this point the rise and spread of dispensationalism. Dispensationalism, though premillennial, must be distinguished from the more credible and older historical premillennialism.[19] It is a more recent development, 'invented' by one of the most formative influences among those who founded the Plymouth Brethren in Great Britain, John Nelson Darby, towards the middle of the nineteenth century. It was popularized in America through a series of prophetic conferences, the growing number of Bible institutes, and through prophetic periodicals and popular expositions. In the twentieth century it was given clear articulation, and virtual 'canonical' sanction and wide circulation through the publication of the popular Scofield Reference Bible.[20] Dispensational premillennialists have played an important role in the fundamentalist-modernist struggle in the USA.[21]

Premillennialism's underlying philosophy of history has almost inevitable negative consequences for Christian social responsibility. Not only the previously mentioned external pressures but also its own theology led to an abandonment of worldly affairs. The world is expected to grow worse and worse and there is very little or no hope of improving or reforming it by any human effort.

Within a relatively short time then, there was a significant shift from postmillennial holistic understanding of mission (Edwards and Finney saw preaching of the gospel along with political action and social reform as a means of advancing the Kingdom of Christ) to a premillennial position with its dubious effects in bringing about a *dichotomy* that is so prevalent with conservative evangelicals today.

Donald Dayton in his book *Evangelical Heritage* analyzes it as follows:

> This shift in eschatology had profound, and somewhat mixed, impact on the social involvement of evangelicals. On the one hand, the expectation of the imminent return of Christ freed many from building for the immediate future (social advancement, pension plans, etc.) to give themselves wholeheartedly to the inner cities and foreign missions fields. Resulting contact with poor and oppressed peoples often pushed these devoted souls into relief and other welfare work—and occasionally into reform.
>
> But more characteristic was the tendency to abandon long-range social amelioration for a massive effort to preach the gospel to as many as possible before the return of Christ. The vision was now one of rescue from a fallen world. Just as Jesus was expected momentarily on the clouds to rapture His saints, so the slum worker established missions to rescue sinners out of the world to be among those to meet the Lord in the air. Evangelical effort that had once provided the impulse and troops for reform rallies was rechanneled into exegetical speculation about the timing of Christ's return and into maintenance of the expanding prophecy conference.[22]

(a) 'The Great Reversal'

The rise and spread of twentieth century American Fundamentalism then is closely tied in with the ascendance of Pre-millennialism. The attitude of the fundamentalists was essentially defensive as they saw Christian faith assaulted from various directions. Firstly it was assaulted by liberal theology which was undermining cardinal Christian doctrines; secondly by the general secular climate which was being rapidly created by the new findings and theories of the natural and social sciences. Thirdly, the fundamentalists were threatened—and this is of special connection with our topic—by the so-called 'Social Gospel' movement. The outcome of this controversy between fundamentalism and its opponents was disastrous for evangelical social concern.[23]

This 'Great Reversal' (a phrase coined by Timothy Smith), according to Marsden, had a preparatory stage from 1865–1900 consisting of a transition from the Calvinistic vision of a Christian culture, which 'saw politics as a significant means to advance the kingdom, to a "pietistic" view of political action as no more than a means to restrain evil'. This change also corresponded 'to the change from post-millennial to premillennial views of the relation of the kingdom to the present social and political order'.[24] 'The Great Reversal' actually took place from about 1900–1930 'when all progressive social concern, whether political or private, became suspect among revivalist evangelicals and was relegated to a very minor role'.[25] The stigma of the Social Gospel and its identification with theological liberalism certainly contributed to such a strong and unbalanced reaction by conservatives and to their embrace of premillennialism, and especially to the dispensationalist variety which came to dominate American fundamentalism in the 1920s.

That did not mean, however, that all evangelical premillennialists became passive in relation to social evils. We concur with Timothy Weber, however, who in *Living in the Shadow of the Second Coming: American Premillennialism 1875–1925*,[26] came to the conclusion that Premillennialism, and especially its dispensational variety had a negative effect upon social attitudes.[27] He wrote these words:

> Though not all premillennialists accepted the extreme position on the futility of reform activities, one must finally conclude that premillennialism generally broke the spirit of social concern which had played such a prominent role in earlier Evangelicalism. Its hopeless view of the present order left little room for God or for themselves to work in it. The world and the present age belonged to Satan, and lasting reform was impossible until Jesus returned to destroy Satan's power and set up the perfect kingdom. Consequently, though there were significant exceptions, premillennialists turned their backs on the movements to change social institutions. In time, the social conscience of an important part of American Evangelicalism atrophied and ceased to function. In that regard, at least, premillennialism broke faith with the evangelical spirit which it had fought so hard to preserve.[28]

(b) Saving Souls, not Societies

We have already established the fact that premillennialism is weak on social concern and mentioned some of the historical reasons for such a stance. In addition to these factors, the very pessimistic view of human history is the primary reason for its relative non-involvement when it comes to the political, social, and cultural destiny of the 'planet earth' and its inhabitants. On the one hand the premillennialists seem to take this earth seriously by refusing to spiritualize away prophecies that other views take only symbolically or as fulfilled in the church. On the other hand, however, these promises and the hope for the earth are taken to be completely future in fulfilment. They are not expected to come about by any human effort but solely by the second coming of Christ and his 1000-year rule on this earth. Evil is so deeply entrenched and interlaced in the matrix of human society that only Christ's return in power will be able to overcome it. Since the world, especially in the view of dispensationalists, is expected to grow worse and worse as part of God's programme for the last days, it makes no sense to try to improve society. It would be only a waste of time and energy. Some would even consider involvement as dangerous tampering and somehow detrimental for the Christian hope.

Premillennialists, however, have a strong record in evangelism. 'Urban revivalism and the new premillennialism developed side by side.'[29] Historians of American religion tell us that 'every major American revivalist since Dwight L. Moody has been a premillennialist'.[30]

Premillennialists see this world on a rapid course downward, awaiting judgment. They view it 'as a sinking vessel whose doomed passengers could be saved only by coming one at a time into the lifeboats of personal conversion'.[31] Moody described this position in one of his sermons as follows:

> I look at this world as a wrecked vessel. God has given me a lifeboat, and said to me, 'Moody, save all you can.' God will come in judgement and burn up this world . . . The world is getting darker and darker; its ruin is coming nearer and nearer. If you have any friends on this wreck unsaved, you had better lose no time in getting them off.[32]

Premillennialism's emphasis on the imminent return of Christ provides evangelism with a certain sense of urgency. Since Christ might return at any moment, the time is short both for the evangelists in their labour and for those whom they urge not to wait with their response until it is too late. Dispensational premillennialists see their prophetic scenario fulfilled with precision in our own days in many ways and details and use this 'evidence' of the 'signs of the time' amply as an effective device to bring people to quick decisions.

Another eschatological device frequently employed in dispensational evangelistic appeals is the use of the view of the pre-tribulational rapture of the church. The present author has heard sermons and seen films[33] where this doctrine is used (and abused!) very effectively as a kind of scare-technique to press for decisions. He wonders, however, about the quality and longevity of the results obtained by such methods. The question also needs to be asked whether such presentation of salvation does not border on the betrayal of the gospel ('Good News') and of the biblical understanding of the loving nature of God. This evangelistic technique of 'apocalyptic terrorism', is intended to scare into heaven both the nominal Christian who needs to come out of his 'apostate church' (one of the signs of the last days) and the non-believer who will probably also want to escape the coming horrors he has just heard or seen described in most graphic and terrifying ways. 'Being ready' for the return of the Lord, in pre-tribulational dispensationalism seems, more often than not, to mean being ready for the secret rapture in order to avoid the horrors of the tribulation and the wrath of Antichrist. The results of such a method have negative rather than positive motivation. It is the scare of being 'left behind' more than the longing to see the Lord that underlies this eschatological scheme when applied to evangelism.

This preoccupation with apocalypticism, it seems to me, owes more to certain prevalent Western Cultural moods and fads as well as American conservative politics than to the clear teaching of Scripture. It certainly employs very dubious hermeneutic and unbelievable exegetical gymnastics in its speculative guess-work as verses of Scripture or single phrases are plucked out of their context to prove certain points about developments in modern Russia, China, the European Common Market, World Council of Churches, etc. This sensational eschatology is made attractive and popular as it is often written in the form of science-fiction. One gets the impression that in our age of renewed interest in the occult and in astrology, to many western Christians some of the popular 'last-days' writings serve as a religious substitute for astrology.

A recent edition of a popular American evangelical monthly magazine carried the theme 'Last Days'. It discloses the fact that Hal Lindsey's books sold over 30 million copies. In an interview in the same magazine Lindsey quotes with approval a radio pastor who said: 'God didn't send me down here to clean up the fish bowl but to fish in it.' Such an irresponsible statement is self-explanatory and tempts one to give it more than one interpretation. The same issue provides an annotated bibliography on 'Are We in the Last Days?' Here are some of the titles: The Coming World Crisis; Armageddon; How Close are We? The Beast System—Europe in Prophecy; The Years of the Beast; Countdown to Rapture; Christians Will Go Through the Tribulation—And How to Prepare for it; The Coming World Dictator; World War III and the Destiny of America; Latest Word on the Last Days; Armageddon, Oil, and the Middle East; The Terminal Generation; Russia Invades Israel; Prophecy in the Ring; The Two Jerusalems in Prophecy; 1980s: Decade of Shock; The Final Countdown. No comment needed![33a]

(c) The Missionary Expansion of Premillennialism

'And this *gospel* of the kingdom shall be *preached in all the world* for a witness unto all nations; and *then shall the end come*'. (Matt. 24:14). This statement of Jesus is crucial for our understanding of the premillennialists' motivation for world evangelization and their way of discerning God's time-clock. Though they do not expect any large scale results like the postmillennialists, and despite their pessimistic view regarding the future of humanity, and their strong belief in the power of evil, premillennialists are nevertheless strongly committed to evangelism and foreign missions. This involvement is at times interpreted as 'speeding up' the return of the Lord, thus making it contingent on world evangelization.

Premillennialists played an important role in the Student Volunteer Movement, and were instrumental in the founding of the 'faith missions', Missionary Training Schools and Bible Institutes.[34] By the 1920s they claimed that 'believers in the imminent second coming made up from 75 to 85 per cent of the missionary force worldwide'.[35]

Missionary expansion of the twentieth century is largely marked by the spread of the American version(s) of pre-millen-nialism-dispensationalism.[36] This explains at least partly, why evangelical Christianity in so many third-world countries suffers from the same and similar dichotomies and distortions as in the West, leading to withdrawal from the world, into an escapist position that awaits heaven while the world is going under. Thus they very often represent the defence of the status quo in contexts where change is imperative. By refusing to look at and live out the totality of the teaching of our Lord they seriously undermine the credibility and relevance of the gospel for poor and hungry multitudes as well as for intelligent young people and leaders to whom the mission which is void of social meaning has no meaning at all. No wonder Marxists exploit this weakness of the Christians, for we evangelicals by our behaviour do often validate their criticism of religion. Eschatological outlook that leads to passivist and fatalistic thinking has much to do with their success in certain parts of the world where evangelical Christians have laboured for long times with no great results.

2. The Tension of the Kingdom

New Testament eschatology can in no way be reduced to an apocalyptic fear syndrome. Central to the teaching of Jesus was the announcement of the Kingdom of God. In his person the Kingdom has arrived (Lk. 11:20); it was enacted by his mighty deeds as through exorcisms, healings, and in victory over forces of evil and death he defeated the 'strong man'—Satan (Matt. 12:28–29); its nature was taught in the parables and its ethics exemplified in his person and proclaimed in the Sermon on the Mount. Thus in Jesus the Old Testament promise is fulfilled and the last days have arrived. The Kingdom has been *already inaugurated* with the arrival of the King, although it still *awaits its consummation* and fulness at the time of his second coming.

If this is the focus of the practice and teaching of Jesus, it should also be central to the teaching of evangelicals with their high regard for Scripture and the person of Jesus. In evangelical eschatology, Jesus' teaching about the kingdom, which he enacted in his first coming, should certainly be more central than the millennial debates as mentioned above and the sensational preoccupation with the events surrounding his second coming. This, unfortunately, does not seem to be so, at least when judged by the popular evangelical literary output and the treatment of eschatological themes in mass-media. The millennial question is basically the question of the Kingdom of God. Evangelicals have, by and large, unfortunately taken a limited approach to this important and complex biblical subject, focussing it one-sidedly on the differing interpretations of Rev. 20. It is only more recently that, due to the importance of this concept in modern theological debates, some evangelicals are looking at the Kingdom with greater seriousness. That has hardly, however, filtered down from the biblical theological investigations to the pulpits and has yet to produce a desired change in evangelical behaviour.

A. *The Kingdom: Present and Future*

Conservative Christian theology (as any conservatism) has an inbuilt tendency to oversimplification of complex issues. Evangelicals seem to find it hard to think in dialectical terms and can hardly endure to live with unresolved questions and amidst tensions. They much prefer the clear-cut answers and systematized truth and rules, which offer them assurance that they are right and boldness to communicate their convictions to others.

This may at least partly explain why conservative Christians have problems with the teaching of Jesus on the Kingdom of God. It is not easy to live with the tensions that the Kingdom 'already' brings with not only its offers but also its demands in the present age, while awaiting the 'not-yet' to simplify the issues and make an end to these tensions.

The New Testament teaching is clear. The followers of Jesus live—to use Cullman's familiar analogy—between the D-day and the V-day, in the tension between 'already fulfilled' and 'not-yet completed'. There is both a realized *and* a future eschatology in the New Testament teaching. Not the second but the first coming of Jesus is the decisive event of the gospel teaching. The centre of gravity of Christian faith lies not in the events that come at the end of history, but in the events that have already taken place within history—in the death and resurrection of Jesus and in the outpouring of the Holy Spirit. The decisive event of redemptive history has already taken place. The end-point has been predetermined by the mid-point. The future tense is predicated on the past perfect tense of God's activity in Christ.

> The supreme sign of the *Eschaton* is the Resurrection of Jesus and the descent of the Holy Spirit on the Church. The Resurrection of Jesus is not simply a sign which God has granted in favour of His Son, but is the inauguration, the entrance into history, of *the times of the End.*[37]

With Christ then, the future has already come, or at least begun. As Erickson has said, 'The tendency of some Christians to understand Scriptural eschatology in purely futuristic terms must therefore be regarded as a mistaken, perverted view of Scriptural teaching.'[38] G. C. Berkouwer also has an important warning for many evangelical eschatologists whose emphasis borders on heresy. 'A sharp, dualistic separation between the present and future, as if the eschaton were a reality presently strange and completely unknowable, is definitely unbiblical.'[39] The keystone of the New Testament eschatology is the double advent of Christ, and there is a unique relation between the event of the first coming which predetermines the second coming and makes it inevitable, as that which has already come will be ratified and perfected by what is yet to come. Looking forward to the future coming without looking backward to the implications of the past coming of Jesus is a distortion of the biblical perspective.

The biblical understanding of the Christian faith, W. Manson wrote,

> from the beginning exhibits an essential bipolarity. The End has come! The End has not come! And neither grace nor glory, neither present proleptic fruition nor future perfection of life in God can be omitted from the picture without the reality being destroyed.[40]

This bipolarity of the biblical teaching is lost in much of the evangelical futuristic eschatology. Conservative theology is frequently framed within the 'either/or' rather than 'both/and' thinking. The modernist-fundamentalist controversy in the United States has produced a reactionary conservative ('evangelical') theology, the results of which still predetermine much of the thinking related to our topic. And, of course, such theological thinking is determinative for the kind of, or absence of, Christian involvement and action. Consciously risking some over-simplification I show this tension and differing emphasis as related to the concept of the Kingdom of God in the accompanying diagram. The scheme does assume, of course, that there are differing degrees and shades, as well as possible overlappings, present within evangelical thinking.

TENSIONS BETWEEN 'ALREADY' AND *'NOT YET'*

DOCTRINAL EMPHASIS

Immanentism	*Transcendentalism*
Creation	*Redemption*
Cosmic Redemption	*Individual Salvation*
Whole Man	*'Soul'*
'Jewish'	*'Platonic'*
Eschatology	*Apocalyptic*
Postmillennial	*Premillennial*

RELATION TO EARTH-HEAVEN

Earth	*Heaven*
This-worldly	*Other-worldly*
Present age	*Future age*
Restoration	*Annihilation*
Continuity	*Discontinuity*
Transformation	*Judgement*
'New Earth' =	
Old Earth renewed	
'New Earth' =	
totally new creation (*as if* ex nihilo)	

OUTLOOK/ETHICS/ACTIVITY

Optimistic	*Pessimistic*
Hope	*Despair*
Activistic	*Fatalistic*
Social Involvement	*Evangelism-Proclamation*
Penultimate (hope)	*Ultimate (hope)*

B. *Kingdom-Participation and/or Kingdom-Expectation*

The Kingdom of God has been *already inaugurated* with the first coming of Jesus, his ministry, death and resurrection and with the outpouring of the Holy Spirit upon his followers. This historico-eschatological fact stands against all attempts to overly spiritualize the Kingdom and make it primarily an other-worldly reality. As portrayed in the New Testament, the Kingdom of Christ has strong this-worldly dimensions.

The attitude of expectancy and anticipation as related to the second coming is based on an understanding of the effectiveness and implications of the first coming. It is an active and not a passive attitude; it seeks the present manifestations of the Kingdom in the full spectrum of human existence. For, as T. F. Torrance puts it:

> Through the Church . . . the new humanity in Christ is already operative among men, and it is only through the operation of that new humanity that this world of ours can be saved from its own savagery and be called into the kingdom of Christ in peace and love.[41]

Because of the victory Jesus has already achieved by his resurrection, his followers are never driven to despair even when faced with the most appalling social conditions. They are called rather to an active participation in that new movement in history which takes God's intentions and purposes for mankind as their own. However limited or imperfect his impact may be, a Christian 'knows that every stand he takes for social righteousness and every effort he makes towards social renewal and justice and tolerance is not lost'.[42]

Much of evangelical eschatology, as I have shown earlier, is very pessimistic about the world, and thus marked by a withdrawal from the world. It emphasizes a radical break between the present earth and the awaited 'new heaven and earth'. Such teaching of total discontinuity sees the present completely unredeemable and under judgment of divine destruction, and the 'new earth' to be a kind of a new *creatio ex nihilo*.[43] This view is due to common evangelical neglect or misunderstanding of both the biblical doctrine of creation and the New Testament teaching of the present aspect of the Kingdom of God. It takes literally such apocalyptic statements as 2 Peter 3:10, while at the same time ignoring the implications of Rev. 21:24. This neglected scripture certainly affirms that there will not be total dissolution and annihilation, but rather that there is some continuity between the present and the future age. While not underestimating the biblical emphasis on discontinuity between this age and the next, we must at the same time point out the biblical teaching that there is some continuity as well. We are to work for a better world already here and now, knowing that everything that is noble, beautiful, true and righteous in this world will somehow be preserved and perfected in the new world to come.[44] In this sense, indifference to culture and social involvement, the fatalistic attitude that washes its hands of the world letting it go to further and expected corruption is irresponsible, and a betrayal of entrusted stewardship. This, however, is often true of much of the popular evangelical eschatology.

Hoekema affirms the cultural continuity between the present and the future age,[45] and quotes with approval Berkhof's reminder of biblical figures underscoring the continuity.

> . . . the Bible . . . presents the relationship between now and later as that of sowing and reaping, ripening and harvest, kernel and ear. Paul states that a man can build upon Christ, the foundation with gold or silver, so that his work will remain in the consummation and he will receive his reward (I Cor. 3:14). The book of Revelation mentions the works which will follow the believers in the consummation (14:13), and twice it is said in the description of the new Jerusalem that the glory of the kings of the earth (21:24) and of the nations (21:26) will be brought into it. For us who must choose and labour in history it is of great importance to try to understand more clearly the meaning of this figurative language which speaks so plainly about a continuity between present and future.[46]

The affirmation of this neglected biblical teaching must then serve as an incentive to social involvement. It implies that all of our present work for a better world is of eternal significance. It also implies that we are to appreciate and co-operate with non-Christians where in the areas of science, art, literature, philosophy, and social work they are producing what may well be found on the new earth. As Calvin said: 'All truth is from God; and consequently, if wicked men have said anything that is true and just, we ought not to reject it; for it has come from God.'[47]

Evangelicals tend at times to display not only an escapist but at the same time a triumphalistic and judgmental attitude of superiority over everything that is 'worldly'. They need to hear these lines from Calvin and recognize that, 'in his redemptive activity, God does not destroy the works of his hands, but cleanses them from sin and perfects them, so that they may finally reach the goal for which he created them.'[48] Or, as the medieval theologians used to say: *Gratia non tollit sed reparat naturam*. It is interesting in this connection to note how the Jewish philosopher Martin Buber was critical of the Christian eschatology, especially of its antithesis between heaven and earth and its apocalypticism. As pointed out by Berkouwer, 'Buber seems to look on it as nothing more than a form of dualism, a visionary other-worldliness, a kind of Platonism, which makes God into nothing more than an "idea" with no real relevance for this world.'[49]

Much of the present-day evangelical other-worldly teaching and behaviour seems to justify the criticism of Christianity of both Martin Buber and Karl Marx, as well as of other secular thinkers. We can mention another Jew also who puts his critical finger on the same sore, but from a psychoanalytic perspective. Sigmund Freud in the very title of his work, *Die Zukunft*

einer Illusion (The Future of an Illusion)[50] sums up his theory
that religion, especially the Christian faith, is a wish-fulfilment; a
self-deception by which—as if in a dream—man projects into the
distant and transcendent future all the longings that are unattain-
able in this life. Not surprisingly, Max Warren, the great evangelical missionary statesman, came to a similar conclusion:

> The real reason for the failure of Second Adventism to win support
> lies in the fact that it affronts the moral conscience of the Church by
> its virtual abandonment of responsibility for the things of this world
> in deference to its preoccupation with the imminent return of the
> Lord and the end of history . . . On this view, salvation is salvation
> of the soul alone. No serious attempt is made to consider the soul's
> environment.[51]

Warren goes on to point out that such an attitude gains
popular support in times of despair because 'its despair of the
world *seems to be based on a too thorough-going dualism,*' and he
responds to this perversion of Christian faith by a positive
affirmation. 'This world may indeed be "enemy occupied
territory," but the Enemy has got no property rights in it. He is a
thief and a liar. Our responsibility as Christians is to be *good
stewards* of the King's property . . . There is no room in the true
dialectical process for indifference to the way this world is run.'[52]

Conservative Christians have a tendency to combat one heresy
with another. They confront the 'Social Gospel' with an indivi-
dualized and purely spiritual view of salvation. They oppose a
'realized eschatology' with an other-worldly, futuristic eschatological emphasis. It need not be mentioned that such 'reactionary
theology' does no justice to the complexity and richness of
biblical teaching. And, on the practical level, indifference to the
social problems of the day may have disastrous consequences. As
D. Bosch puts it: 'Where Christianity loses its ability to recreate
the world, other powers will take its place—science and technology, but also atheistic revolution.'[53] Many anti-Christian
political movements in the world today are nothing but a judgment of the sin of indifference displayed by the Christians of
those lands in previous times. 'To be indifferent to the way in
which social life is ordered is in fact to take sides—to take sides
with corruption and tyranny, graft and reaction, since these
social evils feed on the indifference and inactivity of ordinary
folk, and count on it for their continuing existence.'[54]

The Kingdom of God then is the redemptive activity of God in
history through the person of Jesus Christ. It does not arrive by
human achievement. Humans are, however, invited to repentance and faith by which they enter the Kingdom, and are
invited to both the responsible *participation* in the Kingdom-

already-arrived, and to the watchful *expectation* of the Kingdom-still-to-come.

Christians who emphasize Kingdom-expectation and neglect Kingdom-participation, very often reflect a sense of alienation from the world and shrink from this-worldly responsibilities. They lack the biblical emphasis on the sovereignty of God in Christ over the world and display as far as the present age is concerned, a stronger belief in the power and forces of evil than in the victory of Christ achieved by resurrection and operative in the world through the work of the Holy Spirit.

In our consideration of the Kingdom and its implications we need to agree with the summary statement of Donald Bloesch, an evangelical systematic theologian. He concluded his chapter, 'The Personal Return of Christ', with the following paragraph, which I think should be descriptive of a truly evangelical position.

> Our intention has been to construct a doctrine of the millennium that includes the note of victory not only over the world powers at the end-time but also over the world powers within our present age. At the same time, we have tried to stay clear of a false church triumphalism that exempts the church from the judgment of God and from the cross of persecution. We have sought to avoid both a crippling pessimism that sees the church as only a tiny remnant besieged by the hordes of darkness and a too facile optimism that underestimates the continuing power of sin and death in the world. The messianic kingdom of Christ is already realized in the birth and life of the church, but it has yet to be consummated when the church is taken up into the eternal kingdom of God. The new age is present now, though hidden in the community of faith, but it will be manifest throughout all the earth when our Lord comes again in glory.[55]

3. Eschatology and Ethics

Part of the eschatological corrective the Apostle Paul administers in 2 Thessalonians is a warning against idleness (see 2 Thess. 3:6–14) and a withdrawal from the present-day responsibilities, which was probably due to excessive preoccupation with the future and the other-worldly as wrongly conceived in relation to the parousia. Many conceive Christian eschatology in terms of the abandonment of the world and its present sinful world-order, considering it beyond redemption and inevitably doomed for judgment. Those misguided thinkers thus substitute *for* an active involvement in the world a passive expectation of an apocalyptic inbreaking from beyond as the only hope for change, justice, peace, and order. Because of such attitudes, Christian eschatology and Christian ethics have not infrequently been considered as irreconcilable rivals. Does the expectation of the second coming of the Lord take away from the incentive for constructive Christian action in the world? Is it true that, 'All the doctrines of Christian eschatology are rife with ethical content and reality, and . . . of a morally inspirational character,' —as stated by L. S. Keyser?[56] Does Christian hope lead to a passive world-denial or to a fruitful and faithful world-involvement? We have seen in our consideration of millennial views that hope gives an incentive to evangelism. Why is it, when it comes to social responsibility, that it is frequently considered a hindrance rather than an impetus? How is it that some Christians fervently and wholeheartedly evangelize the world even though they know that the results will be limited and not all the world will become Christian? How can they at the same time use a similar limitation as an excuse for non-involvement in facing social evils like poverty, sickness, racism, militarism, etc.?

We have already answered some of these questions by pointing to evangelical imbalance and heretical tendencies in relating—or, to put it more accurately, *failing* rightly to relate—history and eschatology, present and future aspects of the Kingdom of God. Constant preoccupation with apocalypticism tends to show up in evangelical theology in attempts to *de-eschatologize history* or *de-historicize eschatology*. Such a distortion of biblical truth makes it almost impossible to relate eschatology and ethics. Faithfulness to the biblical teaching makes us move beyond such unacceptable dualism. It is here that evangelical theology can be corrected and fruitfully enriched by openly and humbly, even though critically, entering into dialogue with contemporary theologians like Pannenberg, Moltmann, and many others, with their stimulating attempts to relate theology to ethics.

Eschatology has vital implications for the Christian involvement in the world. We agree with the conclusion of the British evangelical theologian Stephen Travis:

> Fortunately, the Christian does not have to choose between his personal immortality and a hope for men's future in the world. Indeed, now that 'theology of hope' and 'political theology' and 'liberation theology' have had some years of attention by theologians, a major task is the creation of a synthesis between these 'worldly hopes' and a theology of immortality in fellowship with God.[57]

A. *The Ethics of Jesus*

The message of the promise of the Kingdom is also a message of warning. Eschatology has unavoidable implications for present experience and action. As Jesus announces the Kingdom, he calls to repentance. 'The summons to repentance in view of the coming Kingdom is characteristic of the entire New Testament ethic . . . The impending Kingdom becomes the sanction of the entire ethical summons. The Beatitudes pronounce a moral universe that is rewarded fully and completely in the future. Main portions of the Sermon on the Mount are validated by eschatology.'[58]

The indicative of the gospel, of the Christ-event, forms an indissoluble unity with the imperative of the ethical teaching of Jesus. The parables of the mustard seed and leaven show that even before the parousia the Kingdom is present in anticipatory form. Christian ethic is an ethic of this new situation, it is the ethic of the new covenant, that does not lead to a world-denial, but rather to a self-denying and faithful discharge of our calling in this present world. In the parable of the talents (Matt. 25:14–30) Jesus commands his servants to 'do business' with the talents he has entrusted to them, and condemns the 'wicked, lazy servant' (NIV) for neglecting his duties. The parable stresses the fact that the absent Lord is still the Lord to be obeyed and served. Paul similarly reminds us that 'while we wait for the blessed hope', the second coming of Christ, we should be 'eager to do what is good' (Tit. 2:13–14).

In the parable of the sheep and the goats (Matt. 25:31–46) Jesus clearly shows that it is impossible to separate service to him from service to those who are in need among fellow human beings, and that the outcome of the future judgment will depend on whether we have recognized him in those who are hungry and naked, sick and enslaved and whether we have responded appropriately to their physical needs.

The problem with some forms of dispensationalism is that in its compartmentalization of Scripture it has to relegate to a future Millennium much of the teaching on the Kingdom that has present relevance. This is done not only with much of the Old Testament prophetic exhortation on social issues, but also with the ethical teaching of Jesus. It is true that when Jesus speaks of the Kingdom of God he uses eschatological language. But dispensational theology

> . . . in its extreme forms also evaporates the present-day relevance of much of the ethics of Jesus. Eschatology is invoked to postpone the significance of the Sermon on the Mount and other segments of New Testament moral teaching to a later Kingdom age. Dispensationalism erects a cleavage in biblical ethics in the interest of debatable eschatological theory. Dispensationalism holds that Christ's Kingdom has been postponed until the end of the Church age, and that Kingdom-ethics will become dramatically relevant again only in the

future eschatological era . . . extreme Dispensationalism holds literally to both eschatology and ethics, but moves both into the future. New Testament theology will not sustain this radical repudiation of any present form of the Kingdom of heaven.[59]

Taking the ethical import of the teaching of Jesus seriously, we concur with René Padilla that:

> In the light of the biblical teaching there is no place for an 'other-worldliness' that does not result in the Christian's commitment to his neighbour, rooted in the Gospel. There is no room for 'eschatological paralysis' nor for a 'social strike'. There is no place for statistics on 'how many souls die without Christ every minute', if they do not take into account how many of those who die, die victims of hunger. There is no place for evangelism that, as it goes by the man who was assaulted by thieves on the road from Jerusalem to Jericho, sees in him only a soul that must be saved and ignores the man.[60]

B. *The Practice of Hope*

Our view of the future is not only information about something we await. It is also a call to participation on the journey toward that future, and it determines the way we live in the present. Christians are called to anticipatory living that produces a proleptic life-style. Proleptic could be taken as meaning an error in chronology, referring to something that occurs before its time. The discovery of the life-style of the Kingdom of God means living in the power of the Kingdom already operative in our lives and in our world since the resurrection of Jesus the King and the giving of the Holy Spirit. It means also living anticipatorily, that is from a hope that sees that which has been inaugurated more and more realized here and now as it approaches its consummation. Proleptic living is a life by faith that takes the promises and commands of God equally seriously and honours Christ by implementing them in the present.

The future makes demands on our living in the present. God's eschatological Kingdom is a radical critique of the present state of things in the world. Christian hope does not lead to an easy acceptance of the status quo. Rather, it 'is a constant disturbance of reality as it is and a call to move ahead to the future. The God of the promise does not sacralize the present.'[61]

While Christian ethics should be an ethics of change, the evangelical ethics often suffers a serious defect in this respect whenever it is nurtured by an other-worldly distortion that conceives salvation as an escape from this world to life in another. Such a view in turn blesses the status quo due to a pessimism about this world. To be eschatologically significant we must regain the vision of both proclamation and action. Christian love that strives for the transformation of the world needs to be engendered by Christian hope, by the promise of the future. We are called to continual realization of the eschatological values that are characteristic of the Kingdom: love, joy, life, justice, peace, freedom, brotherhood, equality, harmony, unity, etc. These future realities of heaven are to be proleptically present as they are practised by the followers of Jesus, and they should motivate us to work toward their greater realization on earth.[62]

Christian ethics as an ethics of change should not be understood only in terms of individual repentance. It must also be extended to the area of social relationships and societal structures. As Christians proclaim and live out the universal values of the Kingdom and in obedience to the coming Lord actively love their neighbours, Christians surely can initiate some significant changes in the world. Even in situations where a Christian may not be able to effect a change, as Max Warren put it, 'his attitude is one of revolutionary expectancy'. When we focus our vision of faith upon the blessed return of our Lord with its assurance of his triumph, we are given new strength to carry on even amidst most hopeless situations.

Christian hope leads to Christian practice. For as Leighton Ford stated, 'The hope of Christ's return is no escapist clause. It is not an out for Christian complacency, nor an alibi for non-involvement.'[63] It is not exclusively other-worldly, but it also pertains to our historical existence as we know that the coming One is already a crucified and risen One. In view of these basic events of the redemptive history both the penultimate hopes and the ultimate hope are to be taken seriously as we pray and obey, hope, and work. We must remember also that this basic two-advent structure of the christocentric redemptive history spells out not only promise but also judgment. It allows for neither utopianism nor other-worldly detachment.

Here evangelicals face a major task to recover the fully biblical view of the future that will enable them to live truly evangelical lives in the present. This will come about only by being responsive to the grave needs for change in our world and not by becoming immobilized by subscribing to a kind of unbiblical 'latter-day fatalism'.[64]

Contemporary evangelicalism needs (1) to reawaken to the relevance of its redemptive message to the global predicament; (2) to stress the great evangelical agreements in a common world front; (3) to discard elements of its message which cut the nerve of world compassion as contradictory to the inherent genius of Christianity; (4) to restudy eschatological convictions for a proper perspective which will not unnecessarily dissipate evangelical strength in controversy over secondary positions, in a day when the significance of the primary insistences is international.

This statement was made thirty-five years ago by Carl Henry in his evangelically epoch-making book, *The Uneasy Conscience of Modern Fundamentalism.*[65] It is equally relevant and even more important today as we evangelicals still have a long way to go in overcoming our weaknesses, limitations and imbalances in order to discover the totality of biblical teaching and practice so that the two petitions of our daily prayer, *Thy Kingdom come,* and *Thy will be done* may equally and fully become a reality as we strive to serve our Lord while awaiting his return.

SELECT BIBLIOGRAPHY

Armerding, Carl E. and Gasque W. Ward, eds: *Handbook of Biblical Prophecy* (Grand Rapids: Baker, 1980). Formerly (1977) published as *Dreams, Visions, and Oracles.*

Bass, Clarence B. *Backgrounds to Dispensationalism: Its Historical Genesis and Ecclesiastical Implications* (Grand Rapids: Eerdmans, 1960). Reprint. Grand Rapids: Baker, 1977.

Boettner, Loraine. *The Millennium* (Philadelphia: Presbyterian and Reformed, 1958).

Berkouwer, G. C. *The Return of Christ* (Grand Rapids: Eerdmans, 1972).

Bloesch, Donald G. *Essentials of Evangelical Theology, Vol. 2: Life, Ministry, and Hope* (New York: Harper and Row, 1978).

Bosch, David J. *Witness to the World: The Christian Mission in Theological Perspective* (Atlanta: John Knox Press, 1980).

Clouse, Robert G., ed. *The Meaning of the Millennium: Four Views.* Chapters by: George E. Ladd, 'Historic Premillennialism'; Herman A. Hoyt, 'Dispensational Premillennialism'; Anthony A. Hoekema, 'Amillennialism' (Downers Grove: Inter-Varsity Press, 1977).

Cullmann, Oscar. *Salvation in History* (New York: Harper and Row, 1967).

Dayton, Donald W. *Discovering an Evangelical Heritage* (New York: Harper and Row, 1976).

Erickson, Millard J. *Contemporary Options in Eschatology: A Study of the Millennium* (Grand Rapids: Baker, 1977).

Hoekema, Anthony A. *The Bible and the Future* (Grand Rapids and Exeter: Eerdmans and Paternoster), 1979.

Kik, J. Marcellus. *The Eschatology of Victory* (Philadelphia: Presbyterian and Reformed, 1971).

Ladd, George E. *The Blessed Hope* (Grand Rapids: Eerdmans, 1956).

Ladd, George E. *Crucial Questions About the Kingdom of God* (Grand Rapids: Eerdmans, 1952).

The Gospel of the Kingdom (Grand Rapids: Eerdmans, 1959).

The Presence of the Future, Grand Rapids: Eerdmans, 1974. Revised edition of *Jesus and the Kingdom* (New York: Harper and Row; London: SPCK, 1964).

Lindsey, Hal, with C. C. Carlson. *The Late Great Planet Earth* (Grand Rapids: Zondervan, 1970. 42nd. printing, 1974).

Marsden, George M. *Fundamentalism and American Culture: The Shaping of Twentieth Century Evangelicalism, 1870–1925* (New York: Oxford University Press, 1980).

Milne, Bruce. *What the Bible Teaches About the End of the World* (Wheaton: Tyndale, 1982).

Moltmann, Jurgen. *Theology of Hope: On the Ground and the Implications of a Christian Eschatology* (London: SCM; New York: Harper and Row, 1967).

Moody, Dale. *The Hope of Glory* (Grand Rapids: Eerdmans, 1964).

Pentecost, J. Dwight. *Things to Come* (Findlay, Ohio: Dunham, 1958).

Ridderbos, Herman N. *The Coming of the Kingdom* (Philadelphia: Presbyterian and Reformed, 1962).

Ryrie, Charles C. *Dispensationalism Today* (Chicago: Moody, 1965).

Sandeen, Ernest R. *The Roots of Fundamentalism: British and American Millennarianism, 1800–1930* (Chicago: University of Chicago Press, 1970).

Sine, Tom. *The Mustard Seed Conspiracy* (Waco, Texas: Word Books, 1981).

Smith, Timothy L. *Revivalism and Social Reform* (New York: Harper Torchbooks, 1957). Reprinted with a new afterword by the author (Baltimore and London: The Johns Hopkins University Press, 1980).

Torrance, Thomas F. *Kingdom and Church: A Study in the Theology of the Reformation* (Edinburgh and London: Oliver and Boyd, 1956).

Torrance, Thomas F. 'The Eschatology of the Reformation,' *Scottish Journal of Theology Occasional Papers*, No. 2, pp.36-62 (Edinburgh and London: Oliver and Boyd, 1953).

Travis, Stephen. *Christian Hope and the Future of Man* (London: Inver-Varsity Press, 1980).

The Jesus Hope (London: Word Books, 1974; Downers Grove: InterVarsity, 1974).

Walvoord, John F. *The Blessed Hope and the Tribulation* (Grand Rapids: Zondervan, 1976).

The Millennial Kingdom (Findlay, Ohio: Dunham, 1958).

Weber, Timothy P. *Living in the Shadow of the Second Coming: American Premillennialism, 1875–1925* (New York and Oxford: Oxford University Press, 1979).

Wilson, Dwight. *Armageddon Now! The Premillennarian Response to Russia and Israel Since 1917* (Grand Rapids: Baker, 1977).

Notes

1. See I. H. Marshall, "Slippery Words": 1. Eschatology *The Expository Times*, Vol. LXXXIX, No. 9, June 1978, pp.264–269.
2. Loraine Boettner, *The Millennium* (Philadelphia: Presbyterian and Reformed, 1958), p.4.
3. George M. Marsden, *Fundamentalism and American Culture* (New York: Oxford University Press, 1980), p.49.
4. Sydney E. Ahlstrom, 'From Puritanism to Evangelicalism: A Critical Perspective,' *The Evangelicals: What They Believe, Who They are, and Where They are Changing*, ed. T. D. Woodbridge and D. F. Wells (Nash-

ville: Abingdon) p.276; see also David Bosch, *Witness to the World: The Christian Mission in Theological Perspective* (Atlanta: John Knox Press), pp.142–147.

5. See Timothy L. Smith, *Revivalism and Social Reform* (New York: Harper Torchbooks, 1957).

6. Bosch, *ibid.*, p.147.

7. James R. Ross, 'Evangelical Alternatives,' in *Handbook of Biblical Prophecy*, eds. C. E. Armerding and W. W. Gasque (Grand Rapids: Baker, 1980), p.125.

8. *ibid.*

9. Marsden, *ibid.*, p.49.

10. G. C. Berkouwer, *The Return of Christ* (Grand Rapids: Eerdmans, 1972), p.307.

11. According to D. H. Kromminga, *The Millennium in the Church* (Grand Rapids: Eerdmans, 1945), p.40: 'a very early millennial type of eschatology'.

12. Ian J. Rennie, 'Nineteenth-Century Roots,' *Handbook of Biblical Prophecy*, p.43.

13. On the eschatological views of the Reformers see T. I. Torrance, 'The Eschatology of the Reformation,' *Scottish Journal of Theology Occasional Papers*, No. 2, pp.36–62; and Heinrich Quistorp, *Calvin's Doctrine of the Last Things* (London: Lutterworth Press, 1955).

14. Millard J. Erickson, *Contemporary Options in Eschatology* (Grand Rapids: Baker, 1977), p.75.

15. George E. Ladd would disagree with that as he claims: 'Sound exegesis of Revelation 20 requires a millennial interpretation; nonmillennialists usually do not appeal so much to exegesis as to theological consistency for support of their position. They interpret such passages as Revelation 20 in a non-millennarian way because they are convinced that the totality of New Testament truth has no room for an interregnum and that there is no alternative in view of the New Testament eschatology as a whole but to interpret Revelation spiritually.' ('The Revelation of Christ's Glory', *Christianity Today*, Sept. 1, 1958, p.13).

16. Donald G. Bloesch, *Essentials of Evangelical Theology, Vol. 2: Life, Ministry, and Hope* (New York: Harper and Row, 1978), p.197.

17. See I. J. Rennie, *ibid.*, p.44.

18. E. R. Sandeen, *The Roots of Fundamentalism* (Chicago: University of Chicago Press, 1970), p.xvii.

19. See the books by George E. Ladd in the bibliography; also C. B. Bass, *Backgrounds to Dispensationalism* (Grand Rapids: Eerdmans, 1960).

20. First published 1909, revised 1917. Now also available in other languages, e.g. German.

21. It is probably because of this strategic and yet coincidental alliance in their own history of struggles against liberalism that many American evangelicals look with some suspicion at non-premillennial evangelicals in Britain and Europe.

22. Donald W. Dayton, *Discovering an Evangelical Heritage* (New York: Harper and Row, 1976), p.127.

23. See David O. Moberg, *The Great Reversal: Evangelism Versus Social Concern* (Philadelphia and New York: J. B. Lippincott Company, 1972);

and by the same author, *Inasmuch: Christian Social Responsibility* (Grand Rapids: Eerdmans, 1965).

24. Marsden, *ibid.*, p.86 in a chapter entitled 'The Great Reversal' (pp.85–93).

25. *ibid.*

26. A revised edition of a doctoral dissertation written at the University of Chicago. New York and Oxford: Oxford University Press, 1979.

27. Paul C. Wilt, *Premillennialism in America, 1865–1918, With Special Reference to Attitudes Toward Social Reform* (unpublished Ph.D. dissertation, The American University, 1970), focuses his study on premillennial views on temperance, the urban poor, labour-management relations, the Negro and foreign missions, and comes to a somewhat more positive conclusion than Timothy Weber: 'Given their pessimism about moral and spiritual improvement they were quite active in certain aspects of social reform.'

28. Weber, *ibid.*, p.183.

29. *ibid.*, p.152.

30. *ibid.*

31. *ibid.*, p.53, see also p.71.

32. D. L. Moody, *New Sermons* (New York: Henry S. Goodspeed, 1980), p.535; quoted by Weber, *ibid.*, p.53.

33. Timothy Weber mentions several of such films in his article 'The Great Second Coming Alert,' *Eternity* (April 1981), pp.19–23.

33a. Evangelical 'eschatologists' would do well to listen to John Stott's call in the exposition of *Lausanne Covenant*, 'not to go beyond the plain assertions of the Bible [but to] retain a humble agnosticism about some of the details of the Lord's return,' while affirming the fundamental truths clearly taught in Scriptures. *The Lausanne Covenant: An Exposition and Commentary*, Lausanne Occasional Papers, No. 3 (Minneapolis: World Wide Publications, 1975), p.35.

34. See Weber, *Living in the Shadow* . . . pp.73–81.

35. *ibid.*, p.81.

36. Cf. Sunhee Kwak, *Eschatology and Christian Mission* (Unpublished D.Miss. dissertation written from Korean perspective at the School of World Mission, Fuller Theological Seminary, Pasadena, USA).

37. W. Manson, 'Eschatology in the New Testament,' *Scottish Journal of Theology Occasional Papers No. 2* (Edinburgh: Oliver and Boyd, 1953), p.6.

38. Erickson, *Contemporary Options* . . . , p.34.

39. Berkouwer, *Return*, p.450.

40. Manson, *ibid.*, p.14.

41. 'Foreword' to Heinrich Quistorp, *Calvin's Doctrine of the Last Things*, p.8.

42. Bruce Milne, *What the Bible Teaches About the End of the World*, p.146.

43. Cf. Berkouwer, *Return*, pp.220ff.

44. 'Whatever is true, whatever is honourable, whatever is just, whatever is pure, whatever is lovely, whatever is gracious, in the whole creation, in heaven and earth, is brought together in the future city of God. But it is renewed, recreated, and developed to its greatest glory. The material for it is present in this creation.' H. Bavinck, *Gereformeerde Dogmatiek* (Kampen, 1911). Vol. IV p.802; quoted by H. Berkhof, *Christ the Meaning of History* p.180.

45. Cf. Anthony A. Hoekema, *The Bible and the Future* (Grand Rapids and Exeter: Eerdmans and Paternoster, 1979), pp.39–40, 73–75, and the chapter 'The New Earth', pp.274–287.

46. Hendrikus Berkhof, *Christ the Meaning of History* (Richmond: John Knox, 1966), p.189.

47. *Commentary on the Epistles to Timothy, Titus and Philemon* (Grand Rapids: Eerdmans, 1948), comment on Titus 1:12, pp.300–301.

48. Hoekema, *ibid.*, p.73.

49. Berkouwer, *ibid.*, pp.228–229.

50. Cf. Sigmund Freud, *The Future of an Illusion* (Garden City, NY: Doubleday, 1957).

51. Max Warren, *The Truth of Vision: A Study in the Nature of the Christian Hope* (London: Canterbury Press, 1948), p.53.

52. *ibid.*

53. Bosch, *ibid.*, p.210.

54. Alexander Miller, *The Christian Significance of Karl Marx* (London: SCM, 1946), p.95.

55. Bloesch, *Essentials . . . Vol. 2*, pp.203–204.

56. *A System of Christian Ethics* (Philadelphia: The Lutheran Publication Society, 1913), p.224.

57. *Christian Hope and the Future of Man* (London: IVP, 1980), p.138.

58. Carl F. H. Henry, *Christian Personal Ethics* (Grand Rapids: Eerdmans, 1957), p.553.

59. *ibid.*, p.551.

60. 'Evangelism and the World' in *Let the Earth Hear His Voice: Official Reference Volume, Papers and Responses*/International Congress on World Evangelization, Lausanne, Switzerland, 1974; ed. J. D. Douglas (Minneapolis: World Wide Publications, 1975), p.132.

61. J. Miguez Bonino in summarizing the argument of J. Moltmann's *Theology of Hope* in *Doing Theology in a Revolutionary Situation* (Philadelphia: Fortress Press, 1975), p.144.

62. Of the many evangelical books on eschatology which I read or perused I found two systematic yet popularly written treatments (both by British authors) containing some discussion about the practical significance and the motivation that Christian hope provides for responsible living and practice, including social involvement. They are: Bruce Milne, *What the Bible Teaches About the End of the World*, and Stephen Travis, *The Jesus Hope*. Very helpful in this regard is also James R. Ross, 'Living Between Two Ages,' in *Handbook of Biblical Prophecy* pp.231–241.

63. *One Way to Change the World* (New York: Harper and Row, 1970), p.118. C. S. Lewis also warned that a belief in the Second Coming should not preclude '. . . sober work for the future within the limits of ordinary morality and prudence . . . For what comes is judgment: happy are those whom it finds labouring in their vocations whether they were merely going out to feed the pigs or laying good plans to deliver humanity a hundred years hence from some great evil. The curtain has indeed now fallen. Those pigs will never in fact be fed, the great campaign against white slavery or governmental tyranny will never in fact proceed to victory. No matter you were at your post when the inspection came.' 'The Christian Hope', *Eternity* (March 1954), p.50.

64. Cf. the stimulating book by the evangelical futurologist Tom Sine, *The Mustard Seed Conspiracy* (Waco, Texas: Word Books, 1981).

65. (Grand Rapids: Eerdmans, 1947), p.57.

RESPONSE

In his response, Dr. Emilio Nunez C. points to the complexity of the relationship for millennial views and social conscience and to the need for intensive research in the fields of theology, secular and ecclesiastical history and sociology. He admits that premillennialism has often contributed to evangelical indifference to social problems. But so have the other eschatological systems. During the time when racial discrimination and negro slavery grew to enormous proportions in the USA, postmillennialism dominated evangelical views. In the case of Latin America, after the Spanish and Portuguese conquests, history and culture have been shaped to a large extent by the amillennialist Catholic Church. Evangelical Christians, whether premillennial or not have tended to avoid political involvement and accept the status quo. Dr. Nunez suggests that the Marxist challenge must be met by a faith in an earthly manifestation of God's Kingdom and one that does not minimize the problem of contemporary society.

'What we need,' he says, 'is to recuperate the balance provided by the Bible in its teaching on the mission of the Church.' He adds, 'It is our Christian duty to communicate in the power of the Holy Spirit, the total gospel for the benefit of the total man in contemporary society.'

7

A Biblical Encounter with some Contemporary Philosophical and Theological Systems

DR. PROF. PETER BEYERHAUS*

Synopsis Dr. Professor Peter Beyerhaus writes as an apologist seeking to defend evangelical Christianity against contemporary philosophies, ideologies and theologies which offer false utopias to the world. He focuses on three, namely messianic Marxism, scientism and liberal ecumenicalism. He sharply delineates the central issues and shows the dangers of an attempted synthesis without biblical faith. Not all will agree with his evaluation of ecumenical trends, but none can ignore the force and implications of his arguments. The response of the Rev. Gordon Moyes is briefly summarized at the end of the chapter.

In the second part of the chapter Dr. Beyerhaus demonstrates his serious commitment to biblical eschatology and argues for the eschatological reality of the Kingdom of God. He notes that the New Testament fulfils the Old Testament promises in surprising new forms. The Kingdom came in Jesus Christ, his resurrection being the bridgehead of the new creation. In our communion with Christ, we live already in the eschatological realm of his divine rule. Dr. Beyerhaus argues that the manifestation of the 'external side' of the Kingdom awaits Christ's coming

Dr. Prof. Peter Beyerhaus is Director of the Institut für Missionswissenschaft und Ökumenische Theologie at the University of Tübingen, West Germany.

165

in glory. Now Christ's reign is recognized only by the Church; at his coming all will confess that he rules the universe.

During this so-called 'interim period', Satan fights to retain his power. Towards the end of this period of struggle between the kingdoms of Christ and of Satan, Satan will inspire 'the man of lawlessness' to unite mankind under his anti-Christian world dominion. Dr. Beyerhaus suggests that the ecumenical utopia of the coming world community of all nations, religions and ideologies must be evaluated against this background.

During this interim period, God rules mankind through civil governments appointed to preserve order and extend the time for repentance. The completion of the task of world evangelization and the conversion of Israel to Christ are two of the necessary conditions for the return of Christ. Therefore Dr. Beyerhaus sees the offering of salvation for eternal life as the given priority within the total ministry of the Church. However, the proof of our Christian hope is the practising of obedience to Christ in all things, including service to the needy. It is further tested in tribulation. Although the author does not directly discuss the relationship of evangelism to social service, there is no doubt as to where he believes our priority lies.

Some points of his argument reflect his strong adherence to Lutheran orthodoxy.

_____

The historical dimension of the future has entered the mind of modern man with new urgency. It constitutes both a fascinating and a frightening force. On the one hand during the sixties we witnessed a strong wave of futurist optimism. This was expressed in a number of philosophic and theological systems, but also in socio-political movements and ecclesiastical events. Early in the seventies, however, the pendulum was swinging back: suddenly one became frighteningly aware that the same forces and attempts that promised to make the future 'the land of unlimited possibilities', might just as easily throw our earth into an ecological disaster. The new question is: how are we to avert this menace?

Both reactions, the enthusiastic hope of the utopia of world change and the worried prognoses associated with cybernetics, have been taken up by the churches as a challenge. For the future is a central perspective in the biblical message. The worries about the safety and wellbeing of threatened mankind, on the other hand, must also stir up Christian responsibility for decisive action. Thus we understand why the topic 'future' has become the first priority for the Ecumenical Movement. At the same time, the difference in eschatology constitutes a central aspect of that fundamental gap which separates evangelical from modernist theologians today as two broad currents of world christianity. Therefore, re-examining our evangelical position over against non-Christian concepts can greatly clarify the spiritual situation.

1. The Future as Fascination and as Nightmare

A. *The Goals of Messianic Marxism*

Amongst the neo-marxists there is one school of thought which has been called 'messianic Marxism'. Its representatives were the first *Marxist*-Communists who were willing to open up a constructive dialogue with Christian theologians. This *Marxist*-Christian conversion reached its climax during the sixties. It suffered a great setback by being condemned by the mouth-pieces of established 'orthodox' Marxism, i.e. by the Communist parties. The hopes set on this dialogue were almost shattered by the invasion of the Red Army of the CSSR in August 1968. Yet the talk is going on, especially through the Paulus Society.[1] At least for the Christian side its significance is still growing, and in Latin America it has given birth to the 'Theology of Liberation'[2] as the dominant school of thought.

The importance of the concept of the messianic Marxists for our theme is this. Although they do cling to the premises of philosophic materialism, they have received decisive new impulses from studying the Bible. In the Old Testament prophets and in the preaching of Jesus about the Kingdom they discovered a peculiar ardent hope for the future, which they saw intimately related to the whole revolutionary history and to the basic concerns of Socialism. Ernst Bloch has called this emotional force the 'Wärmestrom'[3] (warm current) of Marxism. Its complementary parallel is the 'Kältestrom' (cold current), consisting in socio-economic analyses and prognoses of dialectic materialism. Both currents need each other in order to preserve the psychological dynamics as well as the critical realism in Marxism. For this synthesis between reflection and enthusiasm Bloch coins the term 'Realutopie', thereby giving recognized status to the word 'utopia' in marxist ideology. This 'warm current' or 'warm red' is the indestructable hope of a new and better life, for a coming transformation of all things and a golden age on earth. It is the specific concern of 'esoteric Marxism' in general and of the Christian-marxist dialogue in particular to regain those humanistic dynamics.

The most important representatives of messianic Marxism are the late Tübingen professor Ernst Bloch, the two Czechs Vitezslav Gardavsky and Milan Machovec, and the Frenchman Roger Garaudy, former chief ideologist of the French Communist Party. Ernst Bloch is the profoundest philosophical thinker amongst them. In three volumes he presented the 'Principle of Hope'[4] as the decisive motor in human history. Bloch also inspired Jürgen Moltman to write his 'Theology of Hope'[5] and thereby indirectly gained penetrating influence on ecumenical thought. Roger Garaudy,[6] however, was to become the more important partner of dialogue for the WCC. In his writings the new 'Christomarxism', which is spreading with contagious vehemence, has found its classical expression. What are the main thoughts of messianic Marxism?

The starting point is the dissatisfaction with the present state of the world. Garaudy sees contemporary society engulfed by a total crisis: 'Our society is in a process of dissolution. It calls for a radical change not only of property rights and power structures, but also of our culture and education, of religion and faith, of life and its meaning.' Our task is defined by the sub-title of Garaudy's main work: 'Changer la monde et la vie.'[7] This most needed total change can and must take place only on this earth within our human history: 'Human history is the only place where God's Kingdom is to be established',[8] says Garaudy in the first of his three postulates. This implies the rejection of metaphysical transcendence.

The existence of God is rejected, too. Bloch categorically states as basic presupposition, 'that no God remains in the height, since no God is there at all or ever has been'.[9] Atheism is stressed emphatically in order to secure man's responsibility for ushering in the new age. In as far as it is a protest against the Christian quietism in social affairs, this atheism is justified also by Moltmann.[10]

Paradoxically enough, the Bible is not rejected on account of such atheism. On the contrary, it is praised as an unparalleled source document of hope which really carries the force of change. Bloch tries to resolve that contradiction by an incredible manoeuvre: in his book 'Atheism in Christianity' (1968)[11] he develops the thesis that man's emancipation towards the complete denial of God is the secret theme of the Bible itself! The tempting persuasion of the snake, 'You shall be like God' is revaluated into the first promise given to man. This promise, Bloch proposes, was fulfilled by Jesus: 'He who sees me, sees the Father.' At this point the reinterpretation of the biblical message to annex it to a messianic Marxism reveals its blasphemous nature: 'Christ is the symbol of emancipated mankind . . . In him man for the first time invaded the transcendence and set himself in the place of God, a Messiah against God and for man . . . Man becomes God, and the greatest sin henceforth is not willing to be like God!'[12]

With the help of such demythologizing (or rather re-mythologizing!) hermeneutics, the Bible becomes one of the most important textbooks of revolution to Marxist readers. Any passage related to God's intervention in history to bring about his doom and new creation is read as a challenge to man to follow the example of the 'angry Jesus' by siding with the poor and to overturn the present power systems of oppression. This approach has been taken over and developed by some theologians as a new hermeneutical key under the name 'materialistic exegesis'.[13]

More and more statements of biblical faith are being filled with a new ideological content. In particular, the resurrection of Christ is re-interpreted by Garaudy. It becomes the symbol of the new, horizontal transcendence, which in neo-marxist thinking has taken the place of the metaphysical, vertical transcendence: there is no Beyond, no divine reality above us; but there is the historical reality of the future, which lies ahead of us as a possibility to be audaciously seized. Garaudy here speaks of the 'eschatological postulate of hope'. 'Man is a task to be realized; society is a task to be realized; This postulate is congruent with the faith in the resurrection of Christ.'[14] Faith in the resurrection, accordingly, is a mental attitude which by courageous actions makes possible what appeared to be impossible. In this attitude one has to undertake decisive steps into the revolutionary tomorrow. Thus Garaudy recognizes his own convictions in the slogan of the Parisian student rebellion in March 1968: 'Soyons raisonable: demandons l'impossible!'

Thus we see that in messianic Marxism the Kingdom of God has become clearly an entity within history, to be realized by man himself. Nothing can prevent mankind from opening the gate into the 'Kingdom of Liberty' by revolutionary action. The future lies open before us and reality contains unlimited possibilities which man has to grasp in responsible ventures.

B. *The New World Order of Science and Technology*

One of the main reasons why messianic Marxists proclaim their principle of earthly hope so optimistically, is the immense achievements of technology. Indeed, the last century has witnessed a hectic acceleration of scientific break-throughs.

Nothing seems to remain impossible to *homo faber*. 'Anything that can be conceived, can be realized', we are assured by the bestseller 'Future Shock'.[15]

This untameable optimism of scientism suffers a glacial chill from the unexpected warnings of well-known experts in various fields, from nuclear physics to food economy. Extrapolating from an immense amount of data they tell us that our irresponsible exploitation of the earth's resources will drive us into our collective self-destruction.

General alarm was caused by the publication of the two first Reports to the Club of Rome: 'Limits of Growth' by Dennis Meadows (1972) and 'Mankind at the Turning Point' by Mihailo Mesarovic and Eduard Pestel (1974).[16] The Club of Rome (founded in 1968) is an informal association of noteworthy scientists, economists, politicians, sociologists and also philosphers, who share their reflections upon the future of mankind. Based on their research and computer accounts they also produce prognoses about the likely effects of uncontrolled progress on the various sectors of life. This is followed by proposals of how to steer these processes into a more responsible direction.

The vision of the future produced by the two reports to the Club of Rome is gloomy. It could be called a 'negative utopia'. In his remarkable speech to the Nairobi Assembly in 1975 the Australian biologist Charles Birch summarized the results with a shocking illustration: 'The world is like a "Titanic" on collision course. Ahead of us is an iceberg, whose top appears above the water level . . . Only a change of course can prevent the disaster.'[17] Nothing less than the survival of mankind is at stake!

Although the propositions of the two Reports to the Club of Rome were refuted by other futurologists who have a much more optimistic outlook, one important goal was reached. In the years 1972 and 1974 four large world conferences were convened by the United Nations, which dealt with the themes mentioned: the Environment Conference in Stockholm, 1972, the World Food Conference in Rome, the World Population Conference in Bucharest and the World Resource Conference in New York 1974. Further congresses were to follow. Yet none of these meetings has led to constructive resolutions which could radically remedy this alarming situation. At the first global conference of the World Future Society in September 1980 Dr. Aurelio Peccei, founder of the Club of Rome, told the press: 'The world is in a much worse condition than it was ten years ago.' Looking back at the 70s, he challenged anyone to show any major area of human affairs where things are going better than they were ten years ago. Looking ahead he saw increased problems: The world's population will rise to about 6.5 billion by the end of the century, straining still further the planet's declining resources. The economy will decline, the risk of nuclear war will increase, and as forests are cut down, oceans polluted, and deserts expand, the earth's ability to sustain life will be reduced. Commenting on Peccei's statements, the Toronto Star noted: 'The world begins more and more to resemble a ricocheting bullet careening from disaster to disaster . . .' True enough, there are proposals to change the course. The reports to the Club of Rome were not meant just for frightening, but also for suggesting a programme of overcoming the dangers by joint efforts. Charles Birch has mentioned such proposals in Nairobi: zero growth of population; zero growth of products for consumption; zero growth of pollution; and—you could add—zero growth in armaments.

There is one snag in these proposals. They appear rather intriguing, it is true. But they are unrealistic. They break down on account of that opposition which Birch describes as the large invisible part of the iceberg: the social, political and economic structures as well as the spiritual disorientation about the meaning of life. A way to put it even more clearly is to say: they break down on account of the unrestrained desires for possessions, enjoyment and power of individuals and human communities. Under the present conditions the proposals mentioned cannot be implemented. 'No industrialist', says Eduard Ostermann,[18] 'no Government, no politician, no manager will accept the proposals of Meadow voluntarily and implement them. It would mean destruction . . . Some of the effects would be: rise of costs, unemployment, recession, inflation, financial collapse, unrest, social revolution . . .' The members of the Club of Rome are, of course, aware of this problem. Therefore, their plan is made to include two far-reaching major proposals.

One is to abolish the principle of national states and to replace it by a new international frame, usually referred to as a new political *world order* and a *new economic world order*. This was proposed in the third report to the Club of Rome, which was written by 21 international experts on national economics and edited in late 1976 by the Dutch Nobel prize winner Jan Tinbergen. Under the title 'Reshaping the International Order' (the German title says 'We have but one future—Reform of the International Order') the authors suggested replacing the free market economy by a global planning and steering system, for which supra-natural bodies and boards should be created and invested with greater power to decide. 'What is required is a new international order in which all benefit from change.' De facto this means a step towards a world government.

The other basic proposal is to change man's mentality. Indi-

vidualism and nationalism must be replaced by a global awareness, through which each person conceives his role as that of a
world citizen. In fact such change of mentality is already
attempted by the psychotechnical methods of group dynamics,
which are employed in various sections of human life, in industrial management courses no less than in Pastoral Clinical Education and in week-end retreats for congregations.

Now the two utopian proposals have been complemented by a
third one, which to us appears even more sensational. The
Hungarian-American systems philosopher *Erwin Laszlo* in 1977
presented the fifth report to the Club of Rome 'Goals for
Mankind'. Interacting with behaviourists, sociologists, philosophers, theologians and computer specialists he had been
working on a design for a *new world religion*, which should be
composed of the helpful elements of all existing religions and
ideologies.[19] The volume does not contain the results yet, but
it warmly recommends the findings and suggestions of a group
called 'the religion science-led scenario'. Don Hoke remarks:
'The greatest hope for all the world lies in religionists and scientists uniting to awaken the world to its near-fatal predicament
and then leading mankind out of the bewildering maze of international crises into the future Utopia of humanist hope.'[20]

At least at this point an eye which is sensitized by biblical
revelation, discerns the apocalyptic features of this grand
programme. The Dutch Christian journalist J. A. E. Vermaat
writes: 'One day Antichrist is going to push his utopia of unity
against the background of total destruction. The frightful vision
of disaster shall compel the religions and ideologies to unite. The
ideology of the endtime will predominantly be an ideology of
survival.'[21] Many will disagree with this judgment. Are we not
offered here a futurological design which commends itself both
by its responsibility, courage and consistency?

If the survival of mankind is really at stake today, and if all
organisations and rules by which men have ordered their lives up
to now, will only speed up our collective destruction, we need
radical solutions, they would argue. On the premises of the Club
of Rome it appears that only a world state, ruled by a world
government, fed by a planned world economy and inspired by a
united world religion or One World ideology will be able to bring
about that dramatic change of direction which is demanded.

The question put to us, however, is whether we are prepared
to share those premises. In the perspective of the Club of Rome
our planet earth is likened to a spaceship which has lost its
radar connection with its controlling centre on earth, as another
Dutchman, A. Schouten, remarks.[22] The crew of this spaceship,
mankind, alone is responsible for the continuation of the flight.

It must try to grasp hold of its common future and the fate of our earth. But is this the picture which the Bible paints of God's ruling our world and its future?

This question is placed before us by evangelical theologians with great urgency. For today several other political and religious organizations confront us with the same argument and the same goals, offering us their co-operation and asking for ours to solve the problems of our future. We may refer to the World Conference of Religions for Peace, to the United Nations, and, (as an even greater challenge to us) also to the WCC.

C. *The Utopian Vision of the Ecumenical Movement*

The original ecumenical goal was to reunite the separated churches. Today this is regarded by leading ecumenicals as just an intermediate stage, as a functional precondition for a much wider goal: the unification of all mankind. This goal was proposed in Uppsala in 1968 under the names 'world community' and 'new humanity'. The ecumenical movement of Geneva today feels the prophetic calling to be pacemaker of a new world order in which the ancient desire of mankind for peace and justice is realized. Here, too, one sees a re-interpretation of the messianic promises in the Old Testament. Since salvation allegedly has been spiritualized and pushed into the beyond for many centuries, we are asked to rediscover the fuller concept of shalom on earth. This goal is for all influential leaders of the WCC the motive which, according to Ernst Lange, keeps the Ecumenical Movement moving.[23] In this connection they repeatedly speak of the 'ecumenical utopia', the 'utopic vision' or of 'prophetical dreams'. The content is often described by the biblical names of God's Kingdom or the Heavenly Jerusalem. Thus the WCC, too, has become a determinately future-oriented movement, which also lives by a 'principle of hope'.

This utopic vision, as the former chairman of the Central Committee, M. M. Thomas, has called it,[24] is propelled by two wings: we could call the 'left wing' *liberation*, and its nature is basically Marxist inspired. Karl Marx put the 'classless society' as the goal of history, Ernst Bloch, the 'kingdom of liberty'. Likewise the Ecumenical Movement dreams of an emancipated world society from which all structures of exploitation and oppression of class, race, economic systems and sex are removed.

This design was largely inspired by neo-marxist philosophers and sociologists. Their ideas were mediated by their Christian partners in dialogue, theologians like J. C. Hoekendijk, R. Shaull, J. Moltmann, H. Cox, José Miguez Bonino and others.[25] Today there are quite a number of conceptions of how to relate the Christian faith to the marxist ideology of liberation, and to fill biblical key terms with marxist content. We may refer to some of the most commonly known ones: The theologies of revolution, hope and liberation, Black Theology and, since Melbourne 1980, the 'Theology of the Poor'.[26] Everywhere Christ is painted as spearheading human liberation from socio-political oppression. The liberty sought for is taken to be an anticipation, if not indeed the implementation of the Kingdom of God on earth: 'The message of salvation in Christ . . . takes the unavoidable out of our existing national and international institutions and liberates man to the possibility to achieve that new order in which the Kingdoms of the world really become the Kingdom of God and his Christ', wrote Pauline Webb in an introductory article for the 8th World Missionary Conference in Bangkok 1972/73,[27] referring thereby to Roger Garaudy!

The vision of socio-political liberation is not left in the abstract. Since 1970 this type of theology (or ideology) has been embodied in concrete action programmes, into which the real dynamics of the WCC have been channelled. We may mention particularly the Program of Combating Racism and the Program for Education, which the marxist educator Paulo Freire[28] introduced to Geneva's third programme unit 'Education and Renewal'.

More recently, the often criticized leaning of the WCC towards revolutionary marxism has been counter-balanced by a new theme, which we could call the 'right wing' of the ecumenical vision. Its name is 'One World'. That this is the name given to the WCC's popular periodical is not accidental. In Nairobi the class struggle enthusiasm of Geneva's pacemakers seemed to have passed its apex already, and was gently overshadowed by the new theme 'unity of mankind'. Thus Secretary-General Philip Potter in his report only referred in passing to the liberation theme. Instead he used the word 'global' no fewer than seventeen times! Potter attempted a comprehensive analysis of our contemporary world problems, thereby pre-empting the lecture of Charles Birch. His conclusion was: 'Only a global strategy can solve the global problems of mankind.' If, as we saw, the Club of Rome demands the substitution of national by international institutions and tries to awaken a cosmopolitan consciousness, it is gladly assisted by the WCC.

What then should be the specific contribution of the WCC as a religious organization in creating the new international order? First of all it is busy spreading this idea amongst its member churches. Moreover it has become a main concern of the WCC to remove all divisions which still stand between various human communities and which block the establishment of a world fellowship:

Break down the walls that separate us
and unite us in a single body,

was the chorus sung and danced to with growing enthusiasm at
the Fifth Assembly at Nairobi.

The most important activity serving to bring about this unification of mankind is Geneva's Program of Dialogue with Men of
Living Faiths and Ideologies. It is to be noted that this Dialogue
Program was stimulated in Nairobi by an emphasis on the current threat to human survival.

The new element added at the 5th Assembly was the 'spirituality for combat' which M. M. Thomas called for. This
included the variety of traditions in Christian piety—starting
with the Byzantine liturgy and ending with Pentecostal glos-
solalia. But the mysticism of Eastern religions are also being
tapped as 'spiritual resources' in order to sustain the Ecumenical
Movement in its 'wanderings through the wilderness' (Potter)
towards the unity of mankind. Here an attempt is made in
exactly the same direction as that which the leaders of the Club of
Rome perceived as a saving solution in the present world crisis.
A synthesis of all useful elements in the various religions and
ideologies becomes the spiritual fuel which will enable mankind
to move towards the goal of global unity. Thus in the present
hour of destiny the WCC is allotted an unsought task of highest
relevancy: As a 'charismatic fellowship', to use Potter's new
description of the WCC, it becomes the crystallizing centre of
uniting humanity. The new spirituality generates that faith,
which according to Thomas Müntzer, the enthusiastic prophet of
the Peasants' Wars in Germany, is the possibility 'to attempt the
things that seem to be impossible and to complete them'. Potter
believes that Christians are 'called joyfully to join in God's process of creating a new order' and to operate 'in concert with
God's purpose of transforming his world into his Kingdom of
love, joy and peace'.[29]

Once more the Kingdom of God and the results of the historic
process of global integration into one humanity are openly
equated here. At the ecumenical wedding altar marxist messianism and futurological doom prophecy are coupled and given a
pan-religious inspiration with the purpose of establishing the
new world order.

The ecumenical vision constitutes a challenge to all Christians,
whether they are affiliated to the WCC or not. Even the 'conservative evangelicals' are urged to join the venture, as can be seen by
all the appeals made to them since Uppsala 1968.

One cannot help being impressed by the ecumenical vision of a
better world being achieved by our united efforts. Its message of

impending doom and passionate hope for the future may even remind us of the Old Testament prophets announcing the coming reign of the Lord. But a closer look reveals that such similarities are misleading.

D. *Some Critical Reflections on the Ecumenical Vision*

The description of the object of ecumenical hope is void of any serious attempt to recognize the authority of the biblical witness and to examine its authentic contents. Instead we are offered general human reflections about the present miseries and the aspirations of modern movements for a better future. Together with scientific analyses and prognoses these are treated as a second source of revelation.

Where the Bible is used, e.g. at ecumenical conferences, it is hermeneutically manipulated by employing the so called 'contextual method'. The socio-political situation of the reader determines his peculiar interest and leads him to discover just such aspects of the text as seem to provide a relevant answer to his problems. This is done on the basic assumption of materialistic exegetes that the Bible is a text-book of historical records about ancient socio-economic and political struggles, where God and Jesus were siding with the poor and oppressed fighting to liberate themselves. Texts contrary to this tendency are invalidated with the help of ideological criticism, which takes the place of the former idealistic 'higher criticism' in the historic-critical method. Since ecumenical hope is estranged from the Bible, it is clearly not fulfilled by the real promises of the prophets. Their place is taken by the idea of an 'open future', into which are inserted whatever utopias may be currently fashionable.

Difference in hermeneutics is not the deepest reason for this approach. The dominating ecumenical way of thought is consistent with the entire modern philosophical trend since Hobbes, Hume and Kant to eliminate divine metaphysical transcendence. The history of the empirical world with its inherent forces is regarded as the only objective reality. In the wake of Hegel's philosophy of history, an eschatological dignity is attributed to progress.

The ecumenical vision and the marxist utopia share the conviction that the Kingdom of God must be realized within this world. Under the influence of Teilhard de Chardin and process philosophy, faith in a personal God who as a sovereign creator and redeemer stands transcendently outside this world, is replaced by a new type of panentheism: God is equated with the creative process in the horizontal dimension. This means that the burden of implementing this great task is put solely on the shoulders of man. Not heeding the warnings of two world wars, of Auschwitz and Gulag, man is regarded as essentially good. To his faith the power of infinite creativity is attributed. Even the 'spirituality for combat' does not really restore the divine dimension, for an analysis shows that the concept of spirituality is a merely anthropological category with syncretistic leanings.

The ecumenical One World utopia is based on a monistic universalism. It does not take into consideration the forces of radical evil which are effective in this world, and which poison every human attempt at progress. It ignores the biblical warning that the present antagonism between God and the Devil will lead to a disastrous climax for world history.

Our short analysis of the ecumenical vision has shown that it builds on ideological premises which are completely unacceptable to biblical thinking. We shall not be able to accept the ecumenical invitation. Rather we are commissioned now to re-examine the testimony of biblical revelation in order to give an authentic response to the futuristic aspirations of modern man.

2. The Biblical Witness of the Coming Kingdom

According to the testimony of the Holy Scripture the Kingdom of God is an eschatological reality. This insight is decisive for our theme, 'History and Eschatology'. In the Old Testament we meet the Kingdom essentially as an object of prophetic promises, in the New Testament as a fulfilled reality, which, however, still has a dramatic history and a grand future.

A. *The Kingdom as a Promise*

That Jahweh as the only God always is and always has been the King of all creation and of the world of nations is the basic creed of Israel. Yet in this dominion he is still going to win a great eschatological triumph over all ungodly and harmful forces. Such was the message of the prophets, by which they dynamically re-inforced faltering faith in times of national and religious crisis (see e.g. Isa. 2:2ff.). God will wash away all sins; he will give new hearts to his people and pour out his Spirit upon all flesh. Then from the Mount of Zion his world-wide Kingdom of peace will be established. This glowing expectation was indeed the peculiar mark of Israel's faith in her election history. Here Bloch and the messianic Marxists have made an observation which from the view-point of the history of ideas and of religious psychology is correct.

Yet the biblical testimony and its modern interpretation are separated by a wide gulf. Biblical Messianism is not an ideology which proposes a historical goal to man and an active programme to be worked out by himself. On the contrary, it is founded on the announcement of a series of extraordinary *acts of God*, which supersede all human expectations and abilities. He is going to interfere from outside and from above in earthly history. 'The Lord will fight for you, and you have only to be still' (Ex. 14:14). This assurance holds true for all acts of salvation which the Bible speaks of. Therefore the date, which cannot be determined by man, is called the Day of the Lord. It is the day on which he will assemble all the nations for the execution of his judgment and for manifesting his rule over all the world. It comprises the totality of all deeds by which God himself at the end will establish the new world order.

This theocentric eschatological view was preserved by Israel on through the inter-testamental period, as can be shown by the study of the different Messianic schools of thought.

When we proceed to the New Testament, we make a double observation: The New Testament confirms the promises of the Kingdom, given by the prophets, but it changes their features as they are being fulfilled. It *confirms* the promise that God will manifest his dominion over his creation. The Kingdom is not wholly ethicized or spiritualized. But the implementation of the promises begins with the soteriological concentration on the restoration of the broken relationship with God. This is the necessary precondition for the visible establishment of the Kingdom. Its coming, therefore, is implemented by two separate acts of God, which Karl Heim distinguishes as 'world reconciliation' and 'world consumption'.[30]

B. *The Kingdom which has come in Jesus*

The New Testament neither simply repeats nor negates the Old Testament promises. Rather it proclaims their fundamental realization in a surprising new form.

All Christ events are fulfilments of eschatological promises. At the birth of Jesus, the heavens are opened and angels proclaim peace on earth. In his Sermon on the Mount he proclaims the divine law of the messianic kingdom. In his miracles, the forces of the Kingdom expel the demons from their usurped positions. On the cross the decisive act of salvation is performed: Jesus offers himself as the expiating sacrifice for reconciling the world to God—the dividing wall between God and world, between heaven and earth, is broken down. 'God was in Christ reconciling the world to himself.' The broken connection between God, who is the fountain of incorruptible life, and the world, which, separated from him, is delivered up to the forces of death, has been re-established. Now there is hope once more for the first creation, hope that is revealed on the third day. For the resurrection of Jesus is the bridgehead of the new creation which enters and transforms the old one. Here is a visible assurance of the coming glory of God's Kingdom.

Garaudy openly declares (and it is hard not to feel that some of his ecumenical colleagues are in secret agreement) that the resurrection is simply a postulate of revolutionary hope, a challenge to change the world, which faith is unable to achieve. But the resurrection is not an imperative; it is a pure, incomprehensible gospel fact. God has intervened in the course of history. By raising his Son from the dead, God has already changed the course of the world from within. The objectivity of the resurrection of Jesus is of cardinal significance to the New Testament. For it is the foundation of our hope that all further promises too, will be fulfilled at the final consummation: 'By his great mercy we have been born anew to a living hope through the resurrection of Jesus Christ from the dead, and to an inheritance which is imperishible, undefiled, and unfading, kept in heaven for you, who by God's power are guarded through faith for a salvation ready to be revealed in the last time' (1 Pet. 1:3–5).

The resurrection of Jesus is far more than an event which concerns his own destiny. From the resurrected Christ emanates the power of life eternal. Through the mystical communion with him which is constituted by our baptism into his death (Rom. 6:3–5), the power of his resurrection gives new life to us also and the assurance of our likeness with him in our own resurrection.

The epistle to the Hebrews speaks of Christians as those 'who have tasted the . . . powers of the age to come' (6:5). The ushering in of the eschatological Kingdom by the Christ event is crowned by his ascension. It is his enthronement on the right hand of God the Father, and the taking over of the royal rule over all powers in heaven and on earth. From now on the uplifted Christ sovereignly directs the course of history towards its victorious completion. On the day of Pentecost he fulfils another important eschatological promise (Joel 3) by sending the gift of the Holy Spirit to his disciples. This establishes the communion between Christ as the head and the Church as his body that empowers her to continue his own saving ministry on earth.

By communion with him we live already now in the eschatological realm of his divine rule. This makes the church his 'Kingdom of grace', as the early protestant dogmaticians rightly called her. It is destined one day at the consummation of all things to be transformed into his 'Kingdom of glory'. Nourished by the Holy Spirit and purified by the test of affliction, Christian hope is able to transcend the horizon of our old world and be assured of the glory of the age to come.

C. *The Kingdom in its coming form of glory*

So far we have looked at the *inner side* of the fulfilment of the messianic prophecies (cf. Jer. 31:31; Ezek. 36:26f.). What is still lacking is the manifestation of the *external side* of the Kingdom. The peace of conscience, given by justification (Rom. 5:1), is not yet complemented by visible social and political peace. Nations still engage in warfare and revolt against God. Satan still battles to retain his usurped positions. The realm of nature is not renewed yet. Together with the rest of creation we still groan under our bodies' 'bondage to decay' (Rom. 8:21) and suffer under affliction, pain and death. That even this fate will be overcome one day, is an important aspect of the Old Testament promise of the Kingdom which is confirmed in the New Testament. This means that the Kingdom which has already arrived in Jesus, still has a real future after his enthronement as Lord over heaven and earth. This future is the content of hope in its New Testament form. The designation of Jesus to be the Christ inseparably ties up the Messianic Kingdom with him. Therefore the New Testament hope for the coming of the Kingdom in glory (Matt. 24:30; 25:31) is hope for the parousia of Jesus, the Son of Man. 'Our Lord will come again', is the core of Christian hope for the future. Here, too, the ancient prophecies of the coming Kingdom, especially as shown by Daniel (7:13) find a christological transformation.

Jesus Christ will come again with all his angels in great power and glory and reveal himself visibly before the whole world. At the end every tongue will have to confess that the rule of the universe is really his.

After the completion of world evangelization (Matt. 24:14) Jesus will take his now fully gathered congregation out of her eschatological warfare. He will unite her, together with those who have already completed their earthly life, to himself. They will receive eternal bliss and also a share in his eternal rule.

During Israel's confrontation with the hostility of the nations in the final world war of this present age, Jesus will manifest himself as the saviour of God's first elected people. The Jews shall 'look on him whom they have pierced' and turn to him as their Messiah in deep contrition and faith (Zech. 12:2-3; 9-10; Rom. 11:26-28). The conversion of Israel to Christ is a decisive condition for the implementation of the holistic aspects of the eschatological reign of God as visualized by the prophets. This condition is, however, overlooked by most theologians—both ecumenical and evangelical—who presently deal with the biblical doctrine of the kingdom. It was left out both in Melbourne and in Pattaya 1980.

Jesus will smite his apocalyptic opponent, the Antichrist, who will be the embodiment of mankind's demonical rebellion. Finally he will also deliver the Devil up to eternal punishment. Now the primal rebellion and the historic antagonism which originated from it, will be overcome forever.

All the dead will rise, and Christ will exercise judgement over all mankind. The harvest of world history with all its deeds and crimes will be manifested in its eternal significance. God's justice, which has so often been veiled, will be made manifest before all generations. Man will have to account for every word and deed and receive his righteous retribution.

Now the stage has been set for the final victory in the history of Christ's messianic conquests (1 Cor. 15:24–26): Death will be destroyed. The first creation, i.e. the whole cosmos, will pass away. A new heaven and a new earth will be the scene of God's Kingdom in glory. The city of God will be with man, and the partition between transcendence and immanence will be removed. 'Christ will deliver the Kingdom to God the Father . . . that God may be everything to everyone' (1 Cor. 15:24, 28), i.e. the whole creation is now liberated from hostility and decay and will be in perfect harmony with the aims of the Creator. Now the whole transfigured nature will reflect the glory of God without distortion or defilement. It will be penetrated by God's own eternal being and participate in his holiness, beauty and beatitude.

Eternity will not consist of a fellowship of disembodied spirits. It is true that our present world is separated from the future one by an abyss of cosmic cataclysm. But still the new creation will be in an ontic continuation of identity with the present one; this is the significance of the message of the resurrection of the dead. Our personal resurrection is corresponded to by the promised liberation of everything created from the bondage of decay to the glorious liberty of the children of God. This means that the whole groaning creation will be transfigured by the glory of eternity.

Here we find the relevance of the biblical promise of the Kingdom for the concerns, hopes and anxieties of our contemporary world. Mankind is not left with illusory consolations or human solutions ending in frustration. At the bottom of every human hope, and even of the cry of the wounded animal, there lies a promise by which God has bound himself to his creation for eternity, and which he himself will fulfil in his own way at the end.

Let us sum up: There is a vast essential difference between the biblical hope for the Kingdom and all contemporary philosophies and theologies of history which re-interpret it ideologically.

(1) The hope for the transformation of the fallen world has its foundation not in psychological projections of a 'principle of hope' which is residing in man, but in the biblical promise of God which was realistically confirmed by Christ's resurrection from the dead.

(2) Its terminal target is not the unreachable 'wandering horizon' of expectation, but the second coming of Jesus Christ.

(3) Its contents are not the 'open future' which we have to work out ourselves positively or negatively. On the contrary, the goal of salvation history is determined, unchangeable and indestructible. It is the reality of the eternal Kingdom, which is already hidden with God, and which will be manifested on the day of the eschatological consummation of the world.

Therefore the epistle to the Hebrews (6:19) describes the hope set before us as the 'anchor of the soul', that enters into the inner shrine behind the curtain, where Jesus has gone as a forerunner on our behalf.

D. *The Kingdom in the tension between arrival and expectation*

The time between the atonement and the consummation of the world is, as we saw, an *interim period* in the history of salvation. Although this was not to be foreseen from the Old Testament perspective, Jesus has predicted it in several of his parables. It is not true that on account of his unfulfilled parousia the early church was forced to change the doctrine of the Kingdom or even to abandon it. But the delay in the manifestation of Christ's glory constitutes a crucial problem in our Christian understanding of history. It is equally important to be mindful both of the conditions and of the meaning of present history qualified as interim.

What are the conditions of this interim in salvation history? According to New Testament affirmations three realities are to be taken into account:

First, Jesus *is* already the invisible ruler over heaven and earth. The course of history, although seemingly steered by secular forces, is firmly under his control, and is made to serve his purposes.

But on earth this rule is recognized only by his church—which is his expanding Kingdom in grace. The rest of mankind does not know yet of Christ's kingship or disobeys it. Therefore it is the object of evangelization.

Second, until the return of Christ, Satan and his demonical forces still fight to retain their position of power over this world, although the Devil has lost his rights upon fallen man already.

He is 'bound' (cf. Lk. 11:21f.), i.e. he has to retreat wherever the victory of Christ is boldly proclaimed and obeyed. Therefore Satan tries to separate the church from her Lord by means of seduction (false prophets) and persecution.

Thus this interval is the period of the struggle between the Kingdom of Christ, heading for final victory, and the kingdom of Satan, facing final destruction. Every nation in which the gospel proclamation has gained a Christian bridgehead is conquered in principle, and it will benefit from divine blessings according to its degree of obedience. Still Satan remains powerful enough to construct new positions. Moreover, towards the end of this interim he will unfold new forces again (Matt. 24:10–12) and inspire 'the man of lawlessness' to unite mankind under his antichristian world dominion (2 Thess. 2:3–12; Rev. 13:5–8; 17:12–14). The ecumenical utopia of the coming world community of all nations, religions and ideologies must be evaluated against this background.

Third, during this interim period God rules mankind, as he did before, through the governing authorities (Rom. 13:1–7). Theirs is the task on the basis of the natural law of caring for external peace, justice and welfare, and punishing evildoers. The governing authorities are representatives of God in the civic realm and must be honoured as such by Christians, too.

The institution of the state is an order of preservation. God has given it to mankind in order to prevent chaos and to extend the time for repentance. The civic order does not, however, belong to the order of salvation. Therefore political changes have no redemptive value. Nor can the governing authorities permanently secure the survival of mankind. On the contrary, the accelerating and magnifying catastrophes in history and nature remind us that we are living in an expiring age without future. This shows that the contemporary plans to secure the survival of mankind by a complete revolution of the present world order are both illusory and deceptive as to their true nature and destination.

What then is the meaning of this interim and of the eschatological delay caused by it? The answer is to be sought in words such as Matt. 28:18f. 'All authority in heaven and on earth is given to me. Go therefore and make disciples of all nations . . .' and 1 Cor. 15:25: 'For he must rule until he has put all enemies under his feet.' The period between the ascension of Christ and his return in glory is not for the establishment of the Kingdom on earth, but for preparation for its coming. This implies the spiritual conquest of that dominion which in virtue of his work of atonement is already his by divine right, but which de facto is still occupied by those 'principalities and powers' that oppose his rule. Karl Heim rightly taught that whilst the *question of guilt* has been answered at the Cross, the *question of power* is still to be answered.

But this is not the only function of Christ's second coming. His parousia qualifies—although in a hidden way—the whole interim period. Our time is related to the coming kingdom in several aspects. In it we are to give proof of our discipleship and Christian hope in a threefold way:

First, during the present period the church is to proclaim the kingship of Christ and his salvation amongst all nations. Only when Satan's power structures have been spiritually broken by the establishment of a messianic bridgehead within each nation, and when the total body of Christ, the church, has grown up to her full stature (Col. 2:19), will the condition for Christ's delivering the kingdom to God the Father have been fulfilled.

Offering salvation for eternal life, not physical survival, therefore, is the given priority within the total ministry of the church.

Second, this is also the time to give proof of our Christian hope by being obedient followers of Christ. Our obedience is to be practised not only in the religious duties of prayer and evangelization, but also within all other fields of human vocation. This insight gives a deeper meaning to honest labour. It is not done as a way of making a living, an unavoidable duty. It is also a service rendered to Christ himself, and thereby it receives a consecration for eternity: 'Whatever you do, in word or deed, do everything in the name of the Lord Jesus' (Col. 3:17). Christians are to be salt and light in the world, and to seek the best for the city. They present themselves as Christ's servants by unselfishly seeking their neighbours' well-being and by continuing in Christian love, where other people have finished their duty. They boldly oppose the forces of seduction, and do not lose patience when all good attempts seem to have been wasted. Hoping for the coming Kingdom, they are assured that every really good deed will be remembered (Rev. 14:13). Thus by the courageous obedience and the winning love of Christians the signs of the coming Kingdom can shine already within this passing world order and inflame the hope for the complete appearance of the heavenly city amongst men.

Finally, during this present tension between the opposing ages, Christian hope is to be generated and tested by tribulation (Rom. 5:2–5; 8:31–39). Temptations and afflictions sift out the true followers of Jesus from the nominal ones. At the same time God singles out that closer circle which shall be united to Christ in a more special way. Those who have overcome tribulation will be deemed worthy both to inherit eternal life and also to participate in the eschatological reign of Jesus Christ. 'He who conquers and who keeps my words until the end, I shall give him power over the nations . . .' (Rev. 2:26); or 'If we endure we shall also reign with him' (2 Tim. 2:12). Those consoling promises, addressed to the early Christian martyrs, are given to inspire Christians in all generations to manifest their hope for the coming glory even in the midst of subtlest temptations and severest tribulations.

Bibliography

1. *Messianic Marxism*
   Bloch, Ernst, *Man on His Own* (New York: Herder & Herder, 1970).
   Bloch, Ernst, *Atheismus im Christentum* (Frankfurt, 1968).
   Garaudy, Roger, *The Alternative Future: A Vision of Christian Marxism* (New York: Simon & Schuster, 1974).
   Garaudy, Roger, *From Anathema to Dialogue* (New York: Vintage, 1966).
2. *Marxist-Christian Dialogue*
   Aptheker, Herbert, *The Urgency of Marxist-Christian Dialogue* (New York: Harper & Row, 1970).
   Klugmann, James, ed., *Dialogue of Christianity and Marxism* (London: Lawrence & Wishart, 1966).
   Oestreicher, Paul, ed., *The Christian Marxist Dialogue* (New York: MacMillan, 1969).
3. *Theologies of Hope, Liberation, etc.*
   Moltmann, Jürgen, *Theology of Hope* (New York: Harper & Row, 1967).
   Alves, Rubém, *A Theology of Human Hope* (St. Meinrad, Ind.: Abbey, 1971).
   Cox, Harvey, *The Feast of Fools* (New York: Harper & Row, 1969).
   Gutiérrez, Gustavo, *A Theology of Liberation* (Maryknoll: Orbis, 1973).
   Dale, Vree, *On Synthesizing Marxism and Christianity* (New York: John Wiley & Sons, 1976).
4. *Futurology*
   Toffler, Alvin, *Future Shock* (London: Pan Books, 1978).
   Meadows, Dennis, *Limits to Growth* (1972).
   Mesarovic, Mihailo, *Mankind at the Turning Point* (1974).
   Tinbergen, Jan, *Reshaping the International order* (1976).
   Laszlo, Ervin, *Goals for Mankind* (1977).
   Hoke, Donald E., *Evangelicals Face the Future* (William Carey Lib., 1978).
   Hoke, Donald E., *An Evangelical Agenda: 1984 and Beyond* (William Carey Lib., 1978).
5. *Ecumenical Utopia*
   Norman, Edward, *Christianity and the World Order* (New York: Oxford University Press, 1979).
   Lefever, Ernest W., *Amsterdam to Nairobi* (Washington D.C.: Ethics and Public Policy Center, 1979).
   Van der Bent, Ans, *The Utopia of World Community* (SCM Press, 1973).
   Lange, Ernst, *Die ökumenische Utopie* (Stuttgart: Kreuz Verlag, 1972).

Beyerhaus, P./Betz, U., ed., *Ökumene im Spiegel von Nairobi* (Bad Lieben-
zell, 1976).
6. *Salvation History*
Cullmann, Oscar, *Heil als Geschichte* (Zürich, 1965).
Conzelmann, Gerhard, *The Theology of St. Luke* (London/New York, 1960).
von Rad, Gerhard, *The Message of the Prophets* (London: SCM Press, 1968).
Heim, Karl, *Jesus der Weltvollender* (Wuppertal: Aussaat, 1978).
Heim, Karl, *Weltschöpfung und Weltvollendung* (Wuppertal: Aussaat, 1977).

Notes

1. Erich Kellner, ed., *Christentum und Marxismus—heute: Gespräche der
   Paulus-Gesellschaft* (Wien: Europa-Verlag 1966).
2. Gustavo Gutiérrez, *A Theology of Liberation* (Maryknoll: Orbis 1973);
   Andrew Kirk, *Liberation Theology. An Evangelical View from the Third
   World* (London: Marshall, Morgan & Scott, 1979).
3. Ernst Bloch, *Atheismus in Christendum* (Frankfurt a.M. 1968) S.350.
4. Ernst Bloch, *Das Prinzip Hoffnung*, 3 Vls. (Frankfurt a.M. 1959).
5. Jürgen Moltmann, *Theology of Hope* (New York: Harper & Row, 1967).
6. Roger Garaudy, *The Alternative Future: A Vision of a Christian Marxism*
   (New York: Simon & Schuster, 1974).
7. To change the world and to change life.
8. Roger Garaudy in: *Marxisten und die Sache Jesu*, eds. Iring Fetcher and
   Milan Machovec (Mainz 1972), p.28.
9. Ernst Bloch, *Works*, Volume V (Frankfurt 1959), p.1524.
10. Jürgen Moltmann, *Das Experiment Hoffnung* (München: Chr. Kaiser
    Verlag 1974), p.50.
11. see Note 3.
12. Ernst Bloch, *Works*, Vol. III, p.335.
13. The pioneers of the school of materialistic exegesis are Fernando Belo,
    Lecture matérialiste de l'évangile de Marc (1974); Michel Clévenot,
    Approches matérialistes de la Bible (1971); Georges Casalis, *Les idées justes ne
    tombent pas du ciel* (1977); cf. P. Beyerhaus, *Aufbruch der Armen* (Bad
    Liebenzell 1981), pp.54–61.
14. Roger Garaudy, *Marxisten* . . . (see Note 8), p.38.
15. Alvin Toffler, *Future Shock* (Pan Books:London 1971).
16. The five volumes of the 'Report to the Club of Rome' (1972–1977) are
    summarized by Donald E. Hoke in *Evangelicals Face the Future* (William
    Carey Library 1978), pp.3–8.
17. Charles Birch, 'Creation, Technique and Survival of Mankind' (German)
    in *Beiheft zur Ökumenischen Rundschau* Nr. 30, p.96; (Eng. in *Ecumenical
    Review*, January 1976).
18. E. Ostermann: *Zukunft ohne Hoffnung?* (Neuhausen: Hänssler 1975), p.52.
19. Ervin Laszlo, 'Goals for Global Society': A Positive Approach to the
    Predicament of Mankind'. A Report to the Club of Rome. Project Descrip-
    tion. Typescript November 1974. The title of the book published in 1977 is
    Goals for Mankind.

20. Don Hoke, *op. cit.,* p.8.
21. J. A. E. Vermaat in *Ökumene im Spiegel von Nairobi '75*, ed. P. Beyerhaus/ U. Betz (Bad Liebenzell 1976), p.213.
22. Quoted by Steven Paas, *Vrede en Eenheid in Europa* Amsterdam: Bujten en Schipperheijn 1973), p.125.
23. Ernst Lange, *Die ökumenische Utopie oder: Was bewegt die Ökumenische Bewegung?* (Stuttgart: Kreuz Verlag 1972).
24. M. M. Thomas, 'Report of the Chairman of the Executive Committee', *Utrecht 1972* (Beiheft zur Ökumenischen Rundschau Nr.23), p.16f. (German).
25. Dale Vree, *On Synthesizing Marxism and Christianity* (New York: John Wiley & Sons Inc., 1976).
26. P. Beyerhaus, *Aufbruch der Armen: Die neue Missionsbewegung nach Melbourne* (Bad Liebenzell 1981).
27. *This Month* No. 33, EPS (Dec. 1972), p.2f.
28. *Von Uppsala nach Nairobi*, epd-Dokumentation Vol. 15 (Bielefeld 1975), p.205.
29. Ph. Potter, 'Report of the General Secretary', in *Breaking Barriers*, Nairobi 1975, ed. David M. Paton (SPCK London/Eerdmans 1976), p.254.
30. Heim, Karl, *Weltschöpfung und Weltvollendung* (Wuppertal: Aussat 1977).

RESPONSE

In his response, here summarised, Gordon Moyes recognizes that Dr. Beyerhaus has made an insightful presentation of messianic Marxism as the most powerful non-Christian philosophy dealing with the future of the world. While expressing his appreciation of Dr. Beyerhaus's presentation of the biblical witness to the coming Kingdom, he regrets the omission of the equally biblical emphasis on the Kingdom of God among us here and now and the Christian involvement in the world in terms of salt, light and yeast. He criticises Dr. Beyerhaus for offering the Church only a 'watered down prophetic ministry with no legitimate voice on matters of human justice, exploitation, warfare, sexual abuse and other socio-political matters which affect Christians just as much as those who reject God'. It is dangerous to dismiss this present time as just 'an interim period in the history of salvation'. This suggestion denies the reality of the presence of the Kingdom, the eternal nature of the presence and promises of Christ, and it removes the cutting edge of our proclamation. Moyes agrees that political changes have no redemptive value, but affirms that they do have human value, as, for example, in the abolition of slavery.

His most severe criticism is reserved for Dr. Beyerhaus's attack on the ecumenical movement. 'I believe he attributes to the

World Council of Churches sinister motives and Marxist philosophy in seeking the social well-being of the oppressed which might be no more than a variety of sincere theological interpretations rooted in the Scriptures.' He thinks Dr. Beyerhaus should limit his sweeping condemnation of ecumenical leaders to 'some theologians connected with some churches in fellowship with the World Council of Churches (who) describe the object of ecumenical hope as void of any serious attempt to recognize the authority of Biblical witness'. He argues that themes such as liberation from oppression, peace and justice on earth, the principle of hope, used by neo-Marxists and futurists, are also biblical and should have a larger place in evangelical theology.

Gordon Moyes is Superintendent of the Wesley Central Mission in Sydney, Australia.

8

Evangelism and Social Responsibility —A Biblical Study on Priorities

VINAY SAMUEL and CHRIS SUGDEN*

Synopsis This controversial chapter raises basic hermeneutical issues of the relationship of text and context, of exegesis and eisegesis.

Seeking to develop a theology of mission grounded in the inseparable relationship of the creation order and the gospel, the authors begin by asserting that historically no missionary society before the twentieth century regarded its only legitimate missionary activity as verbal proclamation. The authors raise the issue of priority in a number of basic relationships and seek for wholistic biblical answers. Beginning with the issue of individual or community, they argue that the Bible begins with the community and family (Abraham). Jesus Christ is the fulfilment of the promises made to Abraham. He establishes the people's new identity as the people of God. From a study of community, covenant and kingdom in the two testaments, Samuel and Sugden conclude that 'neither the community nor the individual were reduced to being a mere function of the other.'

On the issue of the priority of the relationship of the vertical over the horizontal, they contend that the vertical relationship is

Rev. Vinay Samuel is a Presbyter in the Church of South India, serving in Bangalore.
Rev. Chris Sugden is Registrar, Oxford Centre for Mission Studies, Oxford, England.

always expressed in relationship to righteousness (love and justice) with one's neighbour. They criticize as dualistic the traditional evangelical view that man lives in two realms, the inner realm of ideas and language being the locus of the vertical relationship with God and experienced individually, with the outer realm of the physical and material being perceived as the locus of the horizontal relationship with man, its actions always the consequence of prior activity in the inner realm.

The priority of personal or social change is seen as linked to the Genesis interpretation of man, male and female, made in the image of God and the nature of the Fall. According to Jesus, the Pharisees dehumanized the law by divorcing its interpretation from the socio-economic and political context in which it was meant to operate. They made the law bearable for themselves by making loving God a priority and a possibility independent of loving one's neighbour. The authors suggest that the praxis of Jesus' righteousness and justification gives content to Pauline terminology. Since evil is seen in all of man's relationships, the scope of Christ's death and resurrection cannot be limited to individual relationships or personal change. It extends to all of the creation order and to all human history. The kingdom cannot be restricted to the spiritual realm or to the church. Heaven and earth are one integrated whole and thus the final consummation of Christ's rule will be the transformation of both earth and heaven. In the *eschaton* there will be the continuity of the new transforming the old and the discontinuity of God judging all things. The new invades the old, it does not evolve from it. The final kingdom will be the fulfilment of man's stewardship of this world.

Samuel and Sugden conclude that any discussion of priority in the focus of the Church's mission will depend not on the concept of mission, but on the context. The Jericho road sets its own agenda. (This paper is a revision of the paper given at CRESR.)

Introduction

The Lausanne Covenant represents a watershed in evangelical involvement in social responsibility in this century. It identified the fact that increasing numbers of evangelicals have been taking social responsibility seriously. It has provided a stimulus to others who may have hesitated to undertake social responsibility as being 'unevangelical'. The impetus which gave rise to the concern for social responsibility in the Lausanne Covenant has seen a further flowering in the eight years since Lausanne.

Lausanne did not define the mission of the church. But from the manner in which the congress defined evangelism and Christian social responsibility and placed them together in the covenant it would be logical to assume that the covenant includes both in the mission of the church. Statements on the topic of the mission of the church by Lausanne-related evangelical gatherings since then have affirmed that mission includes evangelism and social responsibility. Such statements include the Thailand Statement (June 1980), the Evangelical Commitment to Simple Lifestyle (March 1980), and the Madras Declaration on Evangelical Social Action (October 1979).[1]

The practice of the mission of the church has always included both evangelism and social responsibility. In the New Testament the call to the entire church was for it to be involved in both activities. See for example the pattern of Jesus' words and works followed in Acts 4. Historically, no missionary society before the twentieth century stated its goals by declaring that its only legitimate mission activity was verbal proclamation. In its practice of mission, the missionary church introduced literacy, education, medicine, technology (in the form of books, transport and radio) and opposed such practices as child marriage and drunkenness.

Thus mission in practice has always included activities which seek to bring both personal and social change. By personal change we mean a change in the total relationships of an individual with God, others in society and with the creation. By social change we mean a change in society, a community of peoples. We understand society to be a people in relationships which are expressed in and reinforced by structures, culture and world-view.[2] Social change addresses these relationships in society and their expressions.

The relationship between evangelism and social responsibility in the mission of the church is a question of the relationship between those activities which are aimed at changing people and those activities which are aimed at changing society. Thus discussion of the relationship between evangelism and social responsibility involves an examination of the following relationships: the relationship between the individual and the community; the relationship between the vertical relationship between man and God and the horizontal relationship between man and man; and the relationship between the personal and social change which the gospel brings about. We will examine each of these relationships from a biblical viewpoint.

1. The Relationship Between the Individual and the Community

Both personal change and social change focus on persons. How does the Bible understand the relation between persons and society, the individual and the community? Can persons exist, or be addressed apart from society? Does the call of God come to the individual or to the community?

The biblical focus is on the community. The Bible gives its primary attention to the people of God, Israel, the church.[3] God's answer to the human problem was to create a new community. His way of providing men with the new identity which they need for salvation is to start a family. Salvation is for the seed of Abraham. The New Testament affirms that Jesus is the fulfilment of the promise made to Abraham. (See Matt. 1:1–17; Lk. 3:8; Acts 3:25; Rom. 4; Gal. 3; Heb. 2:26; Heb. 7; Jn. 8:56). As T. Wright and M. Sadgrove say, 'God's way of salvation is to start a family; we are saved by belonging to it.'[4]

The rule of God was also expressed primarily in the community, not just in relation to the individual lives within the community. The power of God as Lord of the nations was demonstrated in his ability to create and deliver the people of Israel. The nature of his rule was to be demonstrated in the corporate life of the nation in relation to other nations.

Jesus came announcing the Kingdom of God and called individuals to join the community of the Kingdom. The Kingdom was the arena of God's rule and also a community where that rule was demonstrated. In entering the Kingdom through allegiance to Jesus, the disciples were entering a community where his rule was demonstrated.

Jesus' principle method of constituting this community was in training disciples. The Gospels do not present Jesus as a prophet on his own, or as the word become flesh on his own. He is master of a group of disciples. In terms of his work in society, Jesus made it clear that the work of the disciples started alongside his work as he sent them on their tour through Israel. When he left them, all his work became theirs.

But Jesus did not form this new community of the Kingdom *de novo*. He fulfilled the hopes and promises of the community established under the old covenant. He came to 'his own' (Jn. 1:12). He wept over Jerusalem. He allowed Israelites to identify him as the Messiah in whom the old covenant was fulfilled. The New Testament writers portray him as the true servant of God (a corporate and individual figure) who sums up the remnant of the old community. Jesus is the true son of God, fulfilling Israel's calling to be God's Son. He is the Son of Man who also represents the saints of the Most High (Dan. 7:13–28). Because they are in union with Jesus, the new people of God receive the fulfilment of the promises given under the old covenant.

Thus in Jesus the Old Testament pattern of the relation between individual and community under the covenant is not abrogated but fulfilled. The Kingdom was expressed first of all in the true Israelite, the true Son of God, the true servant, and then in those who in union with him became the New Israel and sons and servants of God. The focus is on the person of Christ and his Kingdom community.

In calling people to join him and his community, Jesus established people's new identity, as people of God. The emphasis in the New Testament on Christian's identity as children of God is on the community first. The 'children of God' was a phrase for Israel. The children of God are a family and community, not just an aggregate of the sons of God. Just as individuals gained their identity by belonging to the covenant community of Israel, so followers of Jesus gain their identity by allegiance to him and incorporation into his community. This identity is not earned through works. It was the Pharisees' mistake to believe that it was. It was a gift of grace. The security of this identity was the basis of service.

From this material on community, covenant and Kingdom in the two testaments we conclude that neither the community nor the individual was reduced to being a mere function of the other. The community was not merely an aggregate of individuals each possessing a prior relationship to God. Neither were individuals mere ciphers within a monolithic collective. The community and the individual found fulfilment in each other. God's covenant with the community in his purpose for the world was the basis of the identity of the individual. God's laws for the community life required a response from individuals. A vital community life in obedience to God required members who were personally loyal to the community's Lord and to one another.

2. The Relationship Between the Vertical and Horizontal

Personal change and social change are matters of changes in man's vertical and horizontal relationships. The Bible does not separate these from each other. In the covenant and the law, there was no meaningful way in which a person's relationship with God could be sundered from his relationship with his neighbours. The laws for the covenant community were given to

enable the community to express its faithfulness to its righteous
Lord but none of them relates exclusively to individual allegiance
to God. They all relate to love of the neighbour. The vertical
relationship with God is consciously acknowledged but it is to be
expressed in relationships of righteousness (love and justice) with
the neighbour.

Jesus beautifully explicated this understanding of the Old
Testament laws as he reaffirmed them for the new covenant
(Matt. 22:34–40; Mk. 12:28–34; Lk. 10:25–28). In different
ways each evangelist stresses that these two commands are of
equal importance. In Matthew 'to love God' is understood as the
great and first commandment. But the second is said to be 'like
it'. Then both commands are linked together as those upon
which 'all the law and the prophets' depend. In Mark the scribe
asks concerning the first of all the commandments. Jesus replies
with the first and second commandment; in other words no *one*
commandment can be marked as first, both are set over against
all other requirements of the law. The second commandment is
not ranked of second importance; it is listed as comprising, with
the first, the chief commandment about which the scribe had
enquired. In Luke one verb, 'you shall love', joined to the
conjunction 'and', governs the two commands, clearly demon-
strating their equality.[6]

In Mark, Jesus clearly explicated the command to love God in
terms of loving the neighbour in contradistinction to the requirements of the cultic law (Mk. 12:33b). These commands mutually
interpret one another. It is impossible to love God without a
relationship to our neighbour.

Jesus also reinterpreted the meaning of love for the neighbour.
Jewish exegesis understood 'neighbour' in Lev. 19:18 to mean
friends, associates or kinsmen. Jesus gave a new understanding
of 'neighbour' based on his understanding of what truly human
life is under the love of God. In Luke, Jesus followed his
teaching on the Great Commandment with the parable of the
Good Samaritan. He showed how the attempt by the religious
leaders to give priority to religious duties to God (avoiding
contamination with a possibly dead body) was in fact disobedience to God's law.

Finally Jesus set the command to love in the context of the
Kingdom of God. The parables of the Kingdom of God in
Matthew 13 focus on God's love to which man's repentance is a
response. The rule of the God of the Kingdom is the rule of love.
To 'receive Jesus' preaching of God's rule is to receive the proffer
of forgiveness and to accept the claim inherent in the promise is
to allow God's love to qualify one's own life in radical and concrete ways.'[7]

Does the vertical relationship have priority?
We have argued that there can be no separation between man's
vertical and horizontal relationships. Few would disagree. But
many have argued that the vertical relationship has a priority in
that the corruption of man's vertical relationship must be
addressed first before any change can be brought to man's horizontal relationships. Justification is then solely the rectification
of the vertical relationship between God and the individual.

This view is closely allied with the view that men are distinct
individuals and that society plays little or no part in their formation or identity. Society is but the aggregate of individuals. Thus
social change comes about if there are a significant number of
transformed individuals to influence society.

We suggest that one reason why people assign this sort of
priority to man's vertical relationship is that they have a dualistic
understanding of existence assuming that man lives in two
realms, an inner realm and an outer realm. This dualism cannot
be sustained either by biblical teaching or by philosophical
reasoning.

The biblical evidence does not support this position. The
vertical line is first of all a covenant line with the community
which the individual represents. Secondly the individual and the
community are mutually interpenetrating concepts in the Bible.
Thirdly the love of the individual for God is interpreted and
expressed in love for the neighbour. Fourthly, sin as we shall
discuss later, is a violation of the covenant and so is expressed in
actions which threaten the harmony of the covenant relationships
in the community. It is not purely a matter of a fractured vertical
relationship with God independent of other relationships.

Since this dualistic position cannot be sustained by the biblical
evidence why have dedicated and sincere Christians held this
view?

We suggest that the roots of such a stress lie in a philosophical
presupposition which posits that man lives in two realms. The
inner realm is the locus of the vertical relationship with God. It is
a realm of unchanging spiritual realities within which people
immediately apprehend God. Here God meets man face to face.
It is a realm of religion, ideas, concepts and language. This realm
can be experienced only individually. There is no 'corporate'
inner realm. Entrance into the life of this realm is through
receiving words and responding to ideas and concepts. The outer
realm is the locus of horizontal relationships with man. It is the
realm of physical and material existence. Anything that occurs in
the outer realm is a consequence of prior activity in the inner
realm. The outer realm cannot be acted on directly, it can be
truly changed only by activity in the inner realm.

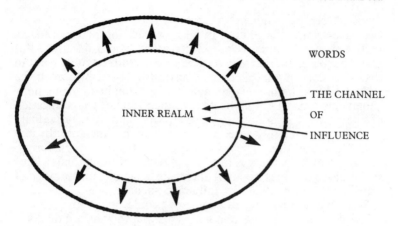

While the inner realm influences the outer realm, there is no traffic the other way. The inner realm is open to transformation only by words, the vehicle of ideas.

This inner/outer realm presupposition acts as a hermeneutical grid for understanding sin, salvation, evangelism and social change. Sin is viewed as an essentially spiritual problem which makes men incapable of relating properly to God. It has various consequences in the individual's life in the material and social sphere, but can be dealt with in the spiritual sphere alone.

Salvation occurs only within the inner spiritual realm. The biblical teaching that the agent of salvation is God, is interpreted to entail first that the arena of salvation must be where God meets man, in the inner realm; and second, that the content of salvation belongs only to this inner realm. It is a spiritual kingdom that is not of this world.

Social sin is primarily caused by individual sins, which are in turn consequences of an essentially inner spiritual problem. The only means of transforming this inner realm is through evangelism understood as the verbal proclamation of a message of justification by faith. Any activity directed at the outer sphere (such as service or relief) without going through the inner sphere of individuals has no transforming effect. It essentially witnesses to the transformed inner life of those who exercise such service and maintains the existence of the outer sphere.

Donald McGavran expresses this view of salvation in these words:

> Salvation is something which the true and living God confers on His creatures in accordance with His once for all revelation in Jesus Christ, God and Saviour according to the Bible. Salvation is a vertical relationship (of man with God) which issues in horizontal

relationships (of man with men). The vertical must not be displaced by the horizontal.

Desirable as social ameliorations are, working for them must not be substituted for the Biblical requirements of/for salvation . . . Paul voiced them . . . to the Philippian jailor: 'Believe in the Lord Jesus, and you will be saved, you and your household.'[8]

This statement demonstrates the separation of inner and outer realms and vertical and horizontal relationships. It locates salvation exclusively in one realm and supposes that any disagreement can mean only a concern to locate salvation exclusively in the other realm which is the realm of man, not of God.

The recognition of the integral nature of man's relationships does not deny that there is an inward aspect to a person's life, thought, feelings, conscience and hopes. The discipline of psychology has examined these in depth. The question whether the inner and psychological has priority in terms of (a) man's relation to God and (b) man's own self is not a psychological question. It is a philosophical one.

Philosophically, a major question mark hangs over the whole idea of whether it is possible to give any meaning to statements about an 'inner realm' which has no reference to any observable behaviour. In other words, suppose someone is sitting in an arm-chair in a perfectly relaxed position and smiles benignly. Suppose then that he says, 'I am in excruciating agony'. It is arguable that he is using language in a totally different sense from normal usage. This is not to pose a behaviourist theory of language. It is to assert that statements about pain, intention to do things, and the continuity of the person are logically tied to bodily behaviour as an irreducible component of such statements rather than to contingent consequences.[9] This means that descriptions of a person's inner experiences are logically tied for their meaning to behaviour, without being reduced to being merely statements about behaviour. 'Inner language' and 'outer language' do not refer to separate realms. They are different languages about one set of human actions viewed from different perspectives.

Therefore it is not possible to separate man's vertical and horizontal relationships, nor establish a priority between them either on biblical or philosophical grounds.

3. The Relationship Between Personal and Social Change

We have argued that the Bible presents an integral relationship between the individual and the community and between the vertical and horizontal relationships of man's life. We will now look at the same integral relationship from the perspective of other categories to examine further the relationship between the personal change and the social change which the gospel brings about. We will examine the nature of man's sin, and the nature of Christ's redemption of man and victory over evil.

A. The Nature of Man

The Hebrew view of man is that man is a unity. D. J. A. Clines writes:

> Recent Biblical scholarship has been well nigh unanimous in reject-ing the traditional view of man as a 'composition' of 'various parts', and has emphasised rather that in the Biblical view man is a unity.[10]

It is sometimes assumed that references to evil proceeding from the heart, and to God's creation of a new heart, are evidence of an inner realm within man which is the locus of his 'spiritual' relationship with God. But Eichrodt makes it clear that in con-trast with such a view common to Greek thought:

> The heart is a comprehensive term for the personality as a whole, its inner life, its character. It is the conscious and deliberate spiritual activity of the self-contained human ego (Eichrodt, *Theology of the Old Testament* Vol II 1967, p. 143).[11]

If then man is a unity, we can learn much about what he is by examining what the Scriptures expect him to be and to do. Man is first presented as the image of God. This sets him apart from other creatures. Since the Old Testament prohibited images, we must gain our understanding of image from its use in the Ancient Near East. The king or the idol in the temple were representa-tives of the absentee god who dwelt on the mountains or else-where. They exercised stewardship or authority over the god's territory on his behalf.

The doctrine of the image of God is about man's role as steward of God's creation. The image is defined in terms of stewardship and dominion in Gen. 1:27-28. 'God created man in his own image . . . male and female . . . and God said to them . . . "be fruitful . . . have dominion . . . over every living thing." '
Man did not lose this image in the fall. The prohibition of murder in Gen. 9:6 is dependent on man being in the image of God. Murder is prohibited because men may have dominion over all creatures except other men.

The doctrine of the image of God is also about man's relation-ships. The image of God is held by male and female together. The image is to be understood in terms of personal relationships, rather than in terms of man's individual psychological make-up. Man is to exercise his role of dominion together with women over the creation as steward of God. Thus people are not isolated individuals, but persons in relationship to God, one another and the material world. And thus a right relationship with God cannot be experienced in isolation from the other relationships.

Man as God's image is fulfilled in Christ. Jesus as the second Adam is the perfection of the image of God (Col. 1:15; Heb. 1:3). He is the demonstration of what manhood is meant to be. He shares his image with his descendants, who are predestined to be conformed to the image of God's Son in order that he might be the firstborn among many brethren (Rom. 8:29). Christ's work in redemption is the fulfilment of the creation of man. It is not only that Christ is the new man, but he also creates one new man from groups which before were divided and hostile. He restores the relationships that characterize the image of God in himself and in the church. Thus in Christ, man becomes 'new man' which is being renewed in knowledge after the image of its Creator. Here there cannot be Greek and Jew, male or female . . . but Christ is all and in all' (Col. 3:10f.; Gal. 3:28). 'He . . . has made us both one . . . has broken down the dividing wall of hostility . . . that he might create in himself one new man in place of the two' (Eph. 2:15). This restoration is not yet complete, for we do not yet see everything in subjection to man as Psalm 8 states. 'But we see Jesus, for a little while made lower than the angels, crowned with glory and honour' (Heb. 2:8).

B. *The Nature of Sin*

Is sin a rupture of the relationship between man and God in the spiritual realm which has consequences in people's individual lives? Or is the broken relationship with God essentially manifested in broken social relationships?

The primordial sin was not disobedience to a whimsical command of God. Adam was persuaded by his partner to misuse their stewardship of nature and use nature for their ends rather than in obedience to God's purpose. Instead of holding each other up to the highest standards God set, Eve exploited Adam and Adam gave in to Eve. Instead of allowing God to determine the standards of right and wrong in using nature, they set those standards for themselves. So the nature of the sin that is described in the fall narrative is a breakdown of all the relationships which characterize man, his relationships with God, other people and nature itself. Because man loses his relationship with God, his ability to carry out his role as God's steward of creation in partnership with his wife is impaired. The model of the marring of man and his image is not the model of a mechanical toy which develops an internal defect leading to more or less aberrant activity. It is a breakdown of the relationships with God which are expressed in being untrue to his relationships with God, people and nature.

Further, in the explication of the fall in Romans 5, Adam is not regarded only as a historical figure. He is understood theologically as a corporate figure embracing all fallen men. He is understood in parallel to Christ who is also a corporate figure, a representative of a race. The perfection of Jesus is the perfection of a corporate person who shares his perfection with his people.

We participate in the sin of Adam because he is a corporate figure, representing and including us all. We all sin in the same way Adam sinned, and we all sin because Adam sinned. Sin is essentially a corporate entity in which the race participates. The individualistic interpretation of sin, as the sundering of the individual's fellowship with God, focuses on the individual dimension of this corporate reality.

This conclusion is substantiated by the biblical evidence. In Romans 1:18 Paul uses the terms 'adikia' and 'asebeia' for human sin. In the LXX these terms refer to offences against the sacral order of divine justice. *Adikia* affected the community whose existence was intimately bound up with the preservation of divine justice. Sin had both theological and social import. It destroyed the community.

In Romans 1:3 Paul does not discuss human sin apart from concrete instances and behaviour which offends God and destroys human community. The broken relationship between man and God is expressed in perversions in human relationships between the sexes and in strife in society.

James states the Old Testament view of sin: 'The person who does not do the good he knows he should do is guilty of sin' (James 4:17). Sin was a clear infringement of known moral law. All the words for sin have this clear connotation: *hamartia* is an offence against law and morals, men or gods; *adikia* is unrighteousness, injustice and unjust deeds; *parabasis* is transgression of the law.[12]

C. *Law and Sin*

We cannot understand sin without reference to the law. Paul asserted that the law brought knowledge of sin (Rom. 3:20). The Old Testament concept of the law was focused on persons in relationship in community. The law was always focused on this life. There are no laws for loving God in the Old Testament which can be broken independently of one's relationship to other people. In fact, idol-worship was singled out for prohibition because it fundamentally threatened the solidarity of the community in its allegiance to its Lord.[13]

The breaking of laws in relationship to other people expresses the breaking of a people's relationship with God. Such breaches have to be atoned for by recompense and reconciliation with the person, and atonement and reconciliation with God.

According to Jesus, the Pharisees dehumanized the law and gave a false priority to its place in man's relationship with God, independent of a relationship to man. He criticized the Pharisees for giving attention to tithing garden herbs as offerings to the temple in faithfulness to God at the expense of justice, mercy and faith.

Jesus' central criticism of the Pharisees was that they dehumanized the law by divorcing its interpretation from the socio-economic and political context in which it was meant to operate. Moses gave the law to protect humanity and promote social justice in the social context of the times. The prophets reasserted that there could be no true obedience to the law if obedience to God was separated from justice in society. Jesus' criticism of the Pharisees was that they separated obedience of the law from its meaning in the social context and made loving God a priority and a possibility independent of loving the neighbour.

Jesus showed his own stance in his discussion on the law with the rich young ruler. The ruler had kept an interpretation of the law divorced from its context of relationships in the community. It was to this obedience Jesus called him when he asked him to sell all he had, give to the poor and follow him.

Jesus also took issue with the Pharisees about where and how cleansing for obedience to the law could take place. The Pharisees divided man into inner and outer realms. They held that cleansing man's relationship with God in the inner realm was assured by the correct observance of rituals of cleansing in the outer realm.

Did Jesus assert that while inner cleansing could not be achieved by outward ritual, it could be achieved by inward attitudes of repentance and faith? He did not join the Essene community who taught precisely this, but in sharp contrast with the Essenes and the Pharisees, taught that it was impossible to love God without loving your neighbour. He did not reverse the roles of inner and outer cleansing. He showed that any distinction between inner and outer realms and inner and outer cleansing was false. For him, as for John the Baptist, repentance was measured by sharing with the poor, giving up exploitation, restoring money taken in fraud and turning from adultery.

In Matthew 23:25–26, Jesus calls the Pharisees to cleanse what is inside the cup first—that is violence and selfishness. This is not a spiritual inner cleansing separate from their relationship with people. It is a holistic cleansing involving, probably, restoration of what they have taken by violence and selfishness. The people of God have always been tempted to separate belief and action into inner and outer realms. It is a way of coping with the inability to live according to God's will. In the prophetic literature, Israel is seen to have separated worship at the temple from the practice of justice in society. The Pharisees made the law bearable for them to obey by making its essential requirement the love of God independent of love of the neighbour. In the early church Paul resisted those who accepted that they were forgiven and took this as a licence for licentiousness. As the church increasingly attracted rich and powerful members, Luke and James had to reassert that belief in Jesus could not be separated from a bias to the poor.

The tendency to separate belief and practice enables us to live with our failures. Jesus did not want people to live with them. He urges them to repent, accept his forgiveness, and as an expression of that to follow him in the power of his Spirit in a life of justice and righteousness as members of God's Kingdom.

It would seem then that Orlando Costas is correct when he states:

> Sin is not an abstract reality but takes concrete form. Sin expresses itself historically in the failure of human beings to relate with one another on the basis of love, or in more positive terms, in the oppression of men and women by their neighbours.[14]

D. *Righteousness and Justification*

God's just character and laws of justice define the sin from which we are justified. Discussion of the meaning of righteousness and justification in their *locus classicus* in Paul's letters is usually focused on the background of the use of the word group in the Old Testament. But the crucial step in the development of the Christian idea of righteousness and justification is the teaching and practice of Jesus. The route from the Old Testament to Paul lies through Jesus. The praxis of Jesus' righteousness and justification should give content to the Pauline terminology.

In his ministry, Jesus established the justice of God. He opposed the current understanding of justice. For example, the Pharisees judged the hated Zaccheus, the chief of the tax collectors, who soiled his hands by daily contact with the Gentiles, took his cut of the taxes he collected and collaborated with the hated Romans. The Pharisees judged him as excluded from the people of Israel. Jesus reached out in forgiveness to Zaccheus, and created justice whereby Zaccheus offered a fourfold restitution to those whom he had cheated. Jesus went further to extend membership of God's people and his kingdom to this outcast and other outcasts. This was blasphemy and led to his death.

Jesus' resurrection was God's 'yes' to his understanding of God's justice. This was what converted Saul the Pharisee, a man obsessed with God's righteousness. The appearance of the risen Jesus showed Saul that God validated Jesus' understanding of how God created right relationships: not by slavish obedience to the law and harsh judgment on defaulters, but by reaching out across all barriers, social, religious, political and sinful to love his enemies and forgive them.

Therefore Paul's own understanding of righteousness reflects Jesus' understanding because he focuses on the religious heart of righteousness which is the reconciliation of people with God and with each other. In his letter to the Galatians he stresses that if Christians accept each other on the basis of merit only then they are failing to express the very meaning of justification by faith. This theme runs through his other epistles and is the key concept he uses to tackle the Jew-Gentile problem in the church.

E. *The nature of evil and of God's victory over it through the life, death and resurrection of Jesus*

Is evil located only in distorted personal wills and personalities, or does evil express itself also in all man's relationships, in his personal and social relationships and in the structures which express and give continuity to them?

God's action in judging and defeating evil reveals its true nature. That action was centred on Christ. The New Testament witness is that the God of the Jews is to be understood as the God and Father of our Lord Jesus Christ: that the work of God in creation and redemption is focused, defined and executed in Christ. Therefore, wherever God works in the world, that work is based on the victory Christ won over sin and evil on the cross. If we say that God works in places and ways in the world that have no reference to this victory of Christ, then we are reducing the New Testament understanding of Christ.

The death and resurrection of Jesus was central to every activity of God in overcoming evil in the world. It is of crucial importance to note that the victory of God over sin, and the lordship of Jesus, are established by the resurrection (Rom. 1:4). God's victory, and Jesus' lordship are not abstract theological truths. They were established by the historical event of the resurrection. Jesus was enthroned as Lord over all creation, with authority in heaven and earth, by the resurrection. Therefore, we cannot limit the scope of his lordship in the present, or of his Kingdom, only to a spiritual realm or to the church. The resurrection enthroned Jesus as Lord of all. What consequences flow from this?

Paul does not limit the scope of Christ's death only to a spiritual inner realm, or to personal change. In Col. 1:15–20 he makes it clear that 'God made peace through his Son's death on the cross and so brought back to himself all things, both on earth and in heaven'. In Col. 2:14–15 he says that on the cross, Christ 'disarmed the principalities and powers and made a public example of them, triumphing over them in him'.

In Paul's thought these powers are demonic forces behind structures in society such as the state and the Jewish religion. Christ triumphed over their rebellion against God on the cross and is sovereign over them. He is continually disarming them by overcoming the injustice in society created by their rebellion. This work is not necessarily exercised only by the church. Whenever justice replaces injustice Christ's victory on the cross is having its effect.

Some evangelicals suspect that this is an attempt to reduce Pauline teaching about supernatural realities to merely humanistic categories, an attempt to demythologize Paul. But such an understanding of principalities and powers does not demythologize Paul, nor does it identify structures with demons, nor does it deny the reality of personal demons. Such an understanding asserts that a category of Jewish apocalyptic which Paul uses, that of demonic forces behind social realities, should be taken in its widest sense and not limited to demonic personal spirits which possess individuals.[16]

One recent evangelical statement asserts the victory of Christ over evil in these terms: 'We affirm the Lordship of Jesus over all demonic powers of evil, which possess persons and pervade structures, societies and the created order.'[17]

From this we conclude that God's work in salvation is centred on and achieved by Christ's death on the cross. But this work is not limited to achieving victory over evil located only in individuals. It is a victory over evil throughout the created order in whatever form it expresses itself.

God's action in Christ addresses the whole creation. It addresses sin and evil in every form. God's action in Christ began with creating all things through him. God reconciled all things by his death (Col. 1:20) thus putting all things under his feet (Eph. 1:22).

Thus God's action in Christ cannot be limited to a spiritual realm within man nor relegated to a realm beyond history. It is taking place on the stage of history as the social relationships of man, the crown of creation, are recreated in Christ.

4. The Relationship Between the Kingdom and History

The overarching concept which enables us to see the linkage between God's redemptive work in persons and in society which shapes them and of which they are a part, is the Kingdom of God. What then is the relationship between God's work in the Kingdom of God and present human history in which society is set? This relationship will determine the mission in society of the community of the Kingdom, the church.

A. *A Spiritual Kingdom?*

Some Christians distinguish the mission of the church from Christian involvement in society because they see the Kingdom as a fundamentally spiritual reality which affects temporal matters. Hence its real home is in heaven beyond the earth and human history. The concept is that heaven comes to influence earth, not that the Kingdom comes to transform the earth. Therefore the consummation is when heaven will totally fill the earth, rather than when the earth finds its consummation in the new earth.

Biblical studies[18] are showing that heaven and earth are one integrated whole. Both are created by the same God. Both were corrupted by the fall (Col. 1:20). The heavenly world is now populated by spiritual forces of wickedness which believers are to fight against (Eph. 3:10; 6:10; 6:12). Both heaven and earth will be redeemed by God in Christ (Col. 1:20; Eph. 1:10, 22; 4:10). Man's response to God's one structure of created reality can, however, take two directions. The sinful response is 'earthly'. The obedient response is 'heavenly'. In using this concept 'heavenly' Paul is expressing in cosmological language man's restored relationship of obedience to and union with the Creator which is part of the total reconciliation of the whole creation. He is not focusing on the cosmology as such. He is not speaking of a sphere of existence in the future which will replace the world, but of a present restored relationship with God which is possible now and which will last forever. This relationship is expressed in a lifestyle which gives precedence to those values which Christ lived, which God vindicated in the resurrection and which will last forever.

The view that the Kingdom is primarily spiritual cites in support John 18:36 where Jesus says to Pilate, 'My kingship is not of this world; if my kingship were of this world, my servants would fight, that I might not be handed over to the Jews; but my kingship is not from this world.' Does this text confirm the assumption that the Kingdom is fundamentally spiritual?

First, Jesus' statement is that his Kingdom does not take its origin from the world. The words *ek* and *enteuthen* denote the source and origin of the Kingdom. It does not arise 'out of' this world. The origin of the Kingdom is the Father, and it enters the world from him.

Secondly, Jesus clearly contrasts his Kingdom with worldly kingdoms by contrasting the behaviour of his servants in this world. His servants do not fight. Jesus had devoted considerable time to training his disciples to serve and suffer in this world instead of fighting. He taught them to serve, to renounce vengeance and to love their enemies such as the Romans and Samaritans. Were Jesus' Kingdom 'other worldly' then the logical behaviour would be withdrawal and passivity, not active service, love and suffering in this world. Jesus' Kingdom takes a different expression in this world from the kingdom of men.

Thirdly, the context of Jesus' statement in John establishes rather than denies Jesus' kingly authority in this world. In John 19:10, 11, Pilate and Jesus have this exchange:

'Do you not know that I have power to release you, and power to crucify you?' Jesus answered him, 'You would have no power over me unless it had been given you from above.'

Jesus' statement is a kingly statement. For who has power over a king except God? John's narrative establishes that Jesus is in kingly command of the whole situation of his trial, crucifixion and death. (cf. also John 10:17–18).

On the contrary, Scripture links the fulfilment of the Kingdom with the transformation of this earth. Many descriptions of the final consummation and its events relate to the earth. 'Blessed are the meek, for they shall inherit the earth' (Matt. 5:5).

The promise to Abraham and his descendants, that they should inherit the world . . . (came) through the righteousness of faith (Rom. 4:13).

The creation itself will be set free from its bondage to decay and obtain the glorious liberty of the children of God. (Rom. 8:21).

'The new heavens and the new earth which I will make shall remain before me' says the Lord (Isa. 66:22).

Then I saw a new heaven and a new earth for the first heaven and the first earth had passed away (Rev. 21:1).

You have made them a kingdom and priests to our God, and they shall reign on earth (Rev. 5:10).

Many biblical images of the relationship between the eschaton and the present earth are in terms of travail and childbirth, harvest, gathering and reaping, the blossoming of spring or summer.[19]

The biblical symbols of the eschaton, the feast, the heavenly city and the promised rest indicate

> the continuity of the social goals of the new age with this-worldly community and ideals. This is not merely because men must use images of the visible to describe the world invisible. It is rather because the goal is seen in relation to the course run, and the new creation to the old.[20]

The biblical presentation of the eschaton is a renewed and transformed earth, the fulfilment of God's purpose in creation, the consummation of God's purpose in history, not the obliteration of history. So the biblical picture can mean that the eschaton is present in all aspects in this world, renewing all man's relationships with God, man and nature.

The Kingdom embraces both heaven and earth. In the Lord's prayer, 'Thy kingdom come' is expanded by the parallel lines 'Thy will be done in earth as it is in heaven'. As the prophet Isaiah longed, there will be 'a new heaven and a new earth' (Isa. 66:22). Heaven and earth will be integrally united. Heaven will not be emptied and earth will not be abandoned.

Therefore the concept of heaven in the Scripture cannot be used to emphasize an eternally existent and perfect sphere with which only the soul has affinity and which will be its final abode. It cannot be used to rule out history and the earth as unimportant spheres scheduled for extinction. It is a mistake to identify man's inner realm by positing its affinity with a destiny in heaven separate from earth. Whatever the exact relationship of the new heavens and new earth will be, man's destiny is to inhabit a kingdom uniting both on a new earth. Thus arguments about a spiritual realm superseding a physical one cannot be based on the biblical material on heaven.

B. *Continuity and Discontinuity*

But the Kingdom of God is not co-terminous with human history, and human history will not evolve into the Kingdom. The Kingdom is importantly distinct from history in a number of ways. Members of the Kingdom are distinguished by their behaviour. They have taken a radical step of repentance in turning away from the values and behaviour of the fallen age. The

contrast between the Kingdom and the old age is between darkness and light, new wine and old. When the final Kingdom
comes those in it will be separated from those outside it, and will
find a dramatic reversal of their experiences on earth. The meek
will inherit the earth, those who hunger and thirst for righteousness will be filled, those who have become homeless, landless or
orphans for the gospel's sake will receive a hundredfold and
eternal life.

The significance of this discontinuity is that the old order
cannot evolve into the Kingdom of God. The Kingdom of God
invades the old order and comes as judgment upon it. Sin is so
deeply rooted in every aspect of creation that the Kingdom will
bring a total transformation which will leave nothing untouched.
For this reason the Kingdom cannot be fully experienced in this
creation as it stands. To experience it fully would entail the
complete transformation of the whole creation.

Any change that the Kingdom brings now is necessarily
limited. None of our activity, even that inspired by the power of
the Kingdom, can bring the final Kingdom. God is the one who
brings the Kingdom. This is the important point of discontinuity.

Discontinuity is not the total biblical picture. There is continuity between the Kingdom and this earth. The Kingdom will
not scrap this creation in favour of another one, or bring an alien
life to take it over. It fulfils the groanings of this creation for
deliverance and fulfilment. The significance of continuity is that
the Kingdom is at work now making human life what it is truly
meant to be.

But how much freight can be carried across the bridge that
links this creation with the coming Kingdom of God? If it will
not come in its completeness until the return of Christ, will not
God then undo all that we can do before ushering in his Kingdom? All our puny efforts, and the structure of God's church
itself, will come under his judgment. Even our bodies will have
to be transformed because flesh and blood cannot inherit the
Kingdom of God. Does it make any difference what we do before
the end comes? It does, because the final Kingdom will be the
fulfilment of man's stewardship of this world. Sons of the Kingdom, conformed to the image of Christ, are proper men, released
from evil's power to fulfil God's command to subdue this world.
They are true stewards of the world God made.

C. *God's Purpose—Stewardship Rewarded*

The basic question then is, what is God's purpose for the world
and for man's stewardship of it? The resurrection gives us some
clues. Our bodies will be transformed. We shall not become

'somebody else'. We shall become more completely ourselves than ever before. Paul and Jesus hint that what we become then bears a distinct relationship to what we are now. Jesus' parable of the talents links entering the joy of the Lord with faithfulness to him now. The man who made ten talents more was given responsibility over ten cities, the man who made five talents was given responsibility over five cities. Paul teaches that the quality of each person's work which he builds on the foundation of Christ, will be tested by fire to show its real quality (1 Cor. 3:14–15). The nature of the reward will be like the intrinsic reward of being able to play and appreciate fine music as a result of rigorous musical training, as opposed to the extrinsic reward of a child practising his musical instrument in order to receive a sum of money promised by his parents.

Until the consummation of the Kingdom Paul urges his readers to be conformed now to the image of God's Son, to grow into mature manhood, to the measure of the stature of the fulness of Christ. He knows that they will finally be transformed by Christ at the resurrection. But he does not for that reason urge that they do nothing which would reflect that transformation now. Similarly with the church. Paul knows that Christ will present it to himself as a spotless bride. But he does not for that reason urge that any transformation now is wasted effort. He urges that Christians should experience as much of that transformation now as possible. He works tirelessly to present every man mature in Christ now, to build up the body of Christ now.

There is therefore clear continuity in the personal sphere. As we have seen, it is a false anthropology and sociology to divorce the personal sphere entirely from the social sphere. Men live in a series of integrated relationships. How is it possible to be a mature man in Christ if one is being mercilessly exploited by others?

Such an understanding of transformation equally applies to our stewardship of creation. Our work will be judged. But it will also be crowned by greater success than we could ever have imagined. Just as we will recognize ourselves in God's Kingdom on earth, so we will recognize the creation which we have stewarded. All the Old Testament concepts of the Kingdom of God are in terms of a renewed earth. The kings of the earth, we are told, will bring into the Kingdom of God the glory and honour of the nations . . . The city which needs no temple, sun or moon is yet open to receive the best of the first creation (Rev. 21:22–24). Only what is unclean is barred. Our work will be carried across that narrow bridge, but only after it has been transformed, purged and crowned by the Lord whose work it is anyway.

The biblical understanding of the new earth and the resurrection would therefore seem to suggest that consummated history will be part of the new reality of the new order. The Old Testament hints that history will be consummated on this earth and not elsewhere. The New Testament takes up the theme of Old Testament history and universalizes the history of Israel. Israel becomes the olive tree into which all Gentile nations are grafted in order to participate in redemption. But what continuity is there in the New Testament between present history and the Kingdom? Is there any relationship between them which is sufficient to enable us to commit ourselves to a present historical project as a project of the Kingdom?

For Paul the good works we do in everyday historical life have a future in that they belong to the new order, the new age, the world of the Kingdom. Yet at the same time they are good works performed within the structural relationships of human history, the relationships of husband and wife, parents and children, masters and slaves. The values expressed in these works are heavenly values which will last for ever. So too the works which express these values inasmuch as they belong to the new age, will find their fulfilment in that age.

In saying this, we are not saying that redeemed men build the Kingdom block by block. The Kingdom comes on God's initiative and by God's grace. It can never come fully before God's intervention to perfect it. But we should not be so afraid of absolutizing any human action as a final action of God that we fail to see the significance of the incarnation. This shows that within fallen human history God can use the ambiguous and imperfect actions of men as vehicles of his Kingdom. The Bible does not restrict the work of God to actions that are perfect. He can be at work in the imperfect. Though the imperfect will pass through the fires of judgment, yet because God has been at work in imperfect human activities, his work will last forever. Ultimately, our faith in the continuity of God's work through human history rests on the sovereignty of God over the whole of creation and history. We must not reduce this sovereignty to merely a spiritual sovereignty in a spiritual sphere, nor demythologize it into the laws of nature and progress. Instead our faith is that Jesus is exalted Lord over all creation. The Kingdom comes wherever Jesus overcomes the evil one. This happens in fullest measure in the church, but it happens in society also. God's rule over human history cannot be separated from the rule of his Kingdom. The New Testament does not know of a general providence apart from the history of God's lordship and saving activity.

Because the community of faith publicly acknowledges the

lordship of Christ it experiences the salvation which the Kingdom brings in a way that is different from the experience of the
larger community where the Kingdom is at work without being
acknowledged. However, the Kingdom activity in society
beyond the church is not just its judgmental activity but also that
which brings promise and grace.[21] The relation between God's
Kingdom activity in the church and beyond it is therefore not
merely a spillover of his work in the church to society, but
essentially the same work of lordship based on the death and
resurrection of Christ moving both the world and the church to
their consummation in the new earth.

4. Implications of the Study for the Relationship Between Evangelism and Social Responsibility

We have seen that in the Bible's view, the individual and the
community are to find fulfilment in each other. God's covenant
with the community is the basis for the identify of the individual,
and a vital community life in obedience to God requires members
who are personally loyal to the community's Lord and to one
another. Thus the very basis for personal change is the establishment of a new society which is in itself an element of social
change.

We have seen that man's vertical relationship with God cannot
be separated from or addressed apart from his horizontal relationship with his neighbours. Thus we can give no conceptual
priority to addressing man's vertical relationship.

We have seen that in bringing salvation, God redeems man as a
unity in all his relationships, and that the restoration of any one
dimension of these relationships must always find expression in
his other relationships. This restoration came through the work
of Christ which is the basis of all God's work of overcoming evil
in the world, both within and beyond the church. This restoration takes place on the stage of human history and will be
consummated in the new heaven and new earth where righteousness dwells.

We can therefore commit ourselves to activities of both personal and social transformation secure in the knowledge that God
is at work amidst the imperfection and provisionality of what we
are able to achieve by his grace and that this work will find its
fulfilment in his everlasting Kingdom.

Therefore conceptually there can be no priority between the
task of addressing personal and social change. The love of God
and the love of the neighbour mutually interpret one another.
Any discussion of priority in the focus of the church's mission

will depend not on the concept of mission, but on its context. The love of the neighbour is affected by the nature of the neighbour's context. This is clearly shown in the parable of the Good Samaritan and the diverse ways in which Jesus addressed the Pharisees, the poor and the dying thief with the good news of the Kingdom. The Jericho road sets its own agenda.

BIBLIOGRAPHY

Carl Armerding (ed.) *Evangelicals and Liberation* (Presbyterian and Reformed Publishing Company 1977).
Bruce C. Birch and Larry L. Rasmussen *The Predicament of the Prosperous* (Westminster 1978).
Orlando Costas *Church Growth: A Shattering Critique from the Third World* (Tyndale 1974).
Orlando Costas *The Integrity of Mission* (Harper and Row 1979).
Samuel Escobar and John Driver *Christian Mission and Social Justice* (Herald Press 1978).
V. P. Furnish *The Love Command in the New Testament* (SCM 1973).
V. P. Furnish *Theology and Ethics in Paul* (Abingdon 1968).
Anthony Hoekema *The Bible and the Future* (Eerdmans, Paternoster 1979).
Arthur Johnston *The Battle for World Evangelism* (Tyndale 1978).
Harold Lindsell *An Evangelical Theology of Missions* (Zondervan 1970).
Leslie Newbiggin *The Open Secret* (Mowbrays/Eerdmans 1978).
René Padilla (ed.) *The New Face of Evangelicalism* (Hodder 1975).
George W. Peters *A Biblical Theology of Missions* (Moody Press 1972).
Waldron Scott *Bring Forth Justice* (Eerdmans 1980).
Vinay Samuel and Chris Sugden *Current Trends in Theology—A Third World Guide* (PIM-Asia 1981).
    Christian Mission in the Eighties—A Third World Perspective PIM-Asia 1981).
    Evangelism and the Poor—A Third World Study Guide (PIM-Asia 1982).
Vinay Samuel *The Meaning and Cost of Discipleship* (PIM-Asia 1981).
Chris Sugden *Social Gospel or No Gospel?* (Grove Booklets on Ethics No. 4, 1977).
    Radical Discipleship (Marshall Morgan and Scott 1981).
Ronald J. Sider (ed.) *Evangelism, Salvation and Social Justice* (Grove Booklets 1977).
    Evangelicals and Development; Towards a Theology of Social Change (Paternoster, Westminster 1981).
    Life Style in the 80's: An Evangelical Commitment to Simple Life Style Paternoster, Westminster 1982).
Max Warren *I Believe in the Great Commission* (Hodder/Eerdmans 1976).
David Watson *I Believe in Evangelism* (Hodder/Eerdmans 1978).
Ralph Winter (ed.) *The Evangelical Response to Bangkok* William Carey 1973).
G. E Wright *The Biblical Doctrine of Man in Society* (SCM 1954).

Notes

1. 'The Evangelical Commitment to Simple Lifestyle' is published in *Lifestyle in the Eighties* ed. Ronald J. Sider (Paternoster/Westminster 1982), and the Madras Declaration on Evangelical Social Action is published in *AIM MAGAZINE*, (November 1979, Evangelical Fellowship of India, 92 Nehru Place, New Delhi 19), and printed in Christopher Sugden, *Radical Discipleship* (Marshall Morgan and Scott 1981).
2. See further, *Dictionary of Sociology* ed. G. Duncan Mitchell (Routledge and Kegan Paul 1968), p.195.
3. See further G. E. Wright, *The Biblical Doctrine of Man in Society* (SCM 1954), pp.18–19.
4. 'Jesus Christ the Only Saviour' by Tom Wright and Michael Sadgrove in *Obeying Christ in a Changing World* Vol 1; *The Lord Christ* ed. John Stott (Collins 1977), p.68.
5. G. E. Wright *op. cit.* pp.82–3.
6. See further Victor Paul Furnish, *The Love Command in the New Testament* (SCM 1973), chapter 1.
7. V. P. Furnish *op. cit.* p.68.
8. 'Salvation Today' by Donald MacGavran in *The Evangelical Response to Bangkok* ed. Ralph Winter (William Carey Library 1973), pp.31–32.
9. See further the writings of P. F. Strawson, *Individuals*, G. E. M. Anscombe, *Intention*, and Gilbert Ryle, *The Concept of Mind*.
10. D. J. A. Clines, 'The Image of God in Man' *Tyndale Bulletin* (1968), p.57; John Goldingay writes: 'While it would be an exaggeration to say that the Old Testament does not distinguish soul and body, it certainly does not make the sharp disjunction between them which characterises Platonic thought and has influenced popular Christian assumptions. The soul is not the true person which can happily survive the loss of the body . . . the physical person is the em-bodi-ment, the incarnation of the true self, and is essential to the true self. In fact a man is lost without a body to "clothe" his self (2 Cor. 5:4).' *Songs from A Strange Land* (Inter Varsity Press 1978), p.138.
11. Colin Brown ed. *Theological Dictionary of the New Testament* (Paternoster Press, Zondervan, Vol II 1976), p.181.
12. See further Colin Brown *op. cit.* Vol II 'Hamartia'.
13. See further G. E. Wright *op. cit.* p.48.
14. Orlando Costas, *The Integrity of Mission* (Harper and Row 1979, p.82).
15. For discussion of these themes see: Jose Miranda *Marx and the Bible* (SCM 1977); Anders Nygren *Commentary on Romans* (Fortress 1974); Brian Wren *Education for Justice* (SCM 1977); Vinay Samuel and Chris Sugden 'Social Justice: Biblical Themes and Practical Expressions' *TRACI Journal* 1980 (E 537 Greater Kailash II, New Delhi 48).
16. For discussion see Ronald J. Sider *Evangelism, Salvation and Social Justice* with a Response by John Stott (Grove Booklets on Ethics No.16, 1977, Bramcote, Nottingham).
17. Statutes of Partnership in Mission (1981).
18. See Andrew Lincoln *Paradise Now and Not Yet* (Cambridge 1981).
19. See Childbirth: Isa. 26:17–18; 66:7–9; cf. 45:10; Mic. 4:9–10; 5:3; Mk. 13:8; Rev. 12:2; Harvest: Rev. 14:15; Jn. 4:36; Gal. 6:8; Blossoming of spring: Isa. 35:1–2; 61:11; cf. 45:8; Mk. 13:28ff.

20. G. E. Wright, *op. cit.* p.115.

21. See for further discussion Vinay Samuel and Chris Sugden 'Towards a Theology of Social Change' in *Evangelicals and Development* ed. Ronald J. Sider (Paternoster Press, Westminster Press, 1981).

RESPONSE

In his response, Dr. Harold Lindsell, editor emeritus, *Christianity Today*, asks for clarification of terms used, such as church, Kingdom of God, justice and injustice and their relationship to each other. He asks, 'Is the mission of the church the same as the mission of the individual Christian? Is it the same as the mission of the Kingdom?' In the discussion on salvation in relation to the eschaton, on the inner and outer life, and on evangelism and social responsibility the respondent misses any direct citation of the sort of eisegesis which the authors reject.

Arguing that the mission of the church is evangelism, Dr. Lindsell observes that those major denominations in the USA that have allocated time and resources to social action have declined in membership and in intent for evangelism. Their praxis shows that their theory is deficient. He fears the same will happen to evangelical churches which include social action in their programmes. If the mission of the church includes social and economic or political action, then the church must be competent to speak on these controversial subjects. Otherwise, it will lead to internal divisions and such conflicts in turn dilute evangelistic enthusiasm. He cites examples from differences of opinion over capitalism, multinational corporations and USA imperialism.

In conclusion Dr. Lindsell asks, 'May not the notion that changed men change society be the key to the problem? May not evangelism do more good than social action? Does social action belong to the mission of the church as church or to believers who make up the churches?' His answer is: 'The mission for the members of the churches describes a number of activities that the Church as Church is not called upon to do in the world.'

(This editor would ask of the respondent one further question for clarification—What does he mean by 'the church as church'?)

9

The Mission of the Church
Theology and Practice

DR. J. CHONGNAHM CHO

Synopsis Dr. Chongnahm Cho discusses recent evangelical thinking about the mission of the church in relation to evangelism and social responsibility. He then explores the biblical mandate for the church's mission and finally suggests some practical implications for both social responsibility and evangelism. In the first part Dr. Cho seeks to clarify the theological position of the Lausanne Covenant and then the Lausanne movement up to the Congress on World Evangelization at Pattaya, Thailand 1980. He concludes that Lausanne recognizes that both evangelism and social responsibility belong to the mission of the church in its corporateness though each is distinct from the other. In comparing the theology of mission at the Berlin Congress of 1966 and the Lausanne Congress of 1974, Cho sees a distinct shift of emphasis. Berlin understood the one task as evangelism. The question of social responsibility was raised but not adequately answered.

In outlining the biblical mandate for the mission of the church, Dr. Cho centres on Jesus Christ as the model and norm of the church's mission. Word and deed are held together in the ministry of Jesus in terms of the command to love God and to love one's neighbour in all his dimensions. 'Love is concerned about the whole man with all his needs', he states. There can be

*Dr. J. Chongnahm Cho teaches at the Seoul Theological Seminary in South Korea.

no dichotomy between obedience to the Great Commission and the keeping of the Great Commandment. Cho deals with three practical implications, namely, that the church's social involvement is through the Christian vocation with its members each exercising the gifts that the Holy Spirit gives to them. He then discusses the church's corporate action and urges caution. Using the four different levels of the church's involvement in social action as described by José Miguez-Bonino, Cho affirms social action at the pastoral and prophetic level but rejects conscientization and direct action. He endorses the Lausanne Covenant's assertion that 'in the church's mission of sacrificial service, evangelism is primary' (par. 6). The urgency of the task of evangelization is outlined against the background of the 2.7 billion peoples of the world who have not yet been reached with the gospel. He warns against the futility of social service without going to the root of the problem of the selfish sinful heart of mankind. He concludes by emphasizing the importance of the spiritual revival of the church by the sanctifying power of the Holy Spirit.

Introduction

The crisis of Christianity in recent decades may be summarized theologically as the problem of the definition of the mission of the church.[1] The church has been faced with two extreme emphases with regard to its mission. One view concentrated on verbally proclaiming the Word and saving individual souls. This view has often been identified as the older and traditional view of mission. Arthur Johnston in *The Battle for World Evangelism*, carefully observes how this traditional view has been challenged by the so-called 'Social Gospel' in earlier decades and in this decade of the twentieth century by an 'ecumenical theology of mission', namely 'holistic evangelism'.[2] In this second view, the emphasis shifted from preaching the Gospel to social action by the church and the christianization of society by socio-political, economic and cultural influences. For the proponents of this view, the task of the church is to initiate action in liberating people from oppression and economic exploitation.[3] This polarization of emphases in mission has confused many people.

How should the mission of the church be defined in relation to evangelism and social responsibility?

In 1974 the International Congress on World Evangelization was convened in Lausanne by evangelicals. One main purpose of the Congress was to 'frame a biblical declaration on evangelism' and 'state what the relationship is between evangelism and social responsibility'.[4]

Participants in the Congress who signed the Lausanne Covenant expressed 'penitence both for our neglect and for having sometimes regarded evangelism and social concern as mutually exclusive'.[5] They affirmed:

> That evangelism and socio-political involvement are both part of our Christian duty. For both are necessary expressions of our doctrines of God and man, our love for our neighbour and our obedience to Jesus Christ . . . The salvation we claim should be transforming us in the totality of our personal and social responsibilities. Faith without works is dead.[6]

But further explication of the Lausanne position and its implications remains necessary. The purpose of this chapter is to explore the position of the Lausanne Covenant and then reflect biblically and practically on the Church's role in the relationship of evangelism and social responsibility.

1. Reflections on the Lausanne Covenant

A. *The Lausanne Position Clarified*

The Lausanne Covenant opens with a paragraph concerning 'the purpose of God'. 'For Mission and evangelism are . . . part of the eternal purpose of God.'[7]

The first paragraph of the Covenant begins with our belief in the one eternal God, 'the Creator and Lord of the world, Father, Son and Holy Spirit, who governs all things according to the purpose of his will' (par. 1). He is also Redeemer. So 'God loves all men, not wishing that any should perish but that all should repent' (par. 3). 'Jesus Christ, being himself the only God-man, who gave himself as the only ransom for sinners, is the only mediator between God and man' (par. 3).

Now, 'Christ sends his redeemed people into the world as the Father sent him and this calls for a similar deep and costly penetration of the world . . . The Church is at the very centre of God's cosmic purpose' (par. 6). The Lausanne Covenant develops its theology of mission on the basis of the purpose and activity of the Triune God. In one place the Covenant defines the mission of the church in terms of 'sacrificial service' (par. 6). It also affirms that 'evangelism and socio-political involvement are both part of our Christian duty, for both are necessary expressions of our doctrines of God and man, our love for our neighbour and our obedience to Jesus Christ' (par. 5). Thus, 'sacrificial service' includes both evangelism and social concern.

This is one of the most significant confessions on mission that evangelicals have ever produced, but it still invites some reactions and questions among evangelicals.

Because the Lausanne Covenant expresses socio-political involvement as a Christian duty so positively, some welcome it as though now evangelicals have recovered their candour. Stott believes it to be a truly biblical understanding of mission.[8]

Others think that this view deviates from the traditional evangelical view of mission, maintained and reaffirmed at Berlin in 1966, and that now the evangelicals have adopted the ecumenical concept of 'holistic mission'.[9]

Some argue that the Covenant means that social concern is the responsibility of the individual Christian, not of the church, while others think that the Covenant meant to include both evangelism and social concern in the mission of the church.

Thus, with regard to the theological interpretation of the Lausanne position and its practical implication, Leighton Ford, the Chairman of the Lausanne Committee admits, 'clearly the house was divided'.[10]

At the Lausanne Congress, Stott presented a paper under the title, 'The Biblical Basis of Evangelism'. He defined the meaning of the words related to mission, which are in the forefront of the recent debate. He said that

> Mission is an activity of God arising out of the very nature of God. The Living God of the Bible is a sending God, which is what 'mission' means. He sent the prophets to Israel. He sent his Son into the world. His Son sent out the apostles, and the seventy and the Church. He also sent the Spirit to the church and sends him into our hearts today.[11]

According to Stott, we are sent into the world as Jesus was himself sent. That is, we are sent into the world to serve.[12] Therefore, the church is to 'be a servant church' after the perfect model of Jesus' service. In a servant role—sacrificial service maintains 'the rightful synthesis of evangelism and social action'.[13]

Stott's position appears to be well represented in the Covenant. The Lausanne (Continuation) Committee reaffirmed this when it stated,

> We recognize that we are coming together on the basis of our common commitment to biblical doctrine and duty, especially as expressed in the Lausanne Covenant . . .[14]

The Committee accepted as biblical the mission of the church as evangelism and social responsibility.[15] More clearly the preamble of 'the Aims, Roles and Functions of the Lausanne Committee for World Evangelization', adopted at the Second Meeting held at Atlanta, January 12–16, 1976, states that the Covenant both defines and defends the biblical doctrine and duty of the Common Evangelical Commitment, and that the committee is determined to communicate biblical doctrine and duty, duty being both evangelism and social involvement.[16] This view appears to have been well echoed in the subsequent evangelism meetings.

The Asian Leadership Conference on Evangelism (ALCOE) was convened from November 1–10, 1978 in Singapore. The Conference issued 'ALCOE Concerns for Study and Action' which stated that evangelism and social responsibility 'belong together like the two wings of a bird. Both are part of the mission for which God sends his people into the world.' 'We encourage all Christians, wherever they can, to be actively involved at all levels of national life. . .'[17] Two years later, the Consultation on World Evangelization (COWE) was held in Pattaya, Thailand, June 16–27, 1980. Eight hundred Christian leaders gathered from around the world. 'The Thailand Statement', understood mission again on the trinitarian basis, and affirmed commitment to both evangelism and social action. It states,

> The exalted Jesus now sends us into the world as His witnesses and servants . . . He has commanded us as His witnesses to proclaim His Good News in the power of the Holy Spirit to every person of every culture and nation, and to summon them to repent, to believe and to follow Him . . . We are also the servants of Jesus Christ. He calls us therefore, not only to obey Him as Lord in every area of our lives, but also to serve as He served.[18]

I conclude that the Lausanne position has been interpreted by the majority of the participants of both ALCOE and COWE in the sense that the mission of the church in the world is both evangelism and social responsibility after the model of Jesus Christ who has been sent into the world.

Another question still remains. Does the Covenant mean that social responsibility belongs only to individual members of the church and not to the body of the church?[19] This question arises because the Covenant did not use the word, 'Church'. It stated that 'evangelism and socio-political involvement are both part of our Christian duty' (par. 5). The Statement of the Lausanne Committee, as well as of the subsequent meetings cited here, did not use the words, 'church's mission'. Did it then mean that only evangelism is the church's mission?

Why should it be taken that one duty, evangelism, belongs to the body of the church and the other duty, social responsibility, to the church's individual members? From the mere context of the sentence, I do not see any particular reason to interpret it in this way. Should the responsibility and duty of a member of the church be different in its essence from that of the whole church although there can be different ways through which the duty is to be executed? Furthermore, the Covenant understood the church in its essence as the people of God rather than as an institution (par. 6). Then the member of the church is to be identified with his 'redeemed people', who are sent by Christ into the world (par. 6). The responsibility of such people could then be understood as that of the church itself. Here, it is worth noticing that the Thailand statement employed the words, 'all God's people', instead of 'we' in par. 5 of the Covenant, for those who 'should share his concern for justice and reconciliation throughout human society'.[20]

From these observations, I would say that the majority of the participants of both ALCOE and COWE, when they endorsed the Lausanne Covenant in its entirety, appear to have taken the broader meaning of the mission.

B. *A Comparison of the Theology of Mission in Berlin and Lausanne*

Before we look into the biblical mandate for mission, it might be good to give some theological comment on this interpretation of the Lausanne position. For the Lausanne Congress marks a significant development in mission theology from Berlin, 1966.

The International Congress on Evangelism in Berlin, 1966 drew 1,200 participants from 100 nations and issued the closing statement, 'One Race, One Gospel, One Task'. In this statement the participants proclaimed their 'determination to carry out the supreme mission of the church'—to 'fulfil the Great Commission'. That is, they saw Christians as sent out by our Lord Jesus Christ, who has all authority in heaven and on earth, 'into the world to be his witnesses'; by 'his witnesses' they emphasized the proclamation of the Good News and disciple-making.

At the Congress John Stott led the Bible study on the great commissions in the Gospels. He deduced that the mission of the church is 'exclusively a preaching, converting and teaching mission'.[21] At Berlin the 'One Task' meant 'an evangelism that was concerned about the church'.[22]

This reflects well what Billy Graham emphasized in his opening Congress address,[23] 'Why the Berlin Congress?' Graham reminded the participants that the primary thrust of evangelism is the winning of people to a personal relationship to Jesus Christ. Berlin made a distinct contribution in defining biblical evangelism, its nature, its message, its greater impact in meeting the social and moral needs of men and even inspiring social movements in history.

This, however, does not mean that Berlin did not express the concern of the Christian for social responsibility. Berlin recognized the importance of the social implication of evangelism but the subject was never adequately handled at the Congress; therefore, there were some reactions from a variety of delegates.[24] 'Christianity Today' reported of the Congress:

> The most common complaint seemed to be that daily discussion groups opened up great issues without striving to arrive at a consensus. The relation of evangelism to social concern . . . to cite the major example . . . was a recurring theme, and many delegates felt that there should have been more of an attempt to crystallize thinking on it.[25]

Consequently Berlin did not establish the theological basis for social action. This was 'the unfinished business of Berlin'.[26] Carl Henry noted that 'evangelical theology concerning pressing social concern reflected significant divisions within the evangelical community'.[27] No wonder that the social concern of the church was taken up seriously at Lausanne. As Graham pointed out, 'this matter—relationship of evangelism to social action—was of vital concern'.[28] A deep and abiding interest in social responsibility on behalf of the poor and oppressed was presented by the participants. The diversity of views was discussed and in-depth analysis was achieved.[29]

As a result of such deliberations, Lausanne theologized the social responsibility of the Christian, which the church was actually carrying out, and which is often thought of, or at least, implied in the biblical mandate for mission. The Covenant affirmed that 'evangelism and socio-political involvement are both part of our Christian duty' (par. 5). This certainly marks a decisive change from the Berlin view which has been traditionally maintained by conservatives. Along with this change, the Lausanne Covenant shifted the emphasis of Christian responsibility from the individual Christian to the church body. The 'individualistic revivalism characteristic of pluralistic, volunteeristic American evangelism'[30] seems to be disappearing from the forefront. As we have already observed, Lausanne developed the theology of mission based on the purpose and activity of a triune God. The mission of the church is seen in Christ's sending his redeemed people into the world after the model of the incarnation of Christ. This approach broadens the understanding of the mission of the church, for 'mission' now describes everything his redeemed people (his church) are sent into the world to do.

This trinitarian understanding of the nature of the missionary task of the church is contrasted with the church-centric understanding of mission. This is important for us to notice. This approach would 'broaden the whole context and perspective of mission from one of looking at the church's work to understanding mission as the participation by the people of God in His work'.[31] This broad view of mission appears to provide a somewhat 'close link' with the theological ideas developed in the ecumenical movement.[32]

At Lausanne, Stanley Mooneyham said,

A great deal has already been said in this Congress about the relationship of evangelism and social concern. The Holy Spirit seems to be showing us that the debate which has gone on for nearly a century is really a non-issue. We thank God for that! There are two mandates in the New Testament. One is witness. The other is service. To ignore or deny either of them is to seriously cripple the church.[33]

But Lausanne made a distinction between evangelism and social action. The Lausanne theology clearly defines evangelism as distinct from social involvement. 'Evangelism itself is the proclamation of the historical, Biblical Christ as Saviour and Lord, with a view to persuading people to come to Him personally and so be reconciled to God' (par. 4). At the same time, the Lausanne Covenant is eager to place the primacy on evangelism in the church's mission. The Covenant reads: 'In the church's mission of sacrificial service, evangelism is primary' (par. 6) . . . 'The church is at the very centre of God's Cosmic purpose and is His appointed means of spreading the Gospel.' Lausanne also avoided the soteriological significance of political liberation, when it stated that 'reconciliation is not reconciliation with God, . . . nor is political liberation salvation' (par. 5). Has this notion of the Lausanne theology of mission deviated from the traditional conservative view maintained from the nineteenth century to Berlin 1966? This seems to be an improvement on Berlin by achieving a right synthesis between evangelism and social action, yet, in the spirit of Berlin. 'The holistic concept may be recent, but the idea is not,' George Peters says. 'It is as old as modern missions.'[34]

We are aware that from the very beginning Christian missions assumed a comprehensive mission—proclaiming the Gospel, teaching and healing according to the example of our Lord (Matt. 9:35). Therefore the church has been involved in the whole life of man, in building culture and in structuring and shaping society and in the quality of political systems throughout the ages. The church did not remain neutral, inactive and indifferent in the course of human development.[35] It is true also that the evangelical church has been engaged in ministries related to social responsibility. We recall 'Acts of the Holy Spirit '74' presented at Lausanne by S. Mooneyham. He made this statement:

> In preparing for this presentation tonight, we surveyed 150 evangelical leaders around the world and asked them to point out significant trends in their areas. From every part of the world came reports that evangelicals are ministering to human needs, as well as spiritual needs in the name of Christ. Concern about medical care, substandard housing, food shortage, illiteracy, political injustice and economic inequality is being translated into Christian action.[36]

In this century, however, it appears that partly because of our reaction against a 'social gospel' of liberal optimism,[37] the evangelical church tended to concentrate almost exclusively on evangelism. Now again reacting against the programme of humanization, evangelicals were somewhat afraid to regard social responsibility as a part of missions, for we could observe without much difficulty that the programme of 'humanization' and 'liberation' of the recent decades of this century is no more successful than was the nineteenth century programme of the 'Social Gospel',—the 'Christianization of the social order'. However, such a note must not lead us to a negative attitude towards the Lausanne position. Furthermore, we should not be afraid if our statement of the concept of the mission of the church sounds the same as that of ecumenical theology, for we have a common doctrinal statement in other areas, too. For example, both we and the Roman Catholics proclaim that Jesus Christ is our Saviour. The difference does not exist in this concept, but in its implication and in its related doctrines, such as the view of faith and works, which creates a wide gap in the soteriology of the two camps. Likewise, it seems to me that some problems and difficulties related to the holistic evangelism (of the ecumenical movement) lie not so much in this concept of mission as in other aspects and implications of mission.

The crucial question would be whether this view is biblically supportive, for we firmly believe that the Bible, the Word of God, as stated in the Covenant (par. 2), is the authority for theology. The Bible is 'the only infallible rule of faith and practice' (par. 2). We shall give our attention to the biblical mandate for mission in the following section.

2. The Biblical Mandate for the Mission of the Church

In the previous section we concluded that the mission of the church in this world is more than 'evangelism'. It is 'sacrificial service' for which Christ sends his redeemed people into the world as the Father sent him out of love and for redeeming love. Jesus Christ is the model and norm for the church's mission because his redeemed people are sent as the Father sent his Son (Jn. 20:21). 'The Word became flesh and dwelt among us' (Jn. 1:14), and took the form of a servant (Phil. 2:5–11). This was God's way to communicate his love for all people whom he created (Jn. 3:16).[38] Jesus manifested in his life the love of God: 'In this the love of God was made manifest among us, that God sent his only Son into the world so that we might live through him' (1 Jn. 4:9). In this love of God Jesus has served and given his life as a ransom for many (Mk. 10:45; Rom. 5:8).

A. *Word and Deed in the Ministry of Jesus Christ*

In his ministry Jesus Christ used both word and deed to minister to people in announcing the coming of God's Kingdom. In Luke 4:18–19, Jesus indicated his own mission in terms of addressing the spiritual and physical needs of people. The Bible records: 'Jesus went about all the cities and villages, teaching in their synagogues and preaching the gospel of the kingdom, and healing every disease and every infirmity' (Matt. 9:35; Acts 10:38). Now Jesus Christ sends his disciples into the world as the Father has sent him (Jn. 20:21).

Therefore the disciples who are sent into the world are to share in his ministry and to follow his example in obedience to his command to love God and one's neighbour (Matt. 22:38), and his commission to make disciples of all nations (Matt. 28:19–20). To the disciples Jesus says, 'This is my commandment, that you love one another as I have loved you' (Jn. 15:12). 'You shall love the Lord your God with all your heart and with all your soul and with all your mind. This is the great and first commandment And a second is like it, you shall love your neighbour as yourself. On these two commandments depend all the law and the prophets' (Matt. 22:37–38). Jesus also says, 'By this all men will know that you are my disciples, if you have love for one another' (Jn. 13:35). 'There is none other commandment greater than these' (Mk. 12:31; Rom. 13:8). Paul exhorts the same in his epistle: 'Walk in love, as Christ loved the church and gave himself for her' (Eph. 5:25). John also admonishes: 'Let us not love in word or speech but in deed and in truth' (1 Jn. 3:17–18). We are thus under the commandment to love others. This certainly implies that the church as a body is also under the commandment to love others, for, as Getz points out, 'The majority of New Testament directives to love others were written to local bodies of believers—not to individual believers per se.'[39] Moreover, this love of God—that Christ died for our sins while we were yet sinners (Rom. 5:8)—compels his people to be ambassadors for Christ (2 Cor. 5:14). 'Surely only a burning heart motivated by the love of Christ and his Word with a zeal to serve God and one another can evangelize this continent . . .'[40]

Here, his love is to be understood as comprehensive as well as complete. Christians are to 'do good to all men' (Gal. 6:10; 1 Thess. 5:15), for everyone is our neighbour. Our love must also be complete as was that shown by Jesus Christ. We must love the whole man. The command of love should manifest concern for man in all of his dimensions. Christ's love should reach out to the unsaved with the gospel (Lk. 19:10). It should be concerned also for man's social needs, for man is a soul-body unit and lives in society. The Christian's concern is to visit those who are imprisoned (Matt. 25:26; Jas. 1:27), and those who are sick and need to be healed (Jas. 5:14). He is concerned with slaves who should be free (Ex. 22:21). 'It is the responsibility of Christian love to oppose oppression. Love is concerned about the whole man with all his needs.'[41] As we take seriously the Great Commandment, to love others, we cannot escape the social responsibility of the church's mission.

We also notice that the risen Lord commissioned his disciples and followers to preach the gospel and make all nations his disciples. This is recorded in all four Gospels (Matt. 28:16–20; Mk. 16:15; Lk. 24:44–49; Jn. 20:21–23). Since the Bible maintains the unity of revelation, the commission recorded in each Gospel should be accepted as 'they beautifully supplement each other. While each of the evangelists presents it with his own unique emphasis, together they make a complete whole.'[42] Therefore it would be an injustice to the missionary purpose of God to say that evangelism (verbal proclamation) is the only task of mission, based only on the Marcan form of the commission, for we see that the Johannine commission (Jn. 20:21) forms a parallel between the Father's sending of Jesus Christ and his sending of the disciples into the world. This helps us to understand mission in the light of the incarnation and broadens the interpretation of the Great Commission. Here mission is a comprehensive task as found in the ministry of Jesus because our task is to follow the mission of God in Christ.

B. *Obeying the Great Commandment and the Great Commission*

Moreover, since we believe in the unity of the Bible, we must say that 'The Great Commission is not an isolated command, (but) a natural outflow of the character of God . . . The missionary

purpose and thrust of God . . .'[43] Thus, we should not take the
Great Commandment and the Great Commission as though they
are mutually exclusive. We should take the Great Commandment—to love others—and the Great Commission—to preach—
together, integrated in the mission of Jesus Christ, for it is the
same Lord, who commanded and commissioned the same
disciples and his followers. Therefore, as Di Gangi says, 'to
communicate the gospel effectively we must obey the great
commandment as well as the great commission. The *disciplining*
of the nations cannot be divorced from the speaking and the
doing of the truth in love.'[44]

When we study the Great Commission more carefully we will
discover also that it does not necessarily exclude the keeping of
the great commandment. From the accounts of the Great Commission recorded in the four gospels, we gather the following
important theological insights and emphases related to evangelism:

1. The dynamics of the Word and the revelational foundation
   of the gospel (Lk. 24:46)—'Thus it is written'.
2. The dynamics of the Spirit and power in evangelism
   (Jn. 20:22; Lk. 24:49)—'Receive the Holy Spirit.' 'Wait
   for the promise (power) of the Father.'
3. The universal need of repentance for the remission of sins
   (Lk. 24:47).
4. The need of Christian presence in the world (Jn. 20:20;
   Lk. 24:48)—'So I send you.'
5. The authority and assurance of the Lord, the sender
   (Matt. 28:18, 20)
6. The importance of teaching and church planting ministry
   (Matt. 28:19, 20)
7. The goal of evangelism (Mk. 16:15; Matt. 28:19)—
   'preach', 'make disciples.'

But the 'all inclusive goal of the Great Commission seems to be
expressed by two imperatives used in the commission: 'make
disciples' (*mathēteusate* Matt. 28:19) and 'preach the gospel'
(*kēryxate* Mk. 16:15). And we notice that these imperatives are
supplemented by the participles, 'going' (*poreuthentes* Matt.
28:19; Mk. 16:15), 'baptizing' (*baptizontes* Matt. 28:19) and
'teaching them to observe' (*didaskontes autous tērein* Matt. 28:20).
While we might discuss at length the implication of, 'going,
baptizing, church planting and teaching' ministries, we will limit
our discussion to our social responsibility in its relation to the
Great Commission.

We call attention to the fact that the process of 'making
disciples' which is evangelism, must be done by 'teaching to

observe' what Jesus Christ has commanded (Matt. 28:19–20)—
to know and obey his commandments. Thus evangelism must
comply with the commandments of Christ. 'In a word,' as
Snyder says, 'evangelism and social concern go together and are
both essential to the one gospel.'[45]

Therefore, it is not helpful to put a dichotomy between the
Great Commission and the Great Commandment, as though the
Great Commandment connotes social concern and the Great
Commission only evangelism.[46] So, 'Failure to teach prospective
believers and new converts that coming to Jesus necessarily
involves a costly discipleship that will confront social, economic
and political injustice constitutes an heretical neglect of the great
commission.' In the same way, if obedience to the Great Commandment—to love one's neighbour—neglects or excludes
telling the neighbour of Jesus Christ, who is the Way, the Truth
and the Life—this cannot reflect a true understanding of the
commandment. Therefore, as Di Gangi reminds us, 'We must
obey the great commission and make disciples, and we must do
so within the context of obedience to the great commandment
which requires love to God and neighbour.'[47] In practice, then,
evangelism and social action are inseparable both in the sense
that the mission of God's people must be sought from the teachings of God, which are summarized in the Great Commandment
to 'love', and also in the sense that the Great Commission is not
an isolated command from God's purpose and character. 'Both
are indicative of our mission.'[48]

This is the pattern of Jesus' ministry for, 'The servant role
fulfilled by the Son of Man demonstrates the proper synthesis
of evangelism and social concern.'[49] This synthesis is clearly seen
in the career of the Apostle Paul. In Romans, Paul said he was
'a minister of Jesus Christ to the Gentiles in the priestly service
of the gospel of God . . . In Christ Jesus, then, I have reason to
be proud of my work for God, for I will not venture to speak of
anything except what Christ has wrought through me to win
obedience from the Gentiles, by word and deed, by the power of
signs and wonders, by the power of the Holy Spirit, so that from
Jerusalem and as far as Illyricum I have preached the gospel of
Christ . . .' (Rom. 15:16–19). Thus, in describing his ministry,
Paul emphasized both what he had said and done. Could we not
say then, with Di Gangi, 'There must be evangelism and social
concerns—obedience to the great commission within the context
of the great commandment—if we would bear witness to our
Lord and serve Him in the world'?[50]

Paul's pattern was followed by Peter and the apostolic church.
In Acts we see that the church had been involved with social
concerns as well as with preaching. This created some problems

and in order to solve these, the church made a functional division of the ministry among the disciples. The twelve apostles were to devote themselves to preaching the Word of God and another group were to 'serve the tables' (Acts 6:1–6). The church made a distinction between evangelism and social responsibility, if we might use contemporary terminology. However, this division does not at all mean to exclude 'serving tables' (social concern) from the task of the church nor to make the two mutually exclusive.

This distinction and division between preaching and social concern is made in response to the existential situation and for practical convenience. This functional division seems to be necessary also because God intends to work through the gifts of the Holy Spirit as given differently to each member of his body (Eph. 4:7). This leads us to consider and discuss the practical implication of the mission of the church.

C. Practical Implications for Evangelism and Social Responsibility

In the previous section, we observed that the Lausanne Covenant developed a broader concept of mission. The mission of the church is seen in the sacrificial service which Christ sends his redeemed people into the world to perform. In this 'service' both evangelism and social concern are included.

I believe that this is a well-balanced, full-orbed scriptural view of the mission of the church. This is a healthy synthesis of the two extremes (polarized view) in the evangelistic spirit and emphasis, which has been maintained by the evangelicals.

Therefore, we should not regard social responsibility as merely a means or preparation for evangelism, nor as a manifestation or by-product of evangelism. Both evangelism and social action are a Christian's duty. Every Christian is a witness and every Christian is also a servant. In principle, every Christian should do both in whatever opportunities he is given. But it does not mean that 'evangelism and social action are such inseparable partners that all of us must engage in both all the time.'[51] In carrying out the mission of the church, we must 'be wise as serpents and innocent as doves' (Matt. 10:16), for different situations will demand a different strategy for the efficacy of the mission and each member of the church has different gifts and callings (Eph. 4:7; 11–22). As we gave seen, in Acts 6 the apostles and disciples appear to be busy in both preaching and serving at table. But the apostles felt a problem arising in the community, so they divided the responsibility among the disciples. The apostles were to be responsible for preaching and another group for 'serving tables'. A distinction between evangelism and social action was made.

This is not a division in essence but for the sake of the practical efficacy of the church's mission and as the solution to a problem which arose in the church. 'This is a necessary deduction from the nature of the church as Christ's body. Although we should resist polarization between evangelism and social action, we should not resist specialization. Everybody cannot do everything. Some are called to be evangelists, others to be social workers, others to be political activists.'[52] There could be occasions when it is legitimate for a Christian to concentrate on one or the other of these two duties; Stephen and Philip only preached (Acts 7; 8) and the good Samaritan rendered only social service (Lk. 10:33–35). What will this mean in practice? For our discussion, I would like to suggest some practical implications.

(a) The Church's Social Involvement through Christian Vocation

The church is involved in social action through the vocation of individual Christians. This suggestion has a theological basis as well as practical advantages. God sends his redeemed people into the world to 'serve'. This is true but there is a difference between the members in the nature of the service which they are called to render. Some are called to be preachers or teachers, others to be social workers, medical doctors and others to be government officials. Through their vocation or life work, the gospel is to penetrate all spheres of human life. The member of the church is sent into the world with his Christian vocation to share God's concern and activity for people and the world.

This is a pattern which the New Testament church applied. Christians were exhorted, 'Whatever your task, work heartily, as serving the Lord and not men, . . . you are serving the Lord Christ' (Col. 3:23). Here we might say with Howe that 'in the work of the dispersed church, which is active in and serving the world, the chief minister is the layman, who in the home or in the office, in the street or in the shop, in the school or in the university, or wherever the work of the world is going on, is the church in that situation and must be the minister of Christ there.'[53] In this case, the effectiveness of this mission will depend on how faithful that Christian is. This service cannot be expected, therefore, without the disciple-making ministry of the church. A disciple-making ministry will result in a remarkable social and political transformation. In this sense, the importance and primacy of evangelism cannot be over emphasized.

Christians are under what I would call 'the Christian mandate'. In this, Christ commands us to 'love others' and commissions us to 'make disciples', therefore Christians with their own vocational callings must be 'the salt of the earth, and the light of

the world' (Matt. 5:13–16). Consequently, we must realize that
a Christian is not merely a member of the human race, but as
a member of the church, which God sends, has social responsibility.

This does not mean that the church should do or compete with
what the civil government does or should do. Protestants believe
that 'in a fallen society God wills civil government as an instrument for the preservation of justice and restraint of disorder'.[54]
Carl Henry says, 'Ideally . . . civil government is the framework
in which the Christian carries forward his struggle for justice.'
But as 'The Basel Letter' declares, '(if) the acts of the state
conflict with the Law of God, we must obey God rather than
man.'[55] Although the state might think it is sovereign and determines what justice is, 'civil government is not the definer of
justice. Civil government is, rather, to be the preserver of justice,
God is the definer of justice.'[56] The Christian, therefore, must
exercise the prophetic ministry wherever he is involved, keeping
his eyes on the contents of justice as defined by God. Admittedly, the Old Testament prophets and the apostles were interested not only in personal righteousness but also in social righteousness.

Furthermore, we ought to know that we share not only the
concern and redemptive interest of God for the world but we also
share in hope with the victory that Jesus Christ has already won
through his crucifixion and resurrection over all the powers of
Satan and all the forces of exploitation and oppression. This is
the victory which also dooms all the powers of evil and oppression. Henry says,

> This victory, moreover, over all the forces of sin, injustice and
> oppression He intends to extend through His body of regenerated
> believers. Through that Body, over which He reigns as crucified,
> risen and ascended Lord, He intends to work ongoingly against sin
> and injustice . . . The ascended Lord wants to extend His victory
> over sin and evil through us, the new society, and enjoins us to be
> light and salt to the world.[57]

Therefore, Christians, i.e. the church cannot escape part of
the responsibility when Christians are silent or inactive when
society is going wrong. As Stott points out, 'When any community deteriorates, the blame should be attached where it
belongs: not to the community which is going bad but to the
church which is failing in its responsibility as salt to stop it going
bad.'[58] This then, naturally, leads us to consider the corporate
action of the church.

(b) Limits to the Church's Corporate Action

The body of Christ carries out her mission through the gifts with which God has endowed its members. It would be desirable if the church could act corporately as a body. The church worships corporately and sometimes all members join together in an evangelistic activity, led by a 'specialized' group, usually of evangelists who are called to evangelism. Should this then be the principle and pattern applied to social concern? Would it not be desirable for the church to express her social concern corporately, guided this time by another 'specialized' group for social concern? This could be done in prayer (Acts 4:24) and protest (Acts 5:29) or in some other adequate form.

If so, as Stott suggests, groups of concerned Christians in the congregation should be encouraged to coalesce into a variety of 'study and action groups'. The 'study and action group', if formed, should grapple with the complexities of the issue and related problems and make recommendations for some course of responsible action to the church council.[59] The church must, then, study it prayerfully and carefully in the light of biblical discernment before taking any corporate action. This could be done either on the local level or national level, depending on the situation.

However, some acute problems and disagreements may arise when we come to the question: in what areas and on what level could we do this? Waldron Scott classifies our social concern into two or three levels: 'Relief,' 'Development' or 'Liberation'. Relief work, in general, deals with symptoms not with causes. By 'development' he means 'the attempt to provide long-term solutions to chronic problems'. This can be the ramification of liberation.[60] Development generally consists of social justice, self-reliance and economic growth.[61] As Peters says, development puts the focus on man. 'It is the rescue, liberation and restoration of man from all that degrades and enslaves him, robbing him of his inherent humanity. It is designed to make man whole and restore him to the dignity of manhood.'[62] Therefore, it might well be called social action or socio-political involvement, being distinguished from mere social service which embraces relief work and other philanthropic activities. Admittedly, there is not much problem when the church is involved in social service, but acute tensions and problems often come to the forefront when we refer to this 'socio-political involvement' or 'social action'.

José Miguez-Bonino mentions four different levels in which the church is involved in social action: the pastoral level, the prophetic level, conscientization and direct action.[63] In the ecumenical movement, especially in Liberation Theology in Latin America, the church is encouraged to engage in 'conscientization' and even be involved in direct action to 'combat racism', and in the human rights movement,[64] using floods of statements on socio-political issues. In Asia, the CCA Assembly in 1973 challenged Christians to recognize that, 'Now is the time for action,'[65] and some churches are complying with this challenge. But we must admit that this practice brought immense difficulties and problems to the church and hindrances to the church's mission. Most of all, when the church, as a whole, is corporately involved in such activities, the identity of the church in society is at stake, because the church, almost inevitably, tends to be identified, at least in the eyes of the public, with particular political parties or slogans. Often in the process of social involvement, the church appears to have, in some situations, a temporal alliance with other secular organizations which have particular goals. This is the reason that, in parts of Asia, a Christian cause, although it claims to be genuinely Christian, is sometimes misunderstood, as if it were aligned with a marxist cause. In this case, the church's mission suffers a great deal. The praxis, it appears to me, does not approve these levels of involvement as an adequate and workable strategy. Thus the church, in her social strategy, must 'be wise as serpents' (Matt. 10:16, cf. 10:23).

The Lausanne Covenant states that 'The church is the community of God's people . . . and must not be identified with any particular culture, social or political system or human ideology' (par. 6). For the church is sent into the world and for the world, yet, 'They are not of the world, even as I (Jesus) am not of the world' (Jn. 17:16, 18). Therefore, out of the four different levels which Miguez-Bonino suggested, we would endorse the adequacy of social action on the pastoral level and sometimes on the prophetic level.

The church is to be involved in creating an informed membership, conscious of Christian social responsibility, alert to the problems of society, committed to Christian discipleship. It must keep challenging such disciples to be involved in necessary socio-political movement. This could be done with the adequate help of a 'study and action group' on particular issues. In this way, the church can maintain oneness along with diversity and also her identity as the salt of the earth and light to the world, while ministering to various, broader ministries as the body of Christ. Here again we realize the importance of the disciple-making ministry in the church.

Along with pastoral involvement, 'The church must be the prophetic voice in the world and function as the conscience of

society. Seldom is there special virtue in silence.'⁶⁶ The church
would need to issue an official statement and direct the attention
of the Christians and the public to their responsibility in meeting
the problems and needs which confront them. Here again, this
activity cannot afford to damage the unity and identity of the
church, which is the dynamic of mission. Therefore the prophetic voice should be restricted lest it cause division among the
congregation and the loss of her identity.

At this point, we must remind ourselves of the fact that the
church is 'a messianic community'. John Driver, in an article
which surveys 'the church's attitude toward and role in the contemporary struggle for social justice in Latin America,' offers a
helpful pointer 'toward a strategy of struggle for social justice'.⁶⁷
According to him, the church is 'a messianic community, which
is in fact the bearer of the real meaning of history, a paradigm of
God's intention for man and the world.' The church, as the
'reconciled and reconciling community,' bears an historical
testimony that this is so by God's grace and work alone, and in
this, God's justice is being concretely realized. This testimony
communicates to the world 'a radically new way' in human social
relationships, which is so different from the attempt to solve
social problems on the world's terms.

It implies, as Driver suggests, that 'the social strategy of the
messianic community is determined by the form which Jesus'
messianic strategy took . . . the messianic community is limited
in the instruments which are at its disposal, those which the
Messiah used, for bringing social change. Violence, defamation,
falsehood, deceit, disrespect for persons, etc. . . . are among the
instruments which society has found to be most effective in
expediting change. . . . But they are not at the disposition of the
messianic community because they do not partake of the essence
of the messianic kingdom.'⁶⁸ The form of social concern which
the church should positively take is 'servanthood'. 'In our identification with Christ and his mission we become servants.'⁶⁹ We
hear 'the call to servanthood' in the Basel letter: 'Dear brothers
and sisters, we affirm that God is calling us, whatever our situation, to recognize that our highest duty and greatest privilege is
to embrace the role his Son embraced. Our Lord Jesus became
the servant of men' (Mk. 10:45).⁷⁰

This directs our attention again to the importance of disciple-
making and spiritual renewal of the members of a Messianic
community. We must learn from Paul. As stated in the Basel
letter, 'Powerless in himself, Paul knew his weapons were
mighty through God to the pulling down of strongholds' (2 Cor.
10:3–5). In his continuous encounter with 'the cosmic powers,
the authorities and potentates of this world, the superhuman

forces of evil in the heavens (Eph. 6:12), Paul relied on the armour God provides'.[71]

(c) Maintaining the Primacy of Evangelism

The Lausanne Covenant asserts that 'in the church's mission of sacrificial service, evangelism is primary' (par. 6). COWE 1980 reaffirmed the primacy of evangelization. To support this primacy, both the Lausanne Covenant and the Thailand Statement acknowledged 'that of all the tragic needs of human beings none is greater than their alienation from their Creator and the terrible reality of eternal death for those who refuse to repent and believe'.[72] The urgency of the task of evangelization was also stressed with particular concern for two billion and seven hundred million (2,700,000,000) people in the world, who are yet to be reached with the gospel. This is true. Jesus often emphasized, in his ministry on earth, the importance of spiritual needs over material needs (Matt. 16:26; Mk. 8:36–37), and so it was with St. Paul (Rom. 9:1–3; 10:1; 2 Cor. 4:11–18). This has been the emphasis of evangelicals. This was and must be so even today, for it is the vital part of the church's mission.

The uniquely important task of evangelism in the church is evident in the Great Commission which the risen Lord gave to the disciples to 'preach the gospel to the whole creation' (Mk. 10:15; Lk. 24:46–49; Matt. 28:18–20; Jn. 20:21–23).[73] We have previously concluded that the commission, recorded in the four gospels and taken as the one integrated commission, indicates that the 'all-inclusive goal is then preaching and making disciples'.

Moreover, we know that the root of the problem in our society lies in the selfish sinful hearts of man, and that relief work, development and even structural change cannot get to the root of this problem. Man must be forgiven and cleansed from his sins, to be reconciled to God and eventually to his neighbour. Without this transformation of man through evangelism, expecting to change society is obviously futile. Here we find 'the urgent and irreplaceable role of evangelism in wholesome social change'.[74]

With the understanding of these factors and this existential context, we could say, reviving the 'Berlin Spirit' with Graham, 'I am convinced if the church went back to its main task of . . . getting people converted to Christ, it would have a far greater impact on the social, moral and psychological needs of men than any other thing it could possibly do. Some of the greatest social movements of history have come about as the result of men being converted to Christ.'[75]

In conclusion, we therefore emphasize the importance of the spiritual revival of the church by the sanctifying power of the Holy Spirit for the further equipping of the disciple, because with the ALCOE participants, we believe that 'only when the church is renewed, purified and mobilized can it hope to fulfil its mission'.[76] Therefore, the Lord charged the disciples, 'Wait for the promise of the Father' . . . 'You shall receive power when the Holy Spirit has come upon you; and you shall be my witnesses in Jerusalem and in all Judea and Samaria and to the ends of the earth' (Acts 1:4, 8).

Notes

1. Arthur Johnston, *The Battle for World Evangelism* (Tyndale House, Wheaton, 1978), p.227.
2. *ibid.*, pp.37–38, 41, 59–62, 229–237, 274–287.
3. *ibid.*, p.286, see also, *International Review of Missions*, April 1973, *Bangkok Report*, p.200.
4. Billy Graham, 'Why Lausanne?, in J. D. Douglas ed., *Let the Earth Hear His Voice*, p.34.
5. *The Lausanne Covenant*, par. 5.
6. *ibid.* (loc. cit.)
7. John Stott, *The Lausanne Covenant: An Exposition and Commentary* (World Wide Publications, Minneapolis, 1974), p.5.
8. John Stott, *Christian Mission in the Modern World* (Falcon Books, London, 1979), p.29.
9. Johnston, *ibid.*, p.297. It is true that Johnston is here criticizing Stott's view. However his word would apply to the Covenant, if we interpret the Covenant along with Stott's view.
10. Leighton Ford, 'Evangelism and Social Responsibility', in *World Evangelization* (March 1982), p.6.
11. J. D. Douglas, *ibid.*, p.66.
12. *ibid.*, p.66.
13. *ibid.*, p.67. Stott, in his later book, *Christian Mission in the Modern World*, further says, 'Social action is a partner of evangelism. As partners the two belong to each other and yet are independent of each other . . . Neither is a means to the other or even a manifestation of the other' (p.87). To support this, he gives the two mandates given by Jesus Christ: 'Love your neighbour'—the great commandment and 'Go and make disciples'—the great commission. Stott believes that 'if we can accept this broader concept of mission . . . then Christians could, under God, make a far greater impact on society, an impact commensurate with our numerical strength and with the radical demands of the Commission of Christ.' (p.34).
14. 'Minutes of the Lausanne Continuation Committee', p.4 (quoted from Johnston, *ibid.*, p.343).
15. Johnston, *ibid.*, p.344.
16. Minutes, quoted from Johnston, *ibid.*, p.346.
17. James Wang, ed., *Asia's harvest*, ALCOE Report, p.68.

18. 'The Thailand Statement 1980' in *International Bulletin of Missionary Research*, Jan. 1981, p.30.
19. cf. Johnston, *ibid.*, p.359.
20. 'The Thailand Statement 1980', in *International Bulletin of Missionary Research* (Jan. 1981), p.30.
21. John Stott, *ibid.*, p.22, Stott admits that he argued it then, but after Lausanne he expressed himself differently on the Mission of the church.
22. Johnston, *ibid.*, p.166.
23. Billy Graham, 'Why the Berlin Congress?' in Carl Henry and S. Mooneyham ed., *One Race, One Gospel, One Task*, Vol. 1, pp.22–34.
24. See Henry & Mooneyham, *ibid.*, Vol. 2, pp.198, 205–206, 256–257, 306, 313, 376–378, 499–501, 523, Vol. 1, pp.281, 306–309.
25. 'The World Congress: Springboard for Evangelical Renewal, 34', quoted from Rodger C. Bassham, *Mission Theology* (William Carey Library, 1979), p.227.
26. Johnston, *ibid.*, p.221.
27. Carl Henry, *Evangelicals at the Brink of Crisis: Significance of the World Congress on Evangelism*, (Word Books, Waco, 1967), p.56.
28. Douglas, *ibid.*, p.29.
29. *ibid.*, p.31, 94, pp.130–131, 144–145, 303–326, 445–446, 698–712, 1163–1182, 1292–1296.
30. Johnston, *ibid.*, p.359, cf. p.175.
31. Bassham, *ibid.*, p.333.
32. *ibid.*, p.222.
33. S. Mooneyham, 'Acts of the Holy Spirit '74' in Douglas, *ibid.*, p.445.
34. George W. Peters, 'The Church and Development: A Historical View', in Robert L. Hancock, ed., *The Ministry of Development in Evangelical Perspective* (William Carey Library, 1979), p.17.
35. *loc. cit.*, pp.7–8.
36. S. Mooneyham, *loc. cit.*, p.445.
37. Stott, *Lausanne Covenant . . .* , p.25.
38. Norman L. Geisler, *The Christian Ethic of Love* (Zondervan 1973), p.54.
39. Gene A. Getz, *The Measure of a Church* (A Division of G/L Pub., Glendale, Ca., 1977), p.33.
40. The ALCOE Commitment, in James Wang, *ibid.*, p.15.
41. Geisler, *ibid.*, p.40.
42. George W. Peters, *A Biblical Theology of Mission* (Moody Press, 1972), p.174.
43. Peters, *ibid.*, p.173.
44. Mariano Di Gangi, *I Believe in Mission* (Presbyterian and Reformed, 1979), p.30.
45. Howard Snyder, *The Community of the King* Inter-Varsity Press, 1977), p.84.
46. Ron J. Sider, *Evangelism, Salvation and Social Justice* (Grove Books, 1977), p.19.
47. Di Gangi, *ibid.*, p.44.
48. *ibid.*, p.51.
49. *loc. cit.*, (*ibid.*).
50. *ibid.*, p.50.
51. Stott, *ibid.*, p.28.
52. Sider, *ibid.*, p..22.

53. R. Howe, *Herein is Love* (The Judson Press, Philadelphia, 1961), p.112.
54. Henry, 'Evangelicals and the Social Scene: God's Plan for Salvation and Justice', in Hancock, *ibid.*, p.100.
55. 'The Basel Letter' in Lionel Holmes, ed., *Church and Nationhood* (WEF, New Delhi, India, 1978), p.9.
56. *op. cit.*, p.100.
57. Henry, *loc. cit.*, Hancock, *ibid.*, pp.98–99.
58. Stott, *ibid.*, pp.31–32.
59. *ibid.*
60. Waldron Scott, *Bring Forth Justice, A Contemporary Perspective on Mission* (Wm. B. Eerdmans, 1980), pp.266–268. Ron Sider gives for social concern three distinct, interrelated activities: relief, development, and structural change (social action), *Asia Theological News* (April–June 1982), p.5.
61. G. Peters, 'The Church and Development: A Historical View', in Hancock, *ibid.*, p.5. This is a definition given at the Montreux Consultation, 1970.
62. *ibid.*, p.6.
63. Jose Miguez-Bonino, 'The Church and the Latin American Social Revolution', in the *Church and Social Revolution* (Perkins School of Theology Senior Colloquy), 1977, quoted from Bassham, *ibid.*, pp.345–346.
64. For an example, see the discussion at Bangkok '78, *International Review of Mission*, Vol. LXII, No. 246 (April 1973), p.198ff. And also, S. Escobar and John Driver, *Christian Mission and Social Justice*, p.86ff.
65. CCA Fifth Assembly, p.52, quoted from Bassham, *ibid.*, p.348.
66. Peters, *loc. cit.*, Hancock, *ibid.*, p.26.
67. John Driver, 'The Anabaptist Vision and Social Justice', in S. Escobar and John Driver, *Christian Mission and Social Justice* (Herald Press, Pa., 1978), pp.102–108.
68. *ibid.*, pp.104–105.
69. *ibid.*
70. Holmes, *ibid.*, p.10.
71. *ibid.*, p.11.
72. 'The Thailand Statement 1980', in *International Bulletin of Mission*, (Jan. 1981), p.30.
73. See this paper in the section of the Biblical Mandate for Mission.
74. L. Ford, *loc. cit.*, in *World Evangelization* (March 1982), p.9. Also see the argument made by Emil Brunner in his book, *Justice & Freedom in Society*, and R. Niebuhr's argument of sin as pride—'Pride of Power' in society, in his book *The Nature and Destiny of Man*, Vol. 1. See also the Bible references to the subject: Gen. 3:17, Rom. 8:17, 1:28, 6:25, 5:12ff., James 1:15, etc.
75. Graham, 'Why the Berlin Congress?' in Douglas, *ibid.*, I, p.38.
76. 'The ALCOE Commitment' in James Wang, *ibid.*, p.15.

RESPONSE

In his response Rev. Tite Tiénou, a pastor and theologian of Upper Volta, asks of Dr. Cho's paper, 'Does it contribute to the clarification of the current debate and does it show us a way towards more obedience in the discharging of our responsibility?' He suggests that the implied ecclesiology of Lausanne could be called *personal corporateness* as opposed to *institutional corporateness* and therefore one should not necessarily look for the word 'church' when looking for statements about the church. 'This is precisely what Cho does when he concludes that the Lausanne position has been understood as one in which the mission of the church includes evangelism and social responsibility.' He thinks that Dr. Cho has moved the present debate forward by proposing that the church's involvement in social action is through Christian vocation. However, Tiénou would prefer to see social action in the wider context of the total ministry of the church. He adds, 'I think there are varieties of ministries in the church for the purpose of accomplishing God's total mission in the world. Therefore, though I believe in the centrality of evangelism, I am not an evangelist. My ministry in the church is elsewhere. Likewise, though I believe in the importance of social action, I am not called to that. Our mistake, I think, is our tendency towards a monolithic ministry in spite of our theoretical adherence to the variety of gifts and ministry.' He wishes that Dr. Cho had been more specific in showing the relationship between evangelism and social responsibility. 'No doubt the variety of our situation calls for variety of possible relationships. In that regard, it may be possible to propose a theoretical solution to our problem.'

Tite Tiénou concludes by raising two questions concerning the outcome of our acts of social responsibility:

Does our social action really contribute to restoring human dignity and wholeness? Or does it create strife, bitterness, and greed? I myself see a strong link between the restoration of human dignity and the wholeness of the person in Christ which comes through the communication of the gospel.

The other question I would conclude with is the matter of institutionalized social responsibility. Institutionalized social action means impersonal involvement and this has disastrous results. Biblical social action means personal commitment, sacrifice, and caring. Another result of institutionalized social action is its effect on some of us on the receiving end. Individuals and churches sometimes seek development and social action programmes for the purpose of increasing their power and respectability within society. This desire may be legitimate, but doing it with outside money certainly defeats the purpose of encouraging the people to engage in personal and corporate social responsibility at their own expense.